RETURN TO
Smith Wigglesworth

RETURN TO
Smith Wigglesworth

a deeper evangelism

Chigbu Okoroafor

TATE PUBLISHING
AND ENTERPRISES, LLC

Published by Tate Publishing & Enterprises, LLC
127 E. Trade Center Terrace | Mustang, Oklahoma 73064 USA
1.888.361.9473 | www.tatepublishing.com

Tate Publishing is committed to excellence in the publishing industry. The company reflects the philosophy established by the founders, based on Psalm 68:11,
"The Lord gave the word and great was the company of those who published it."

Book design copyright © 2011 by Tate Publishing, LLC. All rights reserved.
Cover design by Shawn Collins
Interior design by Joel Uber

Published in the United States of America

ISBN: 978-1-61346-797-8
1. Religion: Christian Life, Spiritual Warfare
2. Religion: Christianity, Pentecostal & Charismatic
11.11.23

Return, O Holy Dove! return
Sweet messenger of rest!
I hate the sins that made Thee mourn
And drove Thee from my breast.
                              –William Cowpe

Acknowledgement

I am very grateful to the men and women of faith whose works and words in different forms were used by the Holy Spirit to bring out the message in this book. My special thanks to all who worked on the manuscript at various stages.

I would like to thank Mr. Mazi Amanze, who introduced me to the Full Gospel Businessmen Fellowship International and, along with Mrs. N. Pius Okeadinma, proofread the drafts of this book

I also wish to acknowledge my staff, Gift Epelle, for her encouragement and assistance in cutting and arranging this work.

Also thanks to my God-given, wonderful daughters, Zyzi, Chumy, China, and Kodi, whose prayers and pressure inspired me to complete this book on schedule.

Preface

This book started as an article I intended for our church magazine, The Christian Messenger. The intended article has become part of the sixth chapter, "The Negative Spirit of Bacchus." My aim was to present to the readers the very fact that the Holy Spirit cannot share a habitation with the spirit of alcohol or Bacchus. On two occasions, I submitted this article to the editor of the magazine, and on those two occasions, he returned back to me the electronics storage I sent to him because he could not open it. The third time, he gave me his removable disc to save the article and avoid the problem of not being able to open mine in his computer. Still he was not able to open the article. That was when the actual instruction of the Holy Spirit began to register to me. Write a book in a layman's language alerting the church of the consequences of her apparent drift from the truth of the Gospel, especially in this end time that the devil has intensified his fight against millenarianism. As the Holy Spirit began to prod me, I started experiencing some strange, logical, and profound insight into some biblical accounts. I started putting them down on paper, and just about this time, I hired a new assistant. Little did I know that she is a staunch born-again

Christian. She became my encouragement. The more I discussed my strange profundity with her, the more I received insight, and to my surprise and delight, she agrees with me in all. Though my task was still not very clear to me, I had begun to appreciate that God wants me to tell the church to wake-up to her challenges and responsibilities, as did Smith Wigglesworth, often referred to as "the Apostle of Faith." He was one of the pioneers of the Pentecostal revival that occurred a century ago. Without human refinement and education, Wigglesworth was able to tap into the infinite resources of God to bring divine grace to multitudes. Thousands came to Christian faith in his meetings, hundreds were healed of serious illnesses and physical infirmities as supernatural signs followed his ministry; hence the title, *Return to Smith Wigglesworth.*

Then the first chapter, "Confidence in the Truth of the Gospel" crystallized in my mind. The objective is to begin by giving the reader confidence in the truthfulness of the Gospel before discussing its subject and characters. The rest followed, and the Holy Spirit responded according to promise. The outcome is this book of seven chapters from a layman whose ability to do the work must only be attributed entirely to His supremacy.

Toward the completion, I realized fully the objective and significance of this assignment: Call the church back to the full gospel. This revelation itself came in a way and manner that established God's intervention beyond any doubt. A member of the Full Gospel Businessmen's Fellowship had been inviting me for some years now. This time, he came with a written invitation and insisted on my coming for their dinner meeting of Monday, 17 March, 2008. I went, and the meeting was rich and fruitful. At the end, I was given a copy of Mr. Demos Shakarian's book, *The Happiest People on Earth.* After reading the book, I called the person who invited me and told him that I had found the meaning of an assignment the Holy Spirit gave to me from the pages of Mr. Demo's book I received at the dinner fellowship he invited me to. It is about sending a message to the church to *return to the full gospel.* That is the message I have come to share with you in this book. The church must believe that the Gospel account is entirely and literally true and correct. The church must see the Lord Jesus Christ as the epitome of God's love and love Him accordingly. The church must see the Holy Spirit as truthful, real, and as active today as on that faithful day of Pentecost. The church must realize that the believer is not called to a life of flamboyance and extravagance, but to a life of modesty and prudence, carrying his or her cross in followership with Jesus. The church must know that nothing has changed between the church of Apostles Peter and Paul and the church of today on the side of the Godhead. What has changed is the attitude of today's church to the gospel of Jesus Christ. The Holy Spirit is very much the same and around as He was then.

Table of Contents

My Testimony

Before I met my Lord Jesus
I habitually challenged Bacchus
Three malevolent punches were a constant
One on my pocket and family
Another on my health and joy
And on my time and peace
Now that I have met Jesus
I have been rescued from Bacchus
I only wished it happened earlier
Before the bruises became indelible scars
Still, better be late than never
Scars than stinking and painful wounds

—Chigbu Okoroafor

Foreword

This book has inserted another very useful device into our evangelical machinery. It makes a delightful reading to any one who genuinely loves Jesus; it is an inspiration to all and a confidence builder to the weak. It agitates the mind like a stream flowing down a stony slop. Some spices interjected into its message provoke some deep theological thought and call for a Holy Spirit-guided insight into some traditional Christian notions and interpretations of some Bible passages. Examples are:

1. Did Saul change his name to Paul at conversion or did he have both names from birth? What did the Bible say? And is it possible he was a Roman citizen from birth without a Roman name?

2. Is it possible to peep into the heart of Paul before his conversion to see why God bypassed many and selected him? Was he aware of the resurrection of Jesus before his conversion but continued to persecute the disciples because it was expedient for him to do so? Was his conscience tormenting him before he met Jesus? Does his first encounter with Jesus Christ suggest something in

a deeper evangelism

this direction? Why the instant recognition of Jesus as Lord, and what is the prick Saul was kicking against? Was it God that sent wise men from the East to honour Jesus, or Satan, to destroy the infant Jesus through Herod? Can their source of information—divination and stargazing—and their route to Bethlehem via Jerusalem (Herod) answer some questions about their mission?

3. Is there any significant insight we can derive from water as a substance that exists naturally (at ordinary temperatures) in all three states of matter in our effort to understand and explain to a sceptical world the conception of the divine Trinity?

4. Can the concept of evolution genuinely qualify as a science theory as generally reputed, or is it an opposing religious belief? Can we find the answer in the Bible and from Charles Darwin's background as a graduate of theology? Was Charles Darwin a spiritualist medium, and can Christianity prove that his evolutionary concept is not a theory but a religious belief, clothed in an academic gown, which the Bible in first Timothy chapter six verse twenty denotes: "*science so falsely called*"?

There are many revelations in this book begging for some further theological investigation. I suggest that we take some profound interest in them.

Chigbu Peter-Okoroafor

Introduction:
The Life and Ministry of Smith Wigglesworth

The exigency of returning the church to the Holy Spirit-filled ministry of the early church and the likes of Smith Wigglesworth is never in greater desire than these last days, when the Word of God is facing new attacks from various quarters, especially the New Age and the politicians. If there ever was any anticipation for assistance in our fight against the devil from the world's doctrinal institutions, the current actions and attitude of Western politicians toward Christianity and its goals have dimmed such prospect beyond the vision of even the most powerful telescope. The church has been invaded by infiltrators who spy into our liberty for materials with which to fight against Christ and Christianity. The same politicians that deny, distort, and destroy the Christians' fundamental beliefs and values are the same occupants of front pews in the churches.

In a natural tendency to seek free information, I stumbled into a shocking discovery. Many websites offering free Internet Christian literatures are not just bogus Christian organizations but are devil's institutions designed to fight Christianity from inside. Their battle plan is to hide their bitter, satanic message in the sweet message of the gospel like a poisonous fruit coated with chocolate—likewise, many so-called churches of the day that were established for the interest and service of their master, Satan. As the Christian begins to eat, he would not know when he has eaten up the sweet chocolate and has started eating the satanic, poisonous fruit hidden inside.

This is the time for the church to really come to terms with the fact that we fight not against flesh and blood. The law courts are not our weapon; neither is the legislature. The Holy Spirit has not left us without examples to follow.

According to Smith Wigglesworth,

> It is impossible to overestimate the importance of being filled with the Spirit. It is impossible for us to meet the conditions of the day, to walk in the light as He is in the light, to subdue kingdoms and work righteousness and bind the power of Satan, unless we are filled with the Holy Ghost… There are many evil, deceiving spirits sent forth in these last days who endeavor to rob Jesus of His Lordship and of His rightful place. Many are opening their doors to these latest devils, such as New Theology and New Thought and Christian Science. These evil cults deny the fundamental truths of God's Word.

This was a statement he made in the early twentieth century but are even more true in this present generation.

Smith Wigglesworth's total surrender to the will of God, derived from faith in the finished work of Jesus Christ, was not a mere belief but a product of absolute belief and trust in the totality and sovereignty of the three-in-one God of the Bible. In a life entirely devoted to the purpose of God, Wigglesworth found that peace of God that passes all human understanding. The fruit of peace is the precursor for the spirit gift of faith. Through obedience to God, Wigglesworth found peace, and the

Holy Spirit baptized him with faith and upon faith. Wigglesworth removed mountains and became known by many Christian faithfuls of his time as the Apostle of Faith. With the gift of faith, Wigglesworth started bearing the fruit of love and joy, the precursors for the gift of the word of wisdom and the word of knowledge (Galatians 5:22 and 1 Corinthians 12). Wigglesworth never attended a formal school due to family circumstance but only learned a plumbing trade in adulthood. He traveled round the world preaching and teaching both learned and unlearned, Christian clergy and the laity the Word of God. That is a clear manifestation of the gift of the word of wisdom and of knowledge. Then compassion became his second name. The ragged and hungry boys and girls of Liverpool, where he moved his plumbing business, were early testimony. With the fruit of kindness came the gift of miracle, including raising the dead and turning water into gasoline.

The story of Wigglesworth turning water into gasoline you may not have heard, but read the account of this miracle of a very practical nature, wrought by Smith Wigglesworth's faith in Christ Jesus. Smith Wigglesworth was already in his eighties during the second World War but continued his Holy Spirit-filled, soul-winning ministry, traveling everywhere the Spirit led him, spreading the Word of God with power, signs, and wonders, despite the difficulties and dangers of traveling in wartime Europe. Like food and clothes, gasoline was a scarce commodity and strictly rationed. A black market for the commodity became a thriving business. Delinquents around military bases made fast and lucrative deals by bribing servicemen for supplies and selling them at inflated prices.

To check this practice and verify the source and origin of fuels such as gasoline, diesel, and paraffin, the government introduced a regulatory policy that required petroleum products for public use to be dyed according to type, source, and location.

Anyone found with a wrong color of fuel, such as red in a green color zone, was arrested. Naturally, genuine Christians would not patronize nor have anything to do with black-market fuel but only depended on their legitimate quota.

It was in this situation that a Christian minister by the name of Harrison, a pastor of a fellowship in Sutton Ashfield, Nottinghamshire, secured the commitment of Smith Wigglesworth, the Apostle of Faith, to come and preach to his congregation on the condition that Harrison would pick him up in a neighboring town after a preaching engagement there.

All went well as the two men headed off to Sutton, until they got to the middle of Sherwood Forest. The tiny Morris Eight, barely enough room for the two men, sighed as the engine juddered, spluttered, and finally went off. The fuel had finished, seventeen miles before they reached their destination.

The location: middle of Sherwood Forest! Time: late at night. Situation: critical, no prospect of any help arriving by that late hour of the night. Poor Harrison, what an embarrassment, while on duty for God! He had succeeded in securing the world's most powerful minister to come and bless his flock. What an anticlimax that he had stranded him in the middle of a dangerous forest in the dark of bomb-blasted England. What would he do? Leave Wigglesworth alone in the middle of this forest and darkness and walk to the nearest house, which was some miles away, and beg for gasoline, or walk to a distant telephone box and ask for rescue? Or should both of them wait for police or military arrival to investigate a vehicle parked suspiciously in the middle of Sherwood Forest?

As Pastor Harrison browsed through options, unable to utter a word, Wigglesworth had already received instructions from the Holy Spirit on the solution.

"Av y' got any water?"

"Yes, I keep a can for topping up the radiator," Harrison answered nervously

"Put it in t' petrol tank," ordered Wigglesworth.

Even with minimal knowledge of auto engine mechanism, anyone would realize that this is absolutely unthinkable.

But when Smith Wigglesworth instructs people to do something, experience, his over-bearing authority, and steadfast faith usually resulted in their speedy compliance. So Harrison was not about to argue the matter. He opened the car door and retrieved a half-gallon can of water from behind the driver's seat, no doubt with clenched teeth, and with whispered prayers, poured the water into his car's fuel tank.

With the starting handle in position, Harrison threaded carefully between the chassis and the radiator to engage a special notch in the crankshaft and braced himself to crank the engine. That was how cars were started then, no battery or ignition key. What a moment. Water inside the hot cylinders would destroy the combustion chamber, crack the valve seats, and ruin his precious vehicle. He was about to murder his own car! What an anxious moment for him. But he obeyed without doubt, because he knew and trusted the person who had instructed him.

In contrast, Wigglesworth was calm and remained in his seat, thanking God for another miracle. He'd been in this kind of situation countless times and knew just how to overcome all obstacles.

Wigglesworth had walked with God for decades at a level of rapport most believers could not comprehend. Smith had learned the truth of the gospel fact Jesus promised His first disciples and that it holds true for all His disciples, then, now, and forever.

Harrison thrust the starting handle through half a turn with all his might. No response. Perhaps an owl cawed mockingly from its treetop roost. Again, he swirled the handle, and the little Morris rocked on its leaf springs: still, silence. Wigglesworth remained impassive yet believing.

On the third cranking, the eight-horse-power engine burbled miraculously into life. Harrison pressed the throttle, the motor hummed happily, and off they went and reached Sutton-in-Ashfield without further incident.

Out of curiosity, Harrison asked his mechanic to make a scoop and withdraw some of the liquid from the car's tank. It was pure gasoline, and not a trace of water! What's more, it was the correct fuel color for Nottinghamshire.

Jesus had not only turned water into gasoline in response to Wigglesworth's faith, but had even ensured it was the legal color too!

Examples of Smith Wigglesworth's miracles demand that the church needs a return to Smith Wigglesworth's kind of faith in Jesus Christ that can open the door of power ministry and save the body of Christ from ridicule as is the case today. After reading transcripts of his sermons, there will be no doubt left in you as to whether the church has need for a return to his faith. Listen to him concerning the miracle of raising a woman from death:

> My friend said, "She is dead." He was scared, and I have never seen a man so frightened in my life. "What shall I do?" he asked. You may think that what I did was absurd, but I reached over into the bed and pulled her out. I carried her across the room, stood her against the wall, and held her up, as she was absolutely dead. I looked into her face and said, "In the name of Jesus, I rebuke this death." From the crown of her head to the soles of her feet, her whole body began to tremble. "In the name of Jesus, I command you to walk," I said. I repeated, "In the name of Jesus, in the name of Jesus, walk." And she walked!

The miracle of raising the dead was just one of the amazing aspects of Smith Wigglesworth's ministry. This great servant of God walked in such an astonishing anointing that the power following his ministry can only be compared to that in the acts of apostles—and with such a simple and unassuming staff of office. Not the papal key to the door of heaven, not the big cross of the evangelicals, the long ropes of the orthodox, the stick of the celestials, the designer suit of the Pentecostals, the moodiness of the Quakers, but a simple conviction: only believe. "I saw that God wants us so badly. He has made the condition as simple as He possibly could: 'only believe.'" This is his usual comment.

Mr. Wigglesworth was born June 8, 1859, in the small England village of Menston, Yorkshire, to Mr. and Mrs. John and Martha Wigglesworth. His father's income was not enough to carter for a family of a daughter and three sons, so he began to work at the age of six, pulling potatoes in a local vegetable field. He therefore could not go to school. Smith became deeply involved in the Wesleyan Methodist church when, at the age of thirteen, he moved with his family to Bradford. At seventeen years of age, Smith met a God-fearing man at the mill where he was working with his father, who taught him the trade of plumbing. Smith was so excellent in the plumbing business that the available job in Bradford was not enough to keep him busy, so he moved to Liverpool. With the power of God mightily upon him, he began to minister to small groups of children of that city. They came in hundreds to the dock shed that had become his sanctuary. Some in rags and hungry looking, the children came, and Smith preached to them and took care of their physical needs. He was good in the plumbing trade and was making good money, but he never spent it on himself. Instead, he would use it to cloth and feed the boys and girls who attended his ministry. Beside these children, Smith and one of his friends also had a hospital ministry.

a deeper evangelism

One of Smith's greatest assets in life was his wife, Mary Jane "Polly" Featherstone. "All that I am today, I owe, under God, to my precious wife. Oh, she was lovely!" he said of her. She came from a good Methodist family, and her father lectured in the Temperance Movement. When her father became heir to a huge sum in inheritance made from the sale of alcohol, he held fast to his deep conviction that alcohol is sin and refused to touch the money, regarding it as a blemish inheritance. Polly watched the lifestyle of her father and translated herself into his strong character and belief in holiness.

As Smith's plumbing business grew, he started going to Leeds to purchase materials to enable him to meet up with schedule. During one of such trips, he attended a church service where healing ministration was featured. He sat through the service in great astonishment and observed the healings that took place. On coming back to Bradford, he went in search of the sick and paid their expenses to go to healing services in Leeds. He hid this gesture from his wife, Polly, thinking she would join other scoffers of that period in branding divine healing as "fanaticism." But as God would have it, when she found out what her husband was doing, Polly became interested and, needing healing herself, followed him to Leeds. Prayers of faith were said for her, and she received her healing. From that day on, the husband and wife became passionate for the truth, and their church in Bradford grew, and they had to look for a bigger place. They found one in a building on Bowland Street and called it Bowland Street Mission (BSM). A large scroll painting on the wall behind the pulpit read, "I Am the Lord That Healeth Thee." Smith continued to take groups of people to Leeds for healing ministry at his own expense. He became known for his great compassion for the sick and the needy. Eventually, the Leeds Healing Ministry propelled Smith to get his own public ministry to grow. They took a decision that compelled Smith to preach in their absence. Away to a convention at Kewick, they asked Smith to conduct the service while they were away. Reluctantly, Smith agreed, hoping that he would just conduct the service while another would take up the pulpit. During the service, Smith conducted, but there was no other to preach. Reluctantly again, Smith began to minister, and at the close of his message, fifteen persons came out for healing call. One man hopped out on a pair of crutches. After Smith prayed for his healing, the man dropped his crutches and ran over the place, obviously healed. No one in that congregation was more surprised than Smith Wigglesworth! From then, he started holding healing services in Bradford. On the first night, twelve people came for healing, and all got healed.

Soon, a major challenge to Smith's faith emerged. The wife of a devoted associate of Smith was on the death list. Doctors had given up on her. Upon hearing the news, compassion swelled up in Smith's heart, and he became determined in faith to save the woman's life. Smith and his minister friend took off for the woman's house. They agreed that the minister should start praying for the woman the moment they got into the house. On arrival, Smith and his friend were confronted with the hopeless condition of the woman, and his friend started praying instantly, though not as they had agreed. From the woman's condition, Smith's friend found no need for healing prayers, but rather started praying for the people she would leave behind. Wigglesworth stopped his friend and instinctively pulled out his bottle of oil from his pocket and emptied the entire bottle on her body in the precious name of Jesus Christ. Standing at the head of the sick woman's bed, Smith experienced a heavenly vision for the first time in his life. This is the way he described the vision. "Suddenly, the Lord Jesus appeared. I had my eyes open, gazing at Him. He gave me one of those gentle smiles.... I have never lost that vision, the vision of that beautiful, soft smile." A few moments after the vision, the woman got up in bed, filled with life, completely healed. She lived and had a good number of children and even outlived her husband.

Smith's hunger for the Word of God was insatiable. He never read anything else, secular or Christian, except the Holy Bible. He argued that all he needed to know was in the Word of God. At a point, Polly, his wife, became concerned over his ignorance. This is what Smith said about it: "She saw how ignorant I was and immediately began to teach me to read properly and write; unfortunately, she never succeeded in teaching me to spell."

His hunger for the full Spirit baptism took him to Sunderland when he heard that a group of people had been baptized in the Holy Spirit and speaking in other tongues. After a number of frustrations, he eventually saw a vision of the empty cross with Jesus exalted at the right hand of the Father. Smith became consumed with worship and praise, and utterances in other tongues began to pour out from his mouth. He became fulfilled, knowing that he had been baptized in the Holy Spirit as it was unto the disciples of Jesus on that faithful day of Pentecost. Smith was so overwhelmed with this development that instead of returning home, he rushed straight to a nearby church where his friend Reverend Boddy was conducting a service and begged to be allowed to speak for a short moment. At the end of his short sermon, fifty people were baptized in the Holy Spirit and spoke with other tongues. The next day, a local newspaper, the *Sunderland Daily Echo*, made the incident headline news.

On a return from one of his many conventions, Smith discovered that almost all of his plumbing business customers had engaged other plumbers to do their work due to his unavailability. A certain widow was waiting for Smith to come because he offered the most affordable price. He went directly to her home and fixed her plumbing and repaired her damaged ceiling also. When he finished, the woman demanded her bill, but Smith replied, "I won't receive any pay from you. I will make this an offering to the Lord as my last plumbing job."

Soon after, while waiting in the train station for a trip to Scotland, Smith received the devastating news of his wife's fatal heart attack on her way from the Bowland Street Mission. Smith rushed to her bedside and found her spirit already gone to the Lord. Refusing in faith to accept the very obvious, Smith rebuked death and brought her spirit back, but only long enough to bid her farewell. That was January 1913. After her death, it was said that Smith asked God for a double portion of the Spirit anointing. What became certain is that his ministry received greater power.

After the death of his wife, Smith started ministering with his daughter, Alice, and son-in-law, James, throughout the United Kingdom. Amazingly, the conservative British press, out of character, carried stories and news of Smith's ministry. *The Daily Mirror* in particular devoted its front page to his power-filled ministry, featuring four photographs of Smith on faith duty.

Smith Wigglesworth did not believe and did not teach that God has favorites. Rather, he believed and taught that there must be something in you and about you that God sees. "There is something about believing God that makes God willing to pass on over a million people just to anoint you," he would always tell believers.

So many people are searching for, and have written about, the secret of Smith Wigglesworth's power. The reason for and source of his power is not any secret at all. His great faith in God came from a perfect understanding of the Word of God and a close relationship with Jesus Christ that brought that peace of God that passes all human understanding into his heart. Faith in God soaked his heart in love, joy, and compassion. These consequently brought the corresponding gifts of the Spirit of word of wisdom from the fruit of love, word of knowledge from the fruit of joy, and the works of miracles from the fruit of kindness. Any search outside of this is in vain, and writing contrary to this is only misleading. This was the centre of his teaching: "God has no favorites—he works through those who believe Him, according to His word," he would always say.

This contradicts the teaching in some Christian quarters that the work of salvation, power ministry, and character molding of a Christian is the sovereign and sole work of the Holy Spirit, that believers should have no contributions as these qualities are bestowed on those God has chosen. Many believers have come to see this teaching that originated from inherited medieval spiritual laxity as false, by courtesy of ministries of the likes of Wigglesworth.

The ministry of Smith Wigglesworth brought a new light to an otherwise very dark horizon. Armed with an unquenchable love for God and humanity and a determination that no one should be lost or denied the height of glory he or she desires through ignorance, Smith began to teach from the Bible that those who received from God had acted upon His word to bear fruit and that those who would receive from Him must act upon His word to produce result. These beliefs became the central theme of his ministry. At the beginning of his altar calls, he would demonstrate this belief by saying, "If you move farther only a foot, you will be blessed: if you move forward a yard, you will get more. If you come up to the platform, we will pray for you, and God will meet your needs with His supply."

Smith Wigglesworth was not just all teaching and believing and acting on faith, but he was also a practical man. As part of his ministry, Smith would read portions of the Bible and act on it himself. A banquet to feed the sick and hungry, with members of his mission in Bowland Street serving the sumptuous meal, was a regular event. During this banquet, he would call for healing testimonies as part of the entertainment, moving those poor folks into solemnity and tears. A precedent he set on the first of these banquets was to draw a program in this form: "We have entertained you tonight, but next Saturday, we are going to have another meeting. You who are bound today and have come in wheelchairs, you who have spent all you have on doctors and are none better, are going to entertain us by the stories of freedom that you have received today in the name of Jesus." And he would add, "Who wants to be healed?" Of course, all would want to be healed. Smith usually took the initiative to stir up the gifts of the Spirit within him by faith. He never waited for the Spirit to spoon-feed him. To Smith Wigglesworth, every action, every operation, and every manifestation of the Spirit stemmed from a strong, absolute faith. "True faith confronts and is ignited by initiative," he had always said.

The power of Smith Wigglesworth is hidden to only those who want to make a myth of it. St. Paul tells us that the product of kindness or charity or compassion is power of miracles from the Holy Spirit. Look at the list of the nine gifts of the Spirit in 1 Corinthians 12, and you will see that miracles is number five in that list. Go to the list of the nine fruits of the Spirit, and you will see that the corresponding number five is kindness. In a plain language, godly kindness in the heart of a Christian earns him the gift of miracles. Smith Wigglesworth was a man of great compassion. As prayer requests poured into his mail from all over the world, Smith would kneel to God in tears on their account. He never ministered to the needy and the afflicted without tears running down his cheeks. He was naturally very tender with children and the elderly. Returning the church of his time to the time of Act of the Apostles, thousands upon thousands were healed as Smith Wigglesworth prayed for those he met, and the ones he could not visit, he sent anointed handkerchiefs to them for healing. An associate of his spoke of the genuine compassion Smith exhibited in this distance ministration in the same way as those present. "When the time for the opening of the letters came, we all had to stop whatever we were doing and get under the burden. There was nothing rushed or slipped in his method. Everybody in the house must join in the prayers and lay hands on the handkerchiefs sent out to the suffering ones. They were treated as though the writers were present in person." Out of compassion for the afflicted, Smith Wigglesworth became positively aggressive in breaking the chains of the devil in a religious determination to free the oppressed. He taught the church not to plead with the devil but to bark at him with command, using the example of a woman he observed at a bus stop trying to get her dog to return home with sweet attempts, but the dog remained. When the dog continued to stay and the bus was approaching, she stamped her foot on the ground and shouted at the dog, "Go home at once!" and the dog ran with its tail tucked. "That is how you have to treat the devil." Smith responded loud enough for everyone at the bus station to hear.

Smith Wigglesworth had his patience for the right things, like when he was searching for the full baptism of the Holy Spirit, but was absolutely impatient with demons, especially when it concerned his operations in the Spirit. In one of his meetings, nothing seemed to be going right. Smith asked from the Lord what the matter was. The Lord revealed to him a line of young men on a row holding hands. Smith knew they were spiritualists who had come to obstruct his ministry. As he was still preaching, he started down the platform and moved toward the direction of the bench where the young men were sitting. On getting there, he took hold of the bench and commanded the devil to get out. The group slumped on the floor into a heap and staggered out of the building.

Persecution was no barrier for Smith, nor did he make any issue over it.

In Sweden in 1920, the medical profession and local authorities prohibited him from laying hands on the people. He was not perturbed. To him, God is interested in faith, not method. He would ask the people to lay their hands on themselves and believe for healing as he prayed. Many received instant manifestation of healing. Smith called the grand-scale healing that took place "wholesale healing." The same year, he was arrested two times in Switzerland under the warrant of practicing medicine without a license. On the third occasion, the officers who came to arrest him at the house of a Pentecostal minister with another warrant for the same charge met his absence. But when the minister took them to the lower part of the town to the home of a woman who had been a nightmare to the officers and who had been restored under the ministry of Wigglesworth, the officers gave their lives to God on seeing the new condition of the woman. It was reported that many received their healing as his shadow passed by them.

Smith Wigglesworth avoided being given praises like a plague. His greatest desire was for people to see Jesus and not Smith Wigglesworth. Toward the end of his ministry, he became suddenly saddened by the fact that people were missing the target. His comment, "Today in my mail, I had an invitation to Australia, one to India and Ceylon, and one to America. People have their eyes on me." With tears, he continued, "Poor Wigglesworth. What a failure to think that people have their eyes on me. God will never give His glory to another. He will take me from the scene." Two months after this statement, Smith Wigglesworth went to meet Polly in the bosom of the Lord. That was March 12, 1947.

a deeper evangelism

Confidence in the Truth of the Gospel

A major obstacle during my early evangelical days was how to convince my audiences that Bible record of events concerning Jesus is a true historical account. Questions that repeated themselves as a stumbling block to my mission were "why should the Bible be my life compass when I am not even sure that it has an authentic historical background? How come that it is only the disciples of Jesus that wrote about him; were they the only people that could write them?" These questions did not only become an obstacle to my evangelical mission but gave me sleepless nights. My analytical mind was drifting along with their faulty reasoning. Faulty because I now know better. If I knew then, what I know now, I probably would have won more souls for Christ and also save myself the agony of those sleepless nights. I am therefore persuaded by my circumstances in the past, to begin this book with information that answers most of these questions.

This book therefore stands firmly on the premise that the Bible is the uncompromising Word of God. And in it, God, through His Son, Jesus Christ, revealed His true nature to man-

a deeper evangelism

kind and delivered man from bondage of captivity into a glorious liberty that guarantees a life in paradise with God forever
when this transient sojourn on earth is over.

An attempt is therefore made in this first chapter to reveal
this Jesus Christ to even skeptics through credible, secular, historical accounts that bear records of Jesus. It is also an attempt to
reinforce the confidence of evangelists by equipping them with
further proof of the infallibility of the Bible for the task of shar-
ing our faith with a cynical world.

Many Christians are ignorant of the existence of much evidence outside the Bible widely accepted by Bible scholars and
secular historians that verify the Bible claims on the life, ministry, death, burial, and resurrection of Jesus.

Knowledge of the deity and person of Jesus Christ were
bequeathed to us through God's inspiration, as recorded in the
Bible by His followers. So it is natural for the cynical to ask
why he or she should believe an account recorded by His followers. My idea is to look at historical accounts as recorded by His
enemies and neutral persons that validate the Bible.

The world has always asked for signs concerning Jesus, even
when in His presence, witnessing His miracles. The same skep-
tical world today still asks for irrefutable proof that the writers of the Bible did not make up the stories. Luckily, our God
has not left us unequipped. He has regularly provided credible
proofs that confirm the Bible events. The Jewish Talmud, Josephus's history books, Pliny's letters, Thallus's books of history,
Phlegon's account of the darkness of AD 33 and so on.

The Jewish Talmud is a Jewish historical collection of events
that include commentaries on Jewish books of the Law and civil
and religious records dating back to before Jesus Christ in flesh.
The record of Jesus in the Talmud was written by His enemies,
the office of the chief priest, the same people who killed Him and
later became afraid of being accused of His murder. The record

of Jesus in the Talmud expectedly is hostile to Jesus and certainly not supportive of Christianity. Its interpretations of Jesus's activities is therefore of no essence but it's merely a record of these events. The account of Jesus in the Talmud was undoubtedly written by those whose sole aim was to obliterate Him. If, therefore, the records of His enemies bear testimony of His events as recoded in the Bible, it must be seen as a highly valuable testimony. The Talmud testified to the many claims of the Bible about Jesus. The Talmud described the trial of Jesus according to the Bible's account and poured praises on those who conducted it. The Talmud gave a vivid record of His conviction and execution. It referred to Jesus as a bastard son of Mary, thereby testifying to the Bible's claim concerning His conception. The Talmud verified the existence of Jesus here on earth, declared that Jesus was a rabbi, and agreed that His trial, conviction, and execution were instigated by the religious leaders. Of importance is that the Talmud recognized that Jesus performed many healings and miracles but claimed that He performed these miracles through the power of sorcery. The Talmud's interpretation of the source of His power is not important here; what is important is the fact that it validates the Bible's account of His conception without any known earthly father, His Ministry, His miracles, His trial, His conviction, and His execution. Though its intentions were mischievous, the writers of the Talmud provided strong supporting testimony to the Bible. The Talmud's interpretation of Jesus's source of power is a further confirmation of the Bible account that the Jewish leaders accused Jesus of sorcery.

> ...If they have called the master of the house Beelzebub,
> how much more shall they called them of his household?
> Matthew 10:25b

Josephus Flavius, a Pharisee and a historian who probably saw Jesus, was born in Jerusalem of both priestly and royal lineage. By AD 66, Josephus had made friends at the court of Emperor Nero, hence changing his name from Joseph Ben Matthias to Josephus Flavius. He recorded in the *Antiquities of The Jews* that Jesus was a great teacher "who wrought many *surprising feats.*" Josephus recorded that Jesus, through miracles, won over many Jewish and Greek followers. He testified that Jesus was condemned under Pilate and "*appeared restored after three days.*" This is a great testimony, more so coming from Nero's friend. Jesus's resurrection found outside the Bible, from no lesser mortal than the greatest Jewish historian, Josephus, who further testified that His followers were called Christians after His "restoration."

Pliny the Younger (AD 62-113), a Roman governor of Syria, left a collection of letters that give a valuable description of life in the first century AD. He was born in Novum Comum and studied in Rome under the famous teacher and rhetorician, Quintilian. Pliny was distinguished both for his literary accomplishments and for his oratorical ability. He held numerous official appointments. At the age of twenty-five years, he had become Quaetor Caesaris. He was married three times but died childless. In one of his letters to Emperor Trajan concerning his policy against the Christians, Pliny testified that Christians were sent off to be executed for "stubbornness and unshakable obstinacy that ought not to go unpunished... They would not recant, and they worshipped and honored Jesus as if he were god."

No normal person can deny the fact that Jesus existed on this earth as recorded in the Bible. Many historical documents hold testimonies that confirm the Bible. We have historical testimonies that verified His conception, His miracles, His crucifixion, His resurrection, and that His followers, both those who witnessed and those who believed through the accounts of the eye witnesses, accepted Him as God and worshipped Him accordingly. Thomas called Jesus God in John 20:28: "...*My Lord and my God*." History has confirmed that all His followers worshipped Him as such.

Thallus, in his *Third Book of History Since Trojan War* AD 52, explained away the darkness of AD 33 as an eclipse of the sun. So it really happened and was recorded in history as also in the Bible. Thallus claimed that the eclipse happened on the noon of the day Jesus died. Believers know that the darkness of that noon was not an eclipse of the sun as fabricated by Thallus, but a sign from God to signify His son's death. Beside mere believe, according to science, it is impossible for eclipse of the sun to occur at that season of the year.

Phlegon, a Greek author from Caria, wrote about the same darkness that occurred in AD 33: "There was the greatest eclipse of the sun. It became as night in the sixth hour of the day so that the stars even appeared in the heavens. There was a great earthquake in Bithynia, and many things were overturned in Nicaca." This is not the gospel according to the Bible but history by an eye witness named Phlegon, an ancient historian. So the darkness of Matthew 27:48 is also recorded in history.

His Resurrection

The message of the resurrection of Jesus is one of the many weapons the devil is using to create doubt in feeble-minded persons over the literalism of the Bible accounts. If Jesus did not bodily resurrect, then He is not God and not a savior, and, of course, Christianity is a lie. His resurrection is not symbolic. It is the proof that He conquered death. It is our assurance that He is the resurrection and that we are partakers in the resurrection if we live in Him. This is the uniqueness of the Christian faith. The devil has manufactured many alternative views to claim that the disciples of Jesus conspired to make Him larger than life. All these conspiracy stories are weak and some too weak to bother about.

It is undeniable that the body of Jesus was no longer in the grave the morning of Easter Sunday. It has been agreed that He lived and died as recorded in the Bible and is confirmed by the Talmud, Josephus, and other historical accounts. It is also very important to remember that Pliny the Younger, the governor of Syria, confirmed that His followers worshipped Him as God. The Jews, the Romans, His disciples, and history concurred that the body of Jesus was missing from the grave. Nobody has ever claimed to have seen the body of Jesus after His resurrection, either in a dream, in a vision, or in reality. This in its own is a miracle. In a world full of deceivers, liars, impostors, and all kinds of evil-minded people, the devil could not give anybody the courage to make such a false claim. If the Jews or the Romans stole the body, nothing could have stopped them from producing it, especially after Peter's Sermon in Acts 2. Of course, Peter would not have dared such a message if he was not sure that Jesus was not dead but had ascended to the Father as they all witnessed.

Come to think of it, all the efforts to crush Christianity would not have been necessary if anybody had pointed toward the direction of the dead body of Jesus. If the Roman soldiers could take money from the chief priest over the story of His resurrection, how much could they have demanded for His body if they had it? If the Jewish religious leaders were not sure that His dead body could never be found, they would have made offers to anybody who could give information about it. An elaborate search for it would have been declared by the authorities. They did not do anything, because they knew the truth but were afraid to admit it for fear of the people's reaction if they found out that their leaders had killed the Messiah out of envy. Saul, who was also called Paul, his Roman name, knew the truth but was determined to cover it up by obliterating its messengers for the interest of the institution he represented—the Sanhedrim. I have made the reference concerning Paul's names to bring to your notice that Saul did not change his name to Paul at conversion as is erroneously believed. Read Acts 13:9 and see that he had both names before his conversion; *Saul that is also called Paul*—or do you suppose that he was born a Roman citizen without a Roman name? Even the Holy Spirit called him Saul in Acts 13:2, seventeen years after his conversion. In the Book of Acts of the Apostles, he was referred to as Saul in the first eighteen years of his apostleship and as Paul in the last seventeen. No wonder he called Jesus Lord in Acts 9:5, when Jesus met him on the way to Damascus to continue the cover-up mission: "*Who art thou, Lord?*" Saul asked. Even the Lord's reply to this in the same verse, five, clearly indicates that Paul knew the truth of the resurrection before his encounter with Jesus. "*…it is hard for thee to kick against the pricks.*" Microsoft Encarta Dictionary gives the meaning of *pricks* as *something that enters the mind painfully; A sudden, unpleasant thought or feeling, often related to some past action or events.* Was Saul tormented in the spirit for killing people who were preaching a message he knew was true? Was Saul remorseful but continued the persecution of Jesus's followers for fear of being thought weak. Was Saul a contrite but yet untamed heart who the Lord did not despise but, rather, perceived docile? What pricks was Saul trying to subdue before he met Jesus? I am convinced that this period of kicking against the pricks in Paul's life was what he brought into philosophical reference in Romans 7.

The earliest, though feeble, cover-up story concerning the body of Jesus, paid for by the office of the chief priest, was that His disciples took it away. Is there any possibility of this? Of course, none. It was the cover-up story manufactured and paid for by the Jewish religious leaders, as recorded in Matthew 28:12-13, and defended with violence, as recorded in history and Acts of the Apostles. Where did they take His body to, and which disciples? The ones who dispersed after His arrest? Jesus had no disciples between the time of his arrest and His resurrection.

> And all His acquaintance, and the woman that followed Him from Galilee, stood afar off, beholding these things.
>
> Luke 23:49

There could be sympathizers and friends, like the people who buried Him and the women who went out that glorious morning to anoint His grave, but far from any disciples because to them, He was no more. Peter was the boldest of them, but his boldness did not take him far. Because of a servant girl's inquisitiveness, Peter started raining curses upon himself to prove that he did not know Jesus. Is this the man to lead the other disciples into such a risky operation of taking Jesus's body away from the Roman soldiers? These were His disciples, who were too afraid to come forward and help Joseph and Nicodemus bury their Master. How come after His burial, they would suddenly become bold enough to risk death by sneaking among Roman guards, breaking the Roman seal, moving the stone without rousing anyone, and taking the body of Jesus, not by car (because there was none then) but on their heads, as was the tradition then? Consider also that the head cloth with which Jesus was wrapped was neatly folded and laid beside the burial cloth (John 27:7). This suggests that whosoever took Jesus out of that grave was not in any hurry. To me, His disciples taking away His body under the circumstances is a more intricate miracle than His resurrection.

We earlier read Pliny's account of the ugly treatments these disciples later received for coming back together to worship Jesus. What would make these disciples rejoice at being beaten, imprisoned, and put through painful deaths? A corpse they took away and disposed of? Of course not, but a living Jesus they all saw ascending into heaven. People may be willing to die for what they know to be true. People may also be willing to die for what they believe to be true. No normal person much less multiple people would be willing to die for what they knew to be a lie. The eleven saw Jesus arrested, and He did not perform to their expectations. They knew He was killed and buried. They had already started counting their individual losses. On gathering back for the gospel of Jesus Christ, they gained absolutely no financial or material gains; instead, they got the opposite. They lost all but the invisible: joy and the hope of salvation. When they were with the human Jesus on earth, their hope was the expectation of an earthly kingdom where they would be the power brokers. If He did not resurrect to His early disciples witness, these men and women would not have reunited to worship someone that had deceived them with such zeal. Because they witnessed that He lives and, by the power of the Holy Ghost, became aware of the kingdom that is theirs for eternity, the flesh which belongs to this earthly kingdom ceased to have meaning to them. All that mattered to them was to be with their Master when life here on earth is over. To them, to live is in Christ and to die is gain. All the apostles were repeatedly beaten and, eventually killed violently, except John who died a natural death.

Is it not a mystery that these men lived through human agony and died so painfully when they had the opportunity of avoiding it by just one sentence? Not one of them recanted in the face of these unimaginably difficult conditions. Not one of them accused the other of bringing him into this. Rather, all of them rejoiced for a reward they were very certain of as they go to meet Him. So what is holding them in the face of tribulation if not that their eyes witnessed His resurrection?

During Jesus's human ministry, the Bible recorded that He was a brother of James and Jude, among others: *"Is not this the son of Mary, the brother of James, and Joses, and Juda, and Simon?"* (Mark 6:3, Matthew 13:55). According to Bible records, Jesus's kinsmen, including His brothers, did not take His claim as the Messiah seriously: "And he (Jesus) marveled because of their unbelief" (Mark 6:6, Luke. 8:19-20).

How come these people who did not believe Him while He was with them became His followers after His death? James, His brother, became the head of the universal church and put his life on line for what he did not believe initially. He wrote an epistle and thought himself unworthy to be called the brother of Jesus, but was instead His servant (James 1:1). Jude, in his own epistle, did the same (Jude 1:1). What brought about this dramatic change in these people? The answer is that they witnessed and experienced several appearances of Jesus after His resurrection. They were present at His ascension at Mount Olivet. The Bible confirmed it.

> These all [those that returned from Mount Olivet after His ascension, Acts 1:12, 13] continued with one accord in prayers and supplication with the women and Mary the mother of Jesus and with His brethren.
>
> Acts 1:14

In conclusion, not one single organization or individual ever questioned the fact that Jesus was killed by the Jewish leaders. Even Islam, the greatest enemy of Christianity, agreed that Jesus was nailed on the cross, but that he was rescued from the cross by God. If Jesus did not die and was not buried, as Islam claims, his disciples would not have mentioned such an important personality as Joseph of Arimathae (Matthew 27:57, Mark 15:43, Luke 23:51), a member of the Jewish Sanhedrim, as the owner of the grave where Jesus was buried. If the story of His burial was made up by His disciples, they certainly would have used an unknown name and not the name of a member of the Sanhedrim. Both Bible and history agree on the personality of Jesus. Josephus, in

his history book *Antiquities of the Jews,* mentioned the following Bible characters: Caiaphas, Pontius Pilate, John the Baptist,
Jesus, and James, whom he described as the brother of Jesus.

Of all the claims of the Talmud concerning Jesus, none inter-
ests me more than the claim that Jesus was a bastard son of Mary.
The Talmud was compiled by the chief priest's office. The Talmud has records of women who were tried and stoned for adultery. How come Mary was not stoned or tried at all? Knowing
how the then-chief-priest's office operated, especially on matters
concerning Jesus, it may not be out of place to consider a possibility of offering money to anybody who could come and claim
responsibility for the fatherhood of Jesus, especially during his
trial, when false witnesses were making rounds. The Talmud has
made the Bible's claim on Jesus's parentage very elegant. How
graceful to have a validation of the Bible that Jesus was not a
biological son of His earthly father, Joseph, yet His mother was
not charged for adultery by the Jewish authority, as was cus-
tomary. Joseph's vision from God (Matthew 1:20) that saved his
marriage from divorce was not enough to save Mary from death
by stoning. This is because her suspected crime of adultery was
not against Joseph as an individual, but God and His people.
So it was no secret, even to the Jewish authorities, the author of
The Talmud, that Jesus had no known earthly, biological father.
Is it not amazing and a further fortification of our believe? Who
would have thought that history, Jewish Talmud, for that matter,
could provide such a wonderful validation to the Gospel?

The literalism of the Book of Revelation has been a question
mark for many. Paul's message in 2 Corinthians, in my Spirit-
guided mind, points to Apostle John and the Revelation.

> I know a man in Christ above fourteen years ago, (whether
> in the body, I cannot tell; or whether out of the body, I
> cannot tell; God knoweth) such a one caught up to the

third heaven....How that he was caught up into paradise, and heard unspeakable words, which it is not lawful for a man to utter. Of such a one will I glory, yet of myself I will not glory, but in my infirmities.

2 Corinthians 12:2, 4-5

If you have been having problems in accepting the factualism of Revelation, read this passage with a sanctified mind and go back to Revelation. You cannot miss the relationship. The passage above talked about words that are unspeakable and words that are not lawful to utter. The Bible tells us that some of what John heard was not lawful to utter. That is why John sealed up and did not write what the seven thunders uttered.

And when the seven thunders had uttered their voices, I was about to write; and I heard a voice from heaven saying unto me, "Seal up those things which the seven thunders uttered, and write them not."

Revelation 10:4

2 Corinthians 12:2 correlates with my findings from Bible time-line of Paul's events that Apostle John was the man Paul knew "in Christ above fourteen years ago." In the Epistle to Galatians, Paul tells us that it took three years from his conversion to the time he visited Jerusalem and saw only Peter, whom he stayed fifteen days with and James, the brother of Jesus. If his conversion was in AD 33, as recorded in Christian history, three years after would make AD 36 the year of this visit. In the first verse of chapter two of the same Galatians, Paul wrote, "Then fourteen years after, I went up again to Jerusalem with Barnabas..." In verse nine, he mentioned John specifically as one of those he met at this visit. So Paul met John for the first time seventeen years into his apostleship. It is therefore within reason to assume that

Paul had known John for only about fourteen years at the time of this writing in early 60s AD.

If Paul died in AD 68, and John's vision was written in the island of Patmos in about AD 96 Paul did not read it, as to say that he made up his own vision of John's Revelation from knowledge. He did not see John again from the time the latter was taken from Ephesus for banishment, which suggests that John didn't communicate this vision to him, Paul. That Paul did not even know whether the person was in body or out of body means that he did not know if John was still alive in the physical or not at the time of this vision, because there was no communication between John and anybody. In the small passage above, Paul is confirming the reality and truthfulness of Revelation.

Further confidence of the factualism of gospel can be found in the prophecies Jesus fulfilled during His stay here in flesh. We have seen and agreed that He was born of Mary without an (identifiable) earthly father. History, the Talmud, and the Gospels agree on it. He had a ministry with signs and miracles—all three agreed: Talmud said it was by the power of the devil, history was neutral, and the gospel said it was by the power of His Father, God. He was arrested by the Jewish leaders and tried by Pilate and found guilty. He was sentenced to death on the cross. He was crucified on the cross. All three agreed there was a total darkness on the day of His death. History and the gospel agreed, so we are now certain that Jesus walked on this earth.

The Old Testament, starting from the promise of God to Abraham (that his seed—just one—shall be the redeemer of the world) and through to the Law and the prophets, tell us about the coming of a divine in human body. The Scripture, through prophecies, tells us all we need to know about this divine coming. Let us look around and see if any one person, or two or more in history and present, met the requirement of this divine as prophesied in the Scripture. In the Old Testament, there are sixty major

a deeper evangelism

prophecies and two hundred seventy ramifications that convey the identity of this divine person called Messiah, which is Christ. All were fulfilled in one person, Jesus, and that is why He is called Christ. With every possible detail the human mind can comprehend, God wrote the description of His Son, the Messiah and Savior of the world, and distinguished Him from anyone who has ever or will ever live in this world. God's description of His Son was documented over a period of a thousand years and contains over three hundred references to His coming.

The message is becoming more interesting now that we are approaching mathematical science, where the possibility of lying is zero, though unbelief must not be ruled out completely, not even in mathematics. Not everybody agrees that one plus one is two, sometimes correctly, because one dollar plus one pound cannot be two of either. Using the science of probability, we determined the chances of only forty-eight of these prophecies being fulfilled in any one person, to give us one in ten to 157th power. Let me also clear the doubt of a possibility that these prophecies were recorded after the time of Jesus to coincide with His life. The devil could bring this thought, but remind him that the Septuagint, the Greek translation of the Hebrew Old Testament, was translated in its entirety as we have it in the Bible today, around 150-200 BC, at least two hundred years *before* the coming of Jesus.

I Am Thomas

I have found the Way
The Way to the Truth
The Truth that leads to Life
The Life that is forever.
Chigbu Okoroafor

If asked to describe the apostle Thomas, many of us will say, "the doubting apostle." That is the Thomas I would like to be: the Thomas of John 11:6; the Thomas of John 14:5; the Thomas of John 20:25; the Thomas of John 20:28.

As a Christian, have you ever asked yourself this question? *Am I ready to die for Jesus?* If your answer is yes, you got it from Thomas. We read of Thomas's resolve to follow his master to death when the other disciples expressed fear over their going to Judah:

> Then said Thomas, which is called Didymus unto his fellow disciples, "Let us also go that we may die with Him."
>
> John 11:16

a deeper evangelism

This is the Thomas I would like to be, the Thomas that is willing to follow Jesus unto death. And all the apostles except Judas Iscariot did followed Jesus unto death, starting with James, who opened the apostolic reunion gate with their Master through martyrdom to John, who closed it through natural death—the two sons of Zebedee, whose mother requested of Jesus that they be given special positions in God's kingdom.

In John 14:6, Jesus revealed to us His three essential personalities: the way, the truth, and the life: "Jesus said to him (Thomas), 'I am The Way, the Truth, and the Life, no man comes to the Father but by me.'"

This is an answer to a question Thomas asked Him: "Thomas said unto Him, 'Lord, we know not whither thou goest and how can we know the way?'" (John 14:6).

F.J. Dake calls this "Life's greatest question." This is the Thomas I would like to be, the Thomas through whom Jesus revealed His fundamental personality. From this answer, we know for sure that no one can receive salvation through any other name, be it religion, works, or whatever. From this answer, we have the boldness to tell the world that only Jesus can save, not religion.

My figurative definition of Christianity is: the way of life in truth. If this definition must make meaning in your life, then consider Charles M. Sheldon's life-control question, *What would Jesus do?* which has come to be abbreviated WWJD. This question has become synonymous with many Christians' way of life. To live in Jesus Christ is to live a way of life that is in truth. That is when you have become a Christian. There are many other ways of life. The Muslim says that Islam is a way of life. But the only way of life in truth that sets free is Jesus. It is an exclusive prerogative of the Christian.

Charles Sheldon was born in Wellsville, New York, in 1857 to a pastor father, who due to health problems relocated to the Dakota Territory in North America. Charles grew up surrounded by Native Americans and American soldiers as well as a practicing Christian family. He became disturbed by how the American Indians were being treated by the local and federal governments of USA; he developed intense hatred for prejudice and oppression in any form. His teachings, and most of all, his books, made him a social crusader and one of the most renowned figures of his time. Many of his reform ideas were based in this simple question: "What would Jesus do?" This question became his guarding principle in all he would do. Whatever sincere answer he found to this question, in all situations, regardless of the circumstance he was facing, he applied and encouraged his congregation to do so.

That should be the way of the Christian. How many times have you asked yourself in any circumstance what Jesus would do if He was faced with your circumstance? He is the way, the truth, and the life. I hope you believe this.

For Charles Sheldon, "What would Jesus do?" became his motto. It was an ingrained theme in his pulpit teaching; it was written on the walls of the church's kindergarten and used as a pledge of accountability in several social organizations. It became the driving force of his social justice and writings.

Who Is Jesus Christ?

We first met Him in Genesis, when God said, "Let us make man in our image, after our likeness..." (Genesis 1:26). He is the "Our" and "Us" in that statement, with the Holy Spirit and the Father; otherwise, God would have said, "Let Me make man in My image, after My likeness..." Later on, still in Genesis, we met Him prefigured in the person of Melchizedek, the prince of Salem, who has neither beginning nor end of life.

> And Melchizedek king of Salem brought forth bread and wine (Sacrament of Eucharist in advance) and he was the Priest of the most high God. And he blessed him and said, "Blessed be Abram…"
>
> Genesis 14:18-19

Moses introduced Him as the coming prophet who the people of God must listen to in all things. David introduced Him as "My Lord." The prophets called Him the Messiah, translated *Christ* in Greek. John the Baptist saw Him as one he was not worthy to loose the latchet of His sandals. The New Testament presents Him as the Redeemer. Mohamed called Him Isa but denied that He is the Son of Allah, Mohammed's god. Muslims believe that their god, Allah, forbids himself from begetting a son. I am not disappointed. Jesus is not and will never be the Son of Allah. So Allah can forbid himself from begetting a son, but the God of Abraham, Isaac, and Israel, the God of the gospel, the mighty Jehovah, begot Himself a Son in Jesus Christ. That is who Jesus is: the Son of the living God, the Messiah and Savior of the world, my God and my Lord.

The founders of the Ibo Nation in Nigeria bore names like Nwachukwu, meaning *son of God*, long before the coming of Christianity in the West African region. General Ike Nwachukwu, a onetime Nigerian foreign affairs minister's great-grandfather, probably was one of such people. How did they know about God and His Son before the arrival of the gospel? The answer is found in the Bible—the Holy Ghost. In the next chapter, we shall meet this third person in the "us and our" of Genesis 1:26. This is one of the essential duties of the Holy Spirit. The Holy Spirit had been and will continue to be a forerunner to the gospel. The Holy Spirit had revealed Jehovah God to this people, and they had differentiated Him from their other petty gods with the name Chukwu, *who lives in heaven*, and His son, whom they did not know, His name they called Nwachukwu— Son of God.

This is how Apostle John introduced Jesus to us:

> In the beginning was the Word [Jesus], and the Word [Jesus] was with God, and the Word was God. The same was in the beginning with God and the Word [Jesus] was with God. All things were made by him; and without him was not anything made that was made. In him was life; and the life was the light of men.
>
> John 1:1-4

John the Baptist bears witness and declared:

> Behold the Lamb of God that taketh away the sins of the world... And I saw and bear record that this is the Son of God.
>
> John 1:27-34

This is what the high priest prophetically said about Him during His trial:

> Now Caiaphas (high priest) was he which gave counsel to the Jews that it was expedient that one man should die for the people.
>
> John 18:14

The King James Version says *expedient*. Encarta Dictionaries defines *expedient* as meaning *Advantageous for practical rather than moral reason*. He spoke from the office of the high priest and not as Caiaphas, because he was not conscious of what he said; otherwise, he would be contradicting his case by admitting that there was no moral justification to murder Jesus.

This is how Paul narrated the earliest creed concerning Him, developed by the council in Jerusalem within the first ten years of Christianity:

> For I delivered unto you first of all that which I also received how "that Christ died, for our sins, according to the scripture: After that he was buried, and that He rose again the third day according to the scripture: and that He was seen of Cephas (Peter), then of the twelve: and that he was seen of above five hundred brethren at once: of whom the greater part remain unto this present, but some are fallen asleep. After that he was seen of James; then of all the apostles." And last of all He was seen of me also, as of the one born out of due time.
>
> 1 Corinthians 15:3-7

One of the most remarkable citations I ever read about the person of Jesus Christ was by the late, great preacher S.M. Lockeridge. He described Jesus in words like these: centerpiece of civilization, unprecedented, supreme, Preeminent, loftiest idea in literature, highest concept in philosophy, fundamental truth in theology, cardinal necessity of religion, king of knowledge, wellspring of wisdom, doorway of deliverance, pathway of peace, roadway of righteousness, the highway of holiness, gateway of glory, the master of the mighty, captain of the conquerors, head of the heroes, leader of the legislators, overseer of the overcomers, King of kings and Lord of Lords, indescribable, irresistible, incomprehensible, invincible.

This is the Christ of my message, the Son of God, the man whose followers turned the world upside down, the power of God and the wisdom of God, the image of the invisible God, and the firstborn of every creature.

My Lord and My God

The apostle Thomas gave us the confidence to call Jesus God. The Apostle John recorded that Thomas called Jesus God and Jesus responded positively. This is our only assurance that the resurrected Jesus accepted the title of God before departing for heaven.

> And Thomas answered and said unto Him, "My Lord and my God." Instantly came the acceptance. Jesus said unto him, "Thomas, because thou hast seen me, thou hast believed [that I am God]; blessed are they that have not seen, and yet have believed."
>
> John 20:28-29

Is there any reason anybody who calls himself a follower of Jesus would be hesitant to call Jesus God? We have even seen that calling Jesus God has its own blessings. If you want this blessing, believe in your heart that Jesus is God. If, because of religion, you harbour doubt in your heart over the deity of Jesus, you will not only deny yourself of this blessing, but you make Him a liar and incur wrath for yourself. The Muslims said that Jesus did not claim to be God but that the church adopted the title for Him. I have also heard Christians express such views. This is the manifestation of the spirit of religion in its fullest. If Jesus is not God, He would have admonished Thomas for calling Him God. He accepted being called God. Why are we, His followers, reluctant to acknowledge Him as such? Why should religion be our standard? There is a purpose for all the apostles, I acknowledge. From Thomas, we have the confidence to call Jesus God; through Thomas, we have the boldness to tell the world that Jesus is the only way to the Father,; the only truth that can set free, and the only life that can be lived with the Father. This is how a hymn titled "The Way, Truth and Life" by G.W. Doane (1797) summarizes it:

> Thou are the way, the truth, and the life;
> Grant us that way to know,
> That truth to keep, the life to win.

YHVH is the Hebrew name of God that is translated *Lord* in English. It is used for *God* in the Old Testament more often than any other name, about seven thousand times. Unfortunately, the English Bible did not make provisions for the different names of God appropriate to the occasion, such as Yahweh, Elohim as found in the original Greek or Hebrew script, but use the general name God in almost all instances. This has brought confusion to many Christians who think that everyone who believes in one god is faithful to God.

This name is referred to as the *tetragrammation*, which Encarta Dictionaries defines as a four-letter Hebrew name for God revealed to Moses:

> And God said to Moses, "I Am That I Am," and he said, "Thus shalt thou say unto the children of Israel, 'I Am hath sent me unto you." God said YHVH [all written in capital letters] is His eternal name and should be preserved for all generations... "This is my name forever and this is my memorial unto all generations."
>
> Exodus 13:14-15

By not adhering to this instruction, we have brought upon ourselves the misunderstanding that anything that answers to *god* is YHVH, pronounced Jehovah or Yahweh. Abuse God to any extent, and the Muslims do not care or get offended; abuse Yahweh or Jehovah, whichever you like to call Him, to any extent, and the Muslim is glad. Try to make a Muslim feel that you have abused his Allah, and see him declare war against you. Because we have become comfortable with the general name *God*, we have been lured into accepting anyone that worships anything that goes by that name as a brother or sister in faith.

The same Lord who revealed Himself as YHVH in the Old Testament has revealed Himself as Yeshua (Jesus) in the New Testament. Jesus shares the same attributes as YHVH and clearly claims to be Him and called Himself so: "Verily, verily, I say unto you, before Abraham was, I Am" (John 8:58). Paul certainly drew his confidence in declaration of Romans 10:9 from this fact that Jesus called Himself *I Am* (YHVH), translated *Lord* in English.

> That if thou shall confess with thy mouth the Lord (YHVH) Jesus and shall believe in thy heart that God [Elohim, God of Power] hath raised Him from the dead, thou shall be saved.
>
> Romans 10: 9

True to character, Paul did not leave us in doubt regarding this powerful declaration but brought into our mind a confirmation by quoting the Old Testament prophecy of Joel in Romans 10:13

> For whosoever shall call upon the name of the Lord (YHVH) shall be saved.
>
> Joel 2: 32

The same Jesus, the way, the truth, and the life, is the Lord, the I Am, the *tetragrammation*—YHVH. Jesus came into this world to reveal YHAH, called Jaweh or Jehovah, the God of the Bible, and also to remove from our memories other native gods that dominated the heart of men. Any deviation from this God, as presented in the Bible, no matter how small, has introduced another god. In A.W. Tozer's book, *Knowledge of the Holy*, we find eighteen characteristics of Yahweh as recorded in the Bible. We shall use them here to examine how Jesus fits into the characteristics of Yahweh and why believers should not entertain any hesitation to call Him such.

Attributes of God: His Characteristics

Wisdom: Encarta Dictionaries defines *wisdom* with the following words:

1. *The ability to make sensible decisions and judgments based on personal knowledge.* Let us look at the case of the woman accused of adultery in the Bible and see how Jesus exhibited sensible decision and judgment without consultation. Did He meet the attribute of God regarding wisdom here or not?

2. *Good sense shown in the way of thinking, judgement, and action.* When the Pharisees came to trap Jesus into offending Caesar or His father over the tribute money after, with their own mouths, they had told Him the coin bears Caesar's head, He answered them, "Give to Caesar what belongs to Caesar and God what belongs to God."

A.W. Tozer says, "Wisdom is the ability to devise perfect ends and to achieve these ends by the most perfect means."

Had Jesus started His ministry with power as the devil wanted, by asking Him to turn stones into bread, the gospel would not have been a gospel of humility, whose weakness in all physical ramifications made manifest the strength of God. The world would have been saying that the gospel of Jesus survived out of physical manifestation of strength if He had come as a conquering Messiah. But unlike Islam, the gospel survived under the greatest odds, in absolute physical weakness, giving the glory of its survival entirely to God. This is wisdom.

Holiness: How many preachers talk about holiness today? You cannot talk about God without holiness, for He is holy. This is the one attribute that sets God apart from all His creation. It refers to His absolute purity in all aspects. No sin can be found in Him. Wherever God establishes His presence becomes holy. This we also see in Jesus. His birth was holy. His death place, a place of abomination, becomes a holy ground. His cross, a curse, becomes a holy relic. His body, the church, become the Holy Catholic.

Faithfulness: Do you have the spirit of discernment to know the difference between the voice of the devil and the voice of God? If you have, you will agree with me that there is never anything God has promised you that did not come to pass. He does not lie. He does not deceive. He does not cheat. Jesus did not only exhibit this attribute but also claimed it when he said that He is the truth. This attribute of Jesus is very important to every true Christian, because it is our hope. Paul reminded us that if our hope is what we are seeing now, that of all men, we are the most miserable. The assurance that our sins are forgiven and of a life with Him in eternity is anchored on His faithfulness.

Omnipotence: Encarta Dictionaries defines this word as *all powerful; possessing complete, unlimited or universal power and authority.* My personal name for Jesus is Power Pass Power. "Have you come to destroy us before our time?" the demons in the legion asked Jesus. He has the power to destroy them at will, but due to His faithfulness, because He had already given them time for their destruction, He let them live in the swine that got drowned. Where are the gods of Ephesus—the great Diana of Acts 19:36; where are the gods of Athens that stirred Paul's spirit in Acts 17:16; where are the gods of Rome, after their encounter with Jesus? This attribute of Jesus is our assurance that we are saved from the hands of the enemy once we turn to Jesus, irrespective of our past. Read this story which I made up from fragments of pulpit messages, and you will appreciate my impression of this power and how it becomes available and effective:

A young man built a nice mansion for himself. He knows Jesus because, like many he goes to church. So one day, Jesus visited him in his mansion. He was glad and offered Jesus a room in his beautiful mansion. In the night, the devil came and knocked on the young man's door. He opened as usual, but instead of their usual monotone dialog, the devil started beating him mercilessly. The next morning, Jesus came down and met him at the sitting room. He asked Jesus why He did not do anything when the devil was beating him last night. Jesus answered him and said, "You have ten rooms in this house with this big sitting room. I came, and you offered me only one room; you have nine, so you are the boss. How can I come to defend you when you have already considered me inferior to you?"

The young man apologized and gave Jesus five rooms and took five and shared the sitting room for both. In the night, the devil knocked, came in, and started beating him mercilessly again. The next morning, he complained to Jesus that He did not come to rescue him when he has already given him half of his house.

Jesus replied to him and said, "But we are equal in your sight, so what do you think that I could have done that you could not do? I have five rooms, and you have five rooms. By your judgment, we are equal, so I could not have helped you."

The young man said, "Okay, Lord, take nine rooms, including the sitting room, but let me keep my master bedroom only."

In the night, the devil came and beat him up again mercilessly. The next morning, he complained to Jesus, saying, "Why didn't you come and rescue me from the devil, when I have given you so much as all my house except my very master bedroom?"

Jesus answered him and said, "How can I come when you have already excluded me from your room? You gave me all the rooms except your room, and I could not come in there to rescue you without being an intruder, which my nature does not allow." The young man now gave Jesus his entire house and asked Him to show him where to sleep. Jesus asked him to sleep in any room he wanted. That night the devil did not come. The next morning, he asked Jesus, saying, "I didn't know when you went out to stop the devil from coming. He didn't come and did not beat me last night."

Jesus said to him, "The devil is wise; he knows that this house belongs to me now and all that are in it, and he dare not show up. As long as this house remains mine, he can never come." This is the kind of power Jesus is associated with, power that scares the devil to hell, his abode.

Omniscience: This attribute means that God is all knowing and does not have need to learn. Jesus knows everything, did not learn from anybody, and never consults anybody. Even the wise men from east that came to see Him as an infant worshipped his knowledge. His community was shocked at His knowledge of all things, more so when they were aware that He had been there with them all along, not learning from anybody. "So where did He learn all these?" they marvelled. A.W. Tozer, in his book *The Knowledge of the Holy*, says, "God possesses perfect knowledge and therefore has no need to learn. God has never learned and cannot learn."

Infinitude: This is an expression of something being infinite in nature. God does not know any boundaries, whether of sex, race, continent, or country. He cannot be quantified or measured. This is an attribute of God that imparts on all other attributes of His. In the Great Commission, Jesus did not draw any boundary, but to all nations of the world.

Sovereignty: The sovereignty of God is in no doubt to any Christian. That is why the Bible tells us to give thanks to God in all situations. We are never to ask Him questions. This command Jesus made very clear to us. The sovereignty of Jesus is not in any doubt. In reply to their accusation that He was acting and encouraging His followers to act in an above-the-law manner, He questioned the Pharisees why they countered the commandment of God by their tradition, irrespective of the fact that he is also a Jew and the same tradition is supposed to be binding on Him. He separated Himself from the Jewish tradition because he is sovereign.

Trinity: Granted, this term is not found in the Bible, but it is greatly implied. It is the wisdom of God that put it into our minds. The Bible clearly shows that the Almighty God, even by name, Elohim is plural in existence. The name *Elohim* is a plural name for one entity; that is why we read in the Bible, "And Elohim said Let us make man in our image..." (Genesis 1:26). Here, God reveals Himself in three persons: the Father, the Son, and the Holy Spirit. The essence of Trinity is that though God reveals Himself in three persons, He is one indivisible God. The function of one is the duty and responsibility of the three.

Self-Existence: The Bible says that God was there from the beginning. That means that He has no *beginning*, in the human sense of the word. The same is said of Jesus in Genesis and Hebrews, concerning Melchizedek, who prefigured Him.

Immutability: This implies that God never changes. And it is said of Jesus: "Jesus Christ is the same yesterday, today, and forever" (Hebrews 13:8).

Self-Sufficiency: The Bible, in John 5:26, tells us that God has life in Himself. He does not need our help in anything, does not need our gifts and sacrifices. But for His desire to relate with us, He permits and encourages us to be part of promoting His work on earth. This is true of Jesus while here on earth. We never read that He solicited for anything except our salvation. When the then authorities asked Him for tax, He never asked for donations, He never asked Judas the treasurer how much they had, but asked Peter to get money from fish and pay. When the multitudes were hungry, He never asked for contributions, but made food abundant for all.

Mercy: Nehemiah described God as slow to anger and merciful. Mercy is the attribute of God that makes Him active in our spiritual and physical healing. It is the compassionate side of God. Mercy is the character of Jesus while here on earth. The New Testament is full of the healing miracles of Jesus. The Bible tells us that most are out of compassion.

Omnipresence: Encarta Dictionaries defines *omnipresence* as *always present every where, continuously and simultaneously throughout the whole creation.* "I am with you always" is repeated twenty-two times in the Old and New Testaments, for both God and Jesus. Have you at any time in a nightmare called out "Jesus"? At that very time, thousands of others did the same, and He answered all, just as He answered you. Any wonder that there is only one Holy Spirit in God, unlike in the kingdom of Satan, who is not omnipresent, where many spirits must exist to represent him at different places and occasions.

Goodness: A.W. Tozer wrote, "The goodness of God is that which disposes Him to be kind, cordial, benevolent, and full of good will toward men." Remember the song "Goodness and Mercy Shall Follow Me All the Days of My Life." This attribute is seen in all the ways Jesus related to people that have had encounters with Him.

Love: Love is such important attribute of God that the Bible, through the Apostle John, informs us that God's other name is Love: "God is Love." Can there ever be any greater expression of love than is found in Jesus? Apart from giving His life as atonement for the sins of others, the ultimate love, we see His entire life as an expression of love—not love of emotion but of action. He even made love a new commandment to His followers. He expressed love in His parable of the Good Samaritan. Who can be a greater love than YHAH, the Lord Jesus?

Gracious: The Bible makes it clear that it is by grace that we are saved. Our righteousness is like a filthy rag before God. Yes, the song by John Newton comes into mind. Go ahead and sing; don't be afraid, for you are not alone; you can hear Paul at the background; you can hear Matthew, the former tax collector at the background. C.S. Lewis has joined the chorus, and I have joined too.

> Amazing grace,
> How sweet the sound,
> that saves a wretch like me
> I once was lost, but now am found:
> was blind, but now I see.
> T'was grace that taught my heart to fear.
> And grace my fears relieved
> How precious did that grace appear
> The hour I first believed.

The remaining two attributes, *Justice* and *Eternal*, have been embodied into the sixteen above.

Let us, at a glance, from one instance in the Bible, take a case study on how Jesus demonstrates the entire attributes of YHAH (Jehovah), which in English is translated *Lord*.

> And the scribes and Pharisees brought unto him a woman taken in adultery, and when they had set her in the midst, they said unto him, "Master, this woman was taken in adultery, in the very act. Now Moses in the Law commanded us that such should be stoned: but what sayest thou?" But Jesus stooped down and with his finger wrote on the ground, as though he heard them not. So when they continued asking him, he lifted up himself and said unto them, "He that is without sin among you, let

him first cast a stone at her." ...When Jesus had lifted up himself and saw none but the woman, he said unto her, "Woman, where are those thine accusers? Hath no man condemned thee?" And she said, "No man, Lord." And Jesus said unto her, "Neither do I condemn thee. Go and sin no more."

John 8: 3-10

This is a very familiar story in the Bible, the story of the woman taken in adultery. Let me first try to list out some significant lessons of this passage, and we shall look at it to see how Jesus divinely demonstrates the characteristics of God.

1. Lessons of the woman taken in adultery, John 8: 3-7:

2. She was caught in the act, according to the passage above. So where was the man? Human prejudice that Jesus could not condone.

3. There was a standing sentence given by Moses; by seeking Jesus's opinion, have the leaders of Israel apparently accepted that Jesus is greater than Moses and could override his judgement, as He did here?

4. Jesus ignored them and continued to write on the ground. Have you not heard people say that Jesus was not lettered? How come He could write? A non-lettered person could read his local alphabets but not write. So from here, we know that Jesus is lettered. I am convinced that if He came into the world today, He would pick up a computer and do whatever anybody can do with computer. He does not need to be thought anything. "And the Jews marvelled, saying How knoweth this man letters, having never learned" (John 7:15).

a deeper evangelism

5. God's Word, according to Moses, says she should be stoned to death, but God's way as revealed by Jesus says she should be shown mercy. Is God's Word in conflict with His way? No, but due to our often-faulty interpretations of His Word, there is need for us to always seek for His way to confirm His Word anytime we are in doubt.

6. We must heed to His way at any time His Word, in our limited understanding, contradicts His Way, because His way is like a picture that cannot be misinterpreted, but His Word is a reference, which is subject to our misinterpretations.

7. *Go and sin no more.* This is the main picture of God's way in this passage—sin no more, forgiveness and sanctification. We can see that there is no contradiction between His Word and His way here. The same Word of God tells us that God is ready to pardon and slow to anger. That is what His way shows here. If not for His character of mercy, she deserves to die. His way demonstrated here another of His character: just; she was caught in the very act. Where is the man? That is the Infinite God.

Now that we have taken the lessons of this passage, let us look at how Jesus demonstrated the entire attributes of God in this one instant.

Wisdom: Let us take the definitions of *wisdom* as we saw in the attributes of God and see how wisdom of God was exhibited by Jesus in this case study. If wisdom is the ability to make sensible decisions and judgements, as according to dictionaries, and the ability to devise perfect ends and to achieve these ends by most perfect means, as according to A. W. Tozer, then Jesus demonstrated this attribute of God perfectly well in our case study. He handed down a judgment based on the wisdom and Way of God rather than that of man—Moses.

Holiness: The fact that the scribes and Pharisees brought this woman to Him is a testimony from them that He is holy. He will not condone sin of adultery or any other for that matter; He will not ask to kill anybody. "Whichever way, we shall fault Him," they must have reasoned.

Faithfulness: What do you think brought these men, no woman, together, apart from those who came to tempt Jesus—the scribes and Pharisees? Not necessarily to hear what Jesus would say on the matter, because they had been conducting themselves in this stoning manner before. What gathered them was their zeal to do the work of God, according to their understanding of Moses's commandment. "For Moses in the Law commanded we that such should be stoned." When their conscience exposed their hypocrisy and prejudice, they disappeared from the scene without any regret. But Jesus remained faithful unto her and granted her forgiveness as promised in God's Word.

Omnipotence. Dictionaries define *omnipotence* as possessing complete, unlimited, or universal power. The scribes and Pharisees were very certain of Jesus's powers, hence consulting Him in matters concerning the Law of Moses. But power cannot be said to be complete, unlimited, and universal if it is limited to what we can see. Jesus here demonstrated the ultimate power: the power to forgive sin, which is the prerogative of God alone.

Omniscience: Have you not heard people refer to Jesus as uneducated because of a comment in Mark's gospel that His people showed surprise about His knowledge because they did not see Him going to school to learn? Jesus, we all agree, is all knowing and was not taught by anybody. Here, Jesus exhibited knowledge of the educated; He was writing on the ground as they struggled for His attention.

Infinitude: The men, no woman, brought the adulterous woman before Jesus. She was caught "in the very act"; that means the man was also caught with her but freed based on human finitude of gender. Jesus is no human like us, but as God, His attitude to the case study here goes beyond finite. "Woman, you did not commit adultery alone; you will not be stoned alone, but your sins are forgiven you. Do not sin again." What about the man, who finitude of man tended to protect? If he was wise, he would have looked for Jesus to seek for his own forgiveness too; otherwise, he remained condemned. Jesus is infinite. No man or woman, no race, no boundaries.

Sovereignty: His judgement was not questioned, even when, to them, it contradicted the Law given to them by Moses. His sovereignty was established.

Trinity: The Law was given to Moses by God the Father, and God the Son put God's face into it in this matter before Him, and the mob received it in obedience through the power of the Holy Spirit; the woman was left free.

Look for the rest of the attributes, self existence, immortality, self-sufficiency, mercy, omnipresence, goodness, love, gracious, and justice, and see if any is missing in Him under this case study. If you found any apparently missing, read the passage over and over, and you cannot miss it.

Attributes of God are not all that merry in heavenly places. There is the bitter side for those who prefer that side of Him.

Wrath. This is God's attribute many Christians will prefer to ignore and rationalize as not consistent with the divine nature of God. We cannot wish it away. The Bible makes this attribute a clear characteristic of God.

> See now that I even I am he and there is no god with me: I kill and I make alive: I wound and I heal: neither is there any that can deliver out of my hand. For I lift up

my hand to heaven, and say. I live forever. If I whet my glittering sword and mine hand take hold on judgment: I will reward them that hate me. I will make my arrows drunk with blood and my sword shall devour flesh and with the blood of the slain and of the captives, from the beginning of revenges upon the enemy.

Deuteronomy 32:39-42

Some Christians will explain away this attribute of God as that of the Old Testament God, as if the God of the New Testament is different. A careful study of a Bible concordance will reveal that there is more reference in both the Old and New Testaments to the wrath, anger, and fury of God than there are His love, mercy, and tenderness. This, more than any other, exposes Him and His nature for our interest; He is holy and abhors sin: "God judgeth the righteous, and God is angry with the wicked every day" (Psalm 7:11).

How could He have defended His other attributes if He shows indifference to sin? How can God, who is infinitely holy, disregard sin? How can God, who delights only in what is pure, loathe and hate not that which is impure? His very nature is a clear indication of the existence of hell. The wrath of God is eternal manifestation of His detestation of all unrighteousness. Wrath is the projection of God's holiness that stirs Him into activity against sin.

For the wrath of God is revealed from heaven against all ungodliness and unrighteousness of men, who hold the truth in unrighteousness."

Romans1:18

This is how Robert Haldane (1764-1842) synopsized Bible account of God's wrath:

It was revealed when the sentence of death was first pronounced, the earth cursed, and man driven out of the earthly paradise: and afterwards by such examples of punishment as those of the deluge and the destruction of the cities of the plain by fire from heaven; by the reign of death throughout the world. It was proclaimed in the curse of the law on every transgression, and was intimated in the institution of sacrifice. In the 8th of Romans, the apostle calls the attention of believers to the fact that the whole creation has become subject to vanity, and groaneth and travaileth together in pain. The same creation which declares that there is a God, and publishes His glory, also proclaims that He is the enemy of sin and the Avenger of the crimes of men… But above all, the wrath of God was revealed from heaven when the Son of God came down to manifest the divine character, and when that wrath was displayed in His sufferings and death, in a manner more awful than by all the tokens God had before given of His displeasure against sin. Besides this, the future and eternal punishment of the wicked is now declared in terms more solemn and explicit than formerly. Under the new dispensation, there are two revelations given from heaven, one of wrath, the other of grace.

Robert Holdane captures the essence of God's wrath in this quote. But more importantly, he highlights a new dispensation in God's relationship with human. He graphically illustrates how the revelation of God's wrath came to a climax by sacrificing His Son to show that He can sacrifice anything against sin. Robert concludes that this supreme sacrifice against sin by God has given individuals the choice between God's wrath and His Grace. This quote stands firm as a synopsis of the Gospel. We have chosen God's Grace, and it is imperative that we must abide by its rules.

Let us see how Jesus demonstrated this attribute of wrath in

The fig tree in Matthew 21:18-19:

1. Now in the morning as he returned to into the city, he hungered. And when he saw a fig tree in the way, he came to it and found nothing thereon, but leaves only and said to it "Let no fruit grow on thee henceforward for ever." And presently the fig tree withered.

This is the kind of wrath we should expect from Him when, instead of bearing fruits as He expects of us, we allow Him to meet us empty.

2. When Jesus entered into the temple in Jerusalem, He was grieved by what He saw and poured His wrath on the offenders. "And Jesus went into the temple of God and cast out all them that sold and bought in the temple, and overthrew the tables of the moneychangers and the seats of them that sold doves" (Matthew 21:12).

3. In Act of Apostles, we saw how the wrath of God was delivered to a husband and wife named Ananias and Sapphira for lying to God the Holy Spirit.

But a certain man named Ananias with Sapphira his wife sold a possession and kept back part of the price; his wife also being privy to it, and brought a certain part and laid it at the apostle feet. But Peter said, "Ananias, why hath Satan filled thine heart to lie to the Holy Ghost and to keep part of the price of the land?" ...Ananias, hearing these words, fell down and gave up the ghost.

Act 5:1-5

Wrath of God in the New Testament is as real as it is in the Old Testament. Don't let anybody deceive you, for God is never mocked.

I Am the Life

Life is a general term used to summarize the activities and characteristics of all organisms, varying from the smallest forms, such as cyanobactria (formerly known as blue-green algal), to plants and animals. This is where we may have thought life to end if Thomas did not get out the real understanding of it from the Master, Jesus Christ.

Apostle John, in his first Epistle General, described this life as what they saw and bore witness of.

> That which was from the beginning, which we have heard, which we have seen with our eyes, which we have looked upon and our hands have handled, of the Word of Life.
>
> 1 John 1:1.

In the next verse, he wrote, "For the Life was manifested and we have seen it, and bear witness and shew unto you that eternal Life."

Paul started his account in Romans 8 with, "There is therefore now no condemnation to them which are in Christ Jesus" (Romans 8:1).

This is to say that a life in the Life is incorruptible even after the physical body has perished.

Cults and religions tend to prosper in times of social and economic instability, as we are witnessing today. They tend to offer members spurious solutions to their many problems, promising them salvation as well as a sense of social security in being a member of a group. The communal lifestyle practiced by these religions usually appeals to people who see it as pleasing to their god. We must be bold to challenge these institutions and religious movements. Members of these movements have been known to drop out of school, abandon career goals, and adopt a full-time life in unfamiliar religious settings. These movements sometimes require their members to wear strange-looking garments, follow unusual habits, chant at specific times, or take new names.

The opposite of Life is death. Paul defined for us those that are in Life and those that are in death.

> For to be carnally mined is death but to be spiritually minded is Life and peace.
>
> Romans 8:6

> Paul defined *death* as *the wage for sin* and *Life* as *the gift of God through Jesus Christ*: "For the wages of sin is death; but the gift of God is eternal life through Jesus Christ" (Romans 6:23).

In the first epistle of John, he writes, "...and the whole world lieth in wickedness" (5:19b).

The people of this world live in wickedness, but the people of God shall overcome their wickedness. This is the promise of God. Earlier in 1 John 2:8, the apostle told us that the true light is already shining, and in verse 13, that those who are following Jesus have overcome this wicked one. In verse 12 of the same chapter 5, he writes, "He that has the Son has life and he that has not the Son of God has no life" (1 John 5:12).

Here he defines the two categories of the people of verse 19. The people who have Jesus have Life, and those who do not have Jesus have death.

> For God so loves the world, that He gave His only begotten son, that whosoever believes in Him should not perish, but have everlasting life.
>
> John 3:16

I cannot remember the source, but I read something some time ago that says, "There is the smell of death in anything that is outside Jesus." That is what John has told us here. There is no in between. Jesus is life; no Jesus equals death without any possibility of survival. That you believe there is God is not enough; who does not?

> Thou believes that there is one God; you do well (thank you, *grazia*), but the devil also believed and trembled.
>
> James 2:19

You may not even have trembled in your belief that there is God, in which case, the devil is one step ahead of you toward God!

So what kind of life are we talking about here? We have mentioned two kinds: *life* as a general term, used to summarize the activities and characteristics of all organisms, and *Life* that only those who are in Jesus Christ are entitled to. The former is for all living things; the latter is for selected or chosen humans only. One can have the former, the latter, or both. He who has the latter only has no less than he who has both.

> In hope of eternal life which God that cannot lie promised before the world began.
>
> Titus 1:2

But he who has the former only has no life at all, because the former started and ended in first Adam, and the latter begins in Jesus Christ, the second Adam: "For as in Adam all die, so in Christ all will be made alive"(1 Corinthians 15:22).

The other day, I saw a caterpillar, on the ground. I picked up a stick and held it above it, but it continued at its sluggish crawl. I brought the stick down almost to its body—no change in movement. And I said, "You think you have life when I could just kill you now without effort." A fly would have darted off. The butterfly would have flown off, but not this. Anyone, anything, would just kill it at will without any form of defense or attempt to escape. That is what we are when our life is as of the former: a vapor. It reminds me of a Jewish adage that says, "If you want to give God a good laugh, tell Him your plans for tomorrow."

If you have the latter, a Life in the Son of God, the Christ, you have life eternal, a life of no end. That is the reason the early Roman Christians called the catacombs *koimeteria*, meaning *sleeping place*. The Christian's body in the catacomb is sleeping and not dead, because he or she lives forever in Christ.

Reminds me again of a woman who queued up on the widows' line in a relief center for Red Cross handouts. The husband saw her on that line and walked to her in surprise and told her that she was on the widows' line. But she replied, "Are you alive?" Think of the embarrassment. Do not let yourself be embarrassed the same way. As a Christian, you must live the Life of Christ. You must not only be alive but let others know that you are.

So what qualifies us for this life? I am not going into the theology of sanctification and all that, but the Bible says that we must be born-again in Christ to receive this life. We must look up to Jesus, the author and finisher of our faith, for it.

The Bible says, "For the wages of sin is death, but the gift of God is eternal life through Jesus Christ" (Romans 6:23).

This brings to my mind the life cycle of the butterfly. A butterfly undergoes metamorphosis that involves four stages: egg, larva or caterpillar, pupa, and adult. The female butterfly lays eggs that hatch caterpillars. The caterpillar eats and grows. That is what I will compare with living here on earth. We are in this present world like the caterpillar in the lifecycle of the butterfly, sluggish and limited in mobility, in vision, and in knowledge of God's will. At a point, the caterpillar metamorphose into pupa, molts, stops growth and eating, looks filthy and dirty as if dead, and, in fact, is inside a cocoon that serves as its coffin. This pupa stage, compares with the end of life of a man in this world. The final stage is the beautiful butterfly, from the immobile eyesore pupa. Those who lived a life in Christ are transformed at the end of their earthly sojourn into a glorious liberty of beauty and freedom into that pavilion of splendor, where they meet face to face with the Master.

The heaviest weight on our foot that works against us in matching into a life in Jesus is pride. C.S. Lewis, in *Mere Christianity*, writes, "A proud man is always looking down on things and people; and of course, as long as you are looking down, you cannot see something that is above."

The Bible tells us the consequence of pride in the story of Nebuchadnezzar.

> But when his heart was lifted up, and his mind hardened, in pride, he was disposed from his Kingly throne, and they took his glory from him.
>
> Daniel 5:20

It was pride that led to the banishment of Nebuchadnezzar into the wilderness, where he dwelled with asses until he knew "the most high God."

We must obtain and preserve this life, just as a soldier in a physical battle field raises up all his senses and weapons to protect his physical life. So must we also take up all spiritual weapons God has provided us in absolute sobriety to protect our life in Christ Jesus. We are in the battle field like any soldier. Our war is not of flesh and blood, but is spiritual. Peter reminded us that we must be sober at all times if we must not lose our guard against the evil one and lose our life in Jesus to the enemy.

> Be sober, be vigilant, because your adversary the devil as a
> roaring lion walking about, seeking whom he may devour.
>
> 1 Peter 5:8

One of the many ways to avoid this roaring lion is to disarm him with the truth. Jesus tells us that we must go beyond the righteousness of the Pharisee if we must meet Him in paradise.

> Except your righteousness shall exceed the righteousness
> of the scribe and Pharisee, ye shall in no case enter into the
> kingdom of heaven.
>
> Matthew 5:20

Your ten percent tithe is not enough; the Pharisees do the same. Church attendance is not enough; you cannot be more regular than the scribes and the Pharisees. Your zeal in the work of God is mere hypocrisy if it carries the same weight as that of the Pharisees. Saul was a typical example of the zeal of a Pharisee toward the work of God. You must be born again; you must be born again in Christ. There is nothing you can give God that He does not have or cannot get without you if He desires it—except your Will.

> For the earth is the Lord's and the fullness thereof.
>
> Psalm 24:1, 1 Corinthians 10:26

As long as you have not given Him your will, which is the only thing He cannot get without your consent, you have not given Him anything.

Our born-again life must reflect on how we conduct our physical life, support, affairs, or our business. We are told in Romans 12:11 not to be slothful in the way we pursue our livelihood. The

Bible warns us of the danger of becoming too familiar with the world and her antecedents.

Paul writes to the Corinthians, "…providing for honest things not only in the sight of the Lord but also in the sight of men"(2 Corinthians 8:21).

The message here is that the devil is not omnipresent like God. He sees us through our interaction with others. He comes to us based on what he heard from others or what he sees when we are in the vicinity of his vision. Then he would size up his target and determine whether or not to attack.

> Submit yourselves therefore to God. Resist the devil, and he will flee from you.
>
> James 4:7

We must be of a balanced mind always, not ever to be influenced by our material surroundings.

> Thou shall not respect persons, neither take a gift (questionable one, I suppose), for a gift do blind the eyes of the wise and pervert the words of the righteous.
>
> Deuteronomy 16:19

> Avoid those described in the Bible as "whose end is destruction, whose God is their belly (greed) and whose glory is in their shame, who mind earthly things."
>
> Phillipians 3:19

Do not envy such persons, for you know not what miseries they are presently passing through as conditions imposed on them by the devil and what awaits them in future under God's judgment. The Bible says: "Be not deceived, God is not mocked for whatever a man soweth, that shall he also reap"(Galatians 6:7).

At all times, remember that Jesus prayed for you while on earth in John 17.

> I pray for them I pray not for the world…(9)
> I pray not that thou shouldest take them out of the world, but that thou shouldest keep them from the evil one (15)
> Neither pray I for these alone, but for them also which shall believe on me through their word. (20)

He is still there at the right hand of the Father praying for you. Above all, we must realize that.

> We wrestle not against flesh and blood, but against principalities, against powers, and against the rulers of the darkness of this world, against spiritual wickedness in high places.
>
> Ephesians 6:12

What are we supposed to do if we must win the battle and continue with life in Jesus Christ? We are more than equipped for the battle.

Ever heard about the Israeli-Arab six-day war of 1967? Look at Israel and look at the whole of Arabia. In six days, Israel humiliated them. That is how swift your victory over the devil will be if you equip yourself with the proper weapons.

> Above all, taking the shield of faith wherewith ye shall be able to quench all the fiery darts of the wicked. And take the helmet of salvation, and the sword of the spirit which is the word of God.
>
> Ephesians 6:16-17

Of all the weapons we are asked to have for our warfare, the only one Paul explained is the Bible, which he called the sword of the Spirit. Can you remember how many battles you have won with the Bible? Uncountable, both the ones you know and the ones you do not know. In one of the services I attended in Latter Rain church, Pastor Tunde Bakare declared that service a thanksgiving service to God for things that did not happen. After that service, I realized the meaning of 1 Thessalonians 4:18: "In everything give thanks, for this is the will of God in Christ Jesus concerning you."

There cannot be a better lesson to the Christian than this, especially when combined with Romans 8:28, that says, "All things work together for good to them that love God, who are called according to his purpose."

Have you ever asked, "Why me?" Then think about the ones that did not happen. Remember the story of the footprints in the sand; you were walking with God, and the four footprints of the two of you showed clearly along the pathway. As you were reviewing the walk, you suddenly noticed that the footprints somewhere on the journey became a pair only. *Where was God at this dangerous point of the journey? Why did He abandon me here?* you asked, and God answered, "At that point, it became so dangerous that I have to carry you. That is why you are seeing only a pair of footprints; they are mine." That is what happens to those who have life in Christ Jesus. God carries them on His shoulder when the going becomes too dangerous. Where do you belong? You will not know how far away you are from Jesus Christ until you give your life to Him. For those of us who were born into real Christian homes, it is usually difficult to draw the line between when we gave our life to Jesus and when we were merely steering at Him in complacency or complete indifference.

In good old Nigeria, a good high school grade automatically secured you a teaching appointment in a secondary school. I was posted to teach mathematics and physics in Hussey College Warri. My salary was about ₦100.00 per month. Don't laugh; that was 1975, a Nigerian *Naira* was about two dollars then. Graduates were earning far higher, about ₦300.00. Even trained grade-two teachers in primary schools were earning higher than we were. I could not understand why we should earn so little in comparison with others who were doing exactly what we were doing. It was only when I got into a higher institution that I realized I was not even qualified to teach because I had not even mastered the subjects I was teaching well enough to effectively impact on another person.

This is what happens to you when you leave your complacent Christian life and enter into Life in Christ. You will realize how far away you have been to the source of Life. You will realize that there was no difference between you and the occult worshipper before you truly became born again. You will realize that your entire past life had been a mere hypocrisy. You will see how you have offended God by following the vain and sometimes fetish traditions of your people.

> Why do you also transgress the commandment of God with your tradition?
>
> Matthew 15:3

> Jesus must have been querying you, while appealing to you to "Absent from all appearance of evil."
>
> 1 Thessalonians 5:18

Don't stay and wait till you are convinced of appearance of evil before you run away. It might be too late.

Hope is not lost at all. The moment you have the boldness to cast away your past, you become a new person. The Bible says:

a deeper evangelism

Therefore, if a man be in Christ he is a new creature; old things are passed away; behold all things are made new.

2 Corinthians 5:17

Let that old man be crucified with Jesus and you will have a new life. "I am crucified with Christ, nevertheless I live yet, not I, but Christ liveth in me."

Galatians 2:20

Some Christians are still keeping one leg on their old relationship with the occult. Nothing can be a greater hindrance to a life in Jesus Christ than the abomination of occult worship. Do not be afraid of your past. Take up your cross and walk with Jesus. Drop any other spiritual relationship. You have become a new person authored by Jesus."Looking unto Jesus the author and finisher of our faith" (Hebrews 12:2).

He is waiting for you. Whatever has held you down will bow to Him at your will to follow Him. For the Bible says: "At the name of Jesus every knee should bow of things in heaven and things in earth and things under the earth" (Philippians 2:10).

It takes primitive boldness to join a cult, but it takes wisdom and courage to come to Jesus. That courage cannot be lacking if you truly look up to Him. The Bible says, "For He has not given us the spirit to fear but of power and love" (2 Timothy 1:7). "Behold, now is the accepted time; behold, now is the day of salvation" (2 Corinthians 6:2).

I Am the Truth

"There is no water in oxygen, no water in hydrogen; it comes bubbling fresh from under the imagination of the living God, rushing from under the great white throne of the glacier" (From *The Truth* by George MacDonald, C.S. Lewis edition).

"What is truth?" Pilate asked Jesus during His trial (John 18:38). This question came after Jesus told Pilate that everyone that is of the truth hears His voice. Different people are bound to respond to the gospel message differently, depending on whether or not one is of the truth. Paul, in his epistle to the Corinthians, wrote:

> But if our Gospel is hid, it is hid to them that are lost; In whom the god of this world hath blinded the minds of them which believe not, lest the light of the glorious gospel of Christ, who is the image of God, should shine unto them.
>
> 2 Corinthians 4:3-4

The truth is in the air, but those that have condemned themselves, not according to the wish of God but according to their own will, cannot hear it. The Pilates of today do not even wait to have an answer to the meaning of truth. Like Pilate, they walk out on Jesus after asking the question, "What is truth?" without waiting for answer. Some, like the Jerusalem mob that murdered Stephen, are annoyed by the truth and will resort to violence. Some, like the Athenians, will chose mockery and will begin to call the bearers of the truth names like they called Paul. Some, like those who stoned Stephen, will block their ears. In all, they who are of the truth find the truth, and the truth sets them free. So what is your relationship with the truth? Being a member of a church does not guarantee one the truth. John warns us in his first epistle, saying, "...if we say that we have fellowship with Him and walk in darkness, we lie and do not have the Truth."

I would like to dwell a little longer on the Athenians' response to the truth, as recorded in the Acts, because it beams a searchlight on the response of the world today and provides a contrast to the response in Berea, an out-of-way town about 70 km from

Thessalonica. From the two examples, you can locate your position, whether you are of Berea or of Athens.

This is how Paul got into Berea and the response to the truth there:

> And the brethren immediately sent away Paul and Silas by night into Berea, who coming thither went into the synagogue of the Jews. These [the Jews] were more noble than those in Thessalonica in that they received the Word with all readiness of mind, and searching the scriptures daily, whether those things were so. Therefore, many of them believed. Acts 17:10-12

This is how the Bible recorded the response of the Bereans to the truth. I would like to emphasize two points here. The Bereans received the truth with "all readiness"; no one of them was persuaded; no banners called them to come and hear the message that would end all their financial and material problems, no hand bills promised them breakthroughs in business or other ventures, no pictures on display with the inscription, "The long-awaited super miracle workers Paul and Silas are in town, come and get your miracle," no promise of lunch or dinner. No, none of these—a lesson I would like to recommend to evangelists.

The second point is their devotion and determination to discover the truth, hence "searching the scriptures daily, whether those things were so." The Bible made so many references as to how we should approach and respond to new witnesses and bearers of strange messages. The response of the Bereans was quite positive, but yet very cautious. They approached Paul and Silas willingly to know what message they came with—that Jesus is the Christ, who the Jews killed, but God resurrected Him from death, and he now is at the right hand of the Father, interceding for those who believe that He is the propitiator for their sins.

Opening and alleging, that Christ must needs have suffered, and raised again from the dead; and that this Jesus whom I preached to you is Christ.

Acts 17:3

This was Paul's response to their approach.

For the Bereans, there was need for caution. So they wanted scriptural evidence that the Christ must pass through these sufferings Paul and Silas told them Jesus went through, which of course, they must also have heard as happened in Jerusalem some few years back, probably as flying news. Paul and Silas gave scriptural references, and the Bereans, with assistance from Paul and the other Jews who were familiar with the scripture, daily searched for and found confirmations:

"… the assembly of the wicked have inclosed me; they have pierced my hands and my feet…they part with my garments among them and cast lots upon my vesture.

Psalm 22:16-18

From the prophet Isaiah, they searched and found; "… he is despised and rejected of men, a man of sorrow, and acquainted with grief; and we hid as it were our faces from Him; He was despised and we esteemed Him not."

Isaiah 53:3

But He was wounded for our transgression, he was bruised for our iniquities; the chastisement of our peace was upon Him; and with His stripes we are healed.

Isaiah 53:5

a deeper evangelism

And he made His grave with the wicked and with the rich in his death; because He had done no violence, neither was any deceit in His mouth.

Isaiah 53:9

From the Scripture, the truth was revealed to the Bereans. There cannot be any better approach than this. The apostles Peter and John require us to investigate any new teaching or doctrine or preacher before we jump along.

Be sober, be vigilant, because your adversary, the devil, as a roaring lion is walking about seeking whom he may devour.

1 Peter 6:8

Beloved, believe not every spirit, but try the spirit whether they are of God, because many false prophets are gone into the world.

1 Jonah 4:1.

This was what the Bereans did, and they received the blessings of the truth, a rich harvest for God from a right approach that illuminated and fortified their minds.

The question may then be why the Jews, whose minds have been illuminated by the same scriptures long before the Bereans were, are still unable to recognize the truth. The Bible gives us the answer. Paul wrote in 2 Corinthians:

Seeing that we have much hope, we use much plainness of speech; And not as Moses, which put a veil over his face, that the children of Israel could not steadfastly look to the end of that which is abolished; But their minds were blinded; for until this day, remaineth the same veil untaken away in the reading of the Old Testament; which

veil is done away in Christ. But even until this day, when
Moses is read, the veil is upon their heart.

2 Corinthians 3:12-15

This passage answers a lot of questions, such as why the Jews
were and still are reluctant in accepting the truth. First, we must
know that God did not instruct Moses to veil himself. Dr. Tunde
Bakere, the pastor of the Latter Rain church, a congregation of
over ten thousand people, described the veil of Moses as a cata-
ract on the hearts of the Jews. How correct and precise. The Jews
have been reading the scriptures hundreds of years before Christ
manifested in flesh. The Jews have been reading the Scriptures
thousands of years after Christ departed this earth. Yet they have
not as a community recognized the truth, so detailed in their
everyday way of life—the Scripture—of the account of Moses
about the Christ, the account of King David concerning the
Christ, and the account of the prophets about the Christ. Paul
said "till this day," meaning that even now, as I am writing this
message, the veil of Moses is still hiding the truth from the collective Jew as a people. Thank God we cannot say this of all Jews,
even at the time of Paul. The reason for this is also in the Bible:
"Nevertheless, when it shall turn to the Lord, the veil shall be
taken away" (2 Corinthians 3:16).

When I first became aware that Benny Hinn is a Jew, I went
into convulsions with joy, and when I recovered, I went straight
to this passage for reassurance. I once listened to Benny Hinn
on TBN and heard him using this scripture; he pointed out that
God does not have a grandchild. You are either a child of God or
not. Your father's position cannot save you. That Abraham is your
father cannot save you. You must be a child of God to be saved.

Now, in contrast to the Bereans, are the Athenians. I will
draw largely from C. Peter Wanger's analysis in his book, *Blazing the Way*, to illustrate the Athens Paul encountered in his

spread of the truth, which goes a long way in explaining their response to the truth. Professor of Church Growth C.P Wanger detailed the environment Paul met in Athens. He described it as "a stronghold of darkness." The Bible described the city as wholly given over to idols: "Now while Paul waited for them at Athens, his spirit was stirred in him when he saw the city wholly given to idols" (Acts 17: 16).

This was Paul's observation and impression of the place he had come to deliver the truth to—a place clothed in falsehood, a place decorated with anything that opposed his mission, a place where the anti-truth had educated everybody and endowed everybody with extra-ordinary wisdom. This was the observation and impression that provoked Paul in the Spirit. This is the only city throughout the New Testament that the apostles, in their missionary work, described with the Greek word *kateidol*, meaning *wholly given over to idol*. It was said that during this time that it was easier to find gods in Athens than to find humans. Ancient literatures describe Athens as a forest of idols, stating that some Athenian streets were so full of idols that pedestrians found it difficult passing through without unlawful contact with the gods. This reality influenced the response of the Athenians to the truth.

Paul's first encounter came shortly on arrival, and his observation and impression were not wrong. When I was still watching American wrestling, God forgive me, Paul's first encounter used to come to my mind at the beginning of each bout. On first encounter, these wrestlers will clash with each other with an unbelievable alacrity for a size up. These use to bring to my mind Paul's first encounter with the Athenian philosophers.

> Then certain philosophers of the Epicureans and of the Stoics encountered him.
>
> Acts 17:18

The Epicureans practiced a system of philosophy based chiefly on the teaching of the Greek philosopher Epicures. Their principal doctrine centered on the fact that intellectual pleasure was the ultimate goal and the overall contentment to life—that serenity resulting from overcoming emotional disturbances such as fear of the gods, fear of death, and fear of what happens after death is the true happiness. The Epicurean philosophy is completely materialistic in concept. It states that sensations are as a result of a continuous stream of "idols" the human body casts out that bear on the senses.

The Stoics were of the Stoic school, established at Athens about 300 BC by Zeno. Theirs was the most influential philosophy during the time of Paul's missionary work in Athens. Like the Epicureans, the Stoics regarded ethics as the ultimate sphere of knowledge. The Stoics believed that the Logos is a rational, divine power that controls the universe and regarded it to be omnipresent. According to them, the human soul is a manifestation of the Logos. Living in conformity with the divine order of the universe, to them, is to live according to reason. Before the advent of Christianity, the Stoics had already recognized the principle of brotherhood of humanity and the equality of all humans.

These were the two sects their members combined to encounter Paul. One thing is certain: these people must have heard of Paul, either while he waited for Silas and Timothy or while disputing in the synagogue or daily in the market, but most probably, the information about Paul that would have attracted these types of men is that they were turning the world upside down with their message. Before Paul arrived in Thessalonica, the Jews who forced him to leave described them as "These that have turned the world upside down have come hither also" (Acts 17:6b). This is a clear indication that the news about their activities must have reached the city of Thessalonica before their arrival. The same is also most likely to be the case in Athens. These men of Epicurean and Stoic sects wanted to know what this "babbler will say" (Acts 17:18b). When Paul delivered the truth to them, it was more than they had bargained for, and they decided to make Paul a public fun.

> And they took him and brought him unto Areopagus, saying, "May we know what this new doctrine whereof thou speakest is?"
>
> Acts 17:19

The Areopagus in Athens was an ancient court that sat on a hill. The court consisted of a council of nobles that met in the open with the accuser and the accused standing on platforms cut from the rocks of the mars hill. The Areopagus could summon any government official to come before it and testify. Because decisions of the court were final, the Areopagus bore overwhelming influence on the state. This was the court Paul was dragged to. We may not have heard the full details of Paul's appearance before this court, but thank God, Who gave him the wits to escape these agents of the power of darkness. Paul was so good that these gifted philosophers had to beg for cover. We are all aware of the Bible story of the unknown god. That was the Holy Ghost at best, not only that Paul escaped from these evil men, but he also left with rewards. The Bible recorded that Dionysius and a woman named Damaris and others went with Paul. Should you find yourself in an environment such as Athens, and the truth comes, will you be mentioned by name as an example for God like Dionysius and Damaris, or will your tradition overtake you? The reason for taking Paul to Areopagus was not to search the Scriptures to see if what he was saying was so, as was the case in Berea, but to entertain them: "For all the Athenians and strangers which were there spent their time in nothing else, but either to tell, or to hear some new thing" (Acts 17:21).

Athens was considered the intellectual center of the then world and the birthplace of philosophical traditions, as we have seen, of the Epicureans and the Stoics. Their response to the truth is a clear indication that their wisdom was not from God but from the forces of darkness that ruled over the city. James, in his epistle, described this type of wisdom like this:

> This wisdom descendeth not from above, but is earthly, sensual, and devilish.
>
> James 3:15

Its purpose is to serve the interest of its master—the devil. Its use is to block the message of the truth by developing alternative truths as those of the Epicureans and the Stoics.

Why should a loving God allow such to befall an entire people of a city? The answer is found in Paul's second letter to the Corinthians:

> But if our gospel (the truth) be hid, it is hid to them that are lost; in whom the god of this world hath blinded the minds of them (with philosophy), which believed not, lest the light of the glorious gospel of Christ, who is the image of God, should shine unto them.
>
> 2 Corinthians 4:3-4

How did Athens fit into the description of those the gods of this world had blinded their mind? The idols of Athens were the visible images of the invisible gods under reference in the Bible passage above. These gods directed all activities of Athens, including but not limited to education, arts, philosophy, and everyday routines of the city. Athens collectively had voluntarily given herself to the gods of this world through a variety of principalities and powers of darkness.

The name of the city was derived from the goddess Athena, and the inhabitants of Athens had given their lives and fate to this so-called "patron god." I understand, though sadly, that the official seal of the state of Californian in the United States of America features this same god. Thank God for Christian satellite TV stations like TBN, for we can, with certainty, say why the truth is suffering hindrances in that state. But I stand before the authority of the Holy Spirit to prophecy that soon, Texas and California will take the lead in returning America to God.

So why didn't Paul and his team go into intercessory prayers on behalf of the city and her inhabitants or bind and cast out this territorial spirits as commanded by the truth? This is another question that is likely to pop up in some minds. The reason they did not is found in the prophecy of Jeremiah: "Therefore pray not thou for this people, neither lift up cry, nor prayer for them; for I will not hear thee" (Jeremiah 7:16).

The physical manifestation of the demonic social life of Athens was in their periodic celebration of festivals in honor of one deity or another. Of the many of these festivals, few can be listed: (1) The festival of Athena (2) The festival of Apollo (3) the festival of Demeter (4) the festival of Poseidon (5) The festival of Anthesterion, in honor of the dead (6) The festival of Dionysus, the jolly Bacchus (7) the festival of Zeus, or Jupiter.

Many cultures and traditions, especially in Africa and Asia, are still similar today to the Athenians of Paul's time. The effect of these traditions on the inhabitants of where they are practiced is the same as was the case with the Athenians.

They mocked Paul, calling him a babbler. The Greek word translated as *babbler* is *spermologos*, meaning *chatter* or *seed-picker*, the name of a small bird that lives by picking up seeds on the road. It is also applied to people who gathered scraps of information from several sources. This was the name these men called Paul, the bearer of the truth.

Beware, therefore, that your tradition does not lead you to the same circumstance as these Athenians.

> If we say that we have fellowship with Him and walk in darkness, we lie and do not have the Truth.
>
> 1 John 1:6

Paul's frustration in Athens could not compare with the prejudice and risk the early European missionaries to Africa faced. At the time of my grandfather's birth, it was an abomination to be a Christian in that part of the world. But today, without any fear of contraction, I can say that 98 percent of the population of this very region where my grandfather was born are Christians, at least by claim. The similarity between the people Paul encountered in Athens and the ones the early missionaries met in Sub-Sahara Africa is that both had a mindset not to accept the message brought by these strangers. Imagine the task of convincing these Africans to worship a man who was hanged on a tree. These were people who would make desolate a village where someone committed suicide by hanging in order to escape from the precarious implications, and their presumed curses associated with death by hanging. The Gospel message, to them, started with an abominable note; that the Christ died by hanging on the cross. Both the Athenians and these Africans were superstitious. There were more gods in Africa at that time than Paul would have met in Athens that stirred his spirit. Almost every tree or strange objects such as anthill were regarded as gods. By any human imagination, the task of these missionaries evangelizing these Africans was impossible. But they came, armed with the Truth "that this man that hanged on the tree, who we have asked you to worship did not die for his own sins but to set you free from your superstitions. You don't have to kill your twins because they are just like you and not evil. Do not waste your God given vegetations thinking that they are habitation for evil spirits. You don't have to kill each other just to prove that you are stronger. Rather if you combine your efforts and resources, you will become richer and more prosperous." This, in my imagination, must have been the type of massage these missionaries deliver in Africa. When some twins that escaped killing due to the missionaries' intervention grew up into normal adult life and did not become evil as they initially thought, these Africans started embracing the message, though with a degree of skepticism. After the missionaries pulled down supposed evil forests and built schools, hospitals and living quarters and did not die, these Africans concluded that the god of the missionaries must be superior and more powerful than all their gods put together if he was able to chase out their own gods. That was how they began to accept the Gospel message and believed without signs and wonders but the Truth. My people, the Ibos of Nigeria in sub Sahara Africa, are today almost totally a Christian population. While the Athenians based their mindset against the Gospel on intellectualism, these Africans based theirs on child-like ignorance. That was the difference and a big lesson on how the Holy Spirit operates. This is how the Bible categorized these Athenians and Africans in Luke 10: 21, "...I thank thee O Father, Lord of heaven and earth, that thou hast hid these things from the wise and prudent and hast revealed them unto babes." Strong's Greek Dictionaries explained the Greek word *nepios* translated babes as meaning a simple-minded person. The human constitutions of both the giver and the receiver of the gospel message, as individuals or a group are very essential to the outcome the Holy Spirit makes of evangelism exercises. This is how the Bible in Romans 2:20 described the equivalent of these early missionaries in Africa. "An instructor of the foolish, a teacher of babes, which has the form of knowledge and the truth in the law." It wasn't the words that these missionaries spoke that convicted these Africans, but the Spirit of God. Paul was never more prepared for his task as a missionary then in Athens. But the outcome was a flop. The giver must see himself as the instructor of the foolish and a teacher of babes. The receiver should be simple minded and not see himself as wise. The wisdom of these Athenians denied them salvation, while the ignorance of these Africans gave them salvation. Probably too, the reason the two results were different could be that Paul prepared himself in Athens as an instructor of the wise while these early African missionaries prepared themselves as instructor of the foolish.

One more note on the Athenian experience. Intellectualism is not a hindrance to the gospel message as we can see from a significant gain Paul made in Athens in the person of Dionysius of the Areopagite (Acts 17:34). The hindrance is the constitution of the individual intellectual. Most intellectuals were good Christians before their learning made them see Christianity as an organization for the simple minded. If you have profoundly felt that Christianity is for the simple or child-like minded and not for an intellectual like you, count yourself lucky, because at that point you are experiencing this feeling, the Holy Spirit is tapping you on the shoulder to open for Him to enter. It is your opportunity to take that ultimate decision and join the likes of CS Lewis, US founding fathers, Bill Graham, and lot of others in an illuminated relationship with God.

I read some time ago in a newspaper that President Obama stated that his two years in office as the president of the United States has afforded him a deeper conviction about God. That was when he joined the child-like minded Christians in a new relationship with God. Before then, Mr. President probably understood God from intellectual view point.

The Bible alerts us in Philippians 3:2 to beware of dogs. Dog is used several times in the Bible figuratively to represent evil-minded people. David lamented in Psalm 22:16, "For dogs have compassed me, the assembly of the wicked have enclosed me." The Gospel according to Mathew 7:6 says, "Give not that which is holy to the dogs." The Athenians of Paul's time were of a particular geographical location, Athens. Today, the equivalent of this people are scattered all over the world. Therefore permit me to borrow from the Bible and call them dogs. Charles Darwin came up with a belief like any other religious conviction, but the dogs accepted it as a theory just to pierce the Christian's hand and feet. I am a practicing chemical engineer and very aware of the processes and requirements for a thought to become a scientific theory. Evolution cannot scale this procedure but has been granted the status of a "scientific" theory by the dogs. Those that are imposing the evolution philosophy on school children are also dogs. I am delighted by this development because God says we should give him thanks in all things, but more importantly because it fulfils in practical terms Paul's prophecy in 1 Timothy 6:20 about "Science falsely so called."

The questions to ask ourselves now are, how do I respond to the truth, and has it set me free? Free from ungodly traditions, free to find the Way?

I Am the Way

Christianity is a way of life—a new way, the Way
   It comes with Jesus
   He dedicated it for general use—threw it open for traffic
   From now on, there were to be no more side paths, or
blind alleys, but an open road
   Christianity is a life to be lived, a path to be trodden, a
work to be done
   Frederic C. Spurr

The followers of Jesus were first called "the Way" in Acts 9:2. Later, in Antioch in Pisidia, they were called Christians, in Acts 13. Apollos of Alexandria was described in Acts 18:25 as an eloquent man and mighty in the Scriptures, a man instructed in the Way. In Acts 19:9, the Bible recorded that Paul established the first Christian theological institution—the school of Tyrannous. Paul separated the church from the synagogue, the worshiping place of the Jews, because the people in the synagogue spoke evil of the Way. The uproar of Acts 19:23, instigated by the silversmiths of Ephesus, arose no small stir about the Way. Paul, in Acts 22:4, claimed to have persecuted this Way to death in his ignorance. In 2 Corinthians, Paul wrote that the veil of Moses, when he delivered the Law, still covered the reading of the Old Testament. No wonder the Jews regarded as heresy Paul's claim that he worshipped the God of his fathers after the Way. Through the doubting Thomas, we know for sure who that Way is—Jesus Christ, the begotten Son of the only living God. Yesterday is gone, tomorrow is still to come, but now is to follow that Way.

The story of the wise men—the Magi—in the Gospel of Matthew is an interesting illustration of the difference between searching for a way to follow and following the Way. These wise men from the east set out following a way—divination—to meet the Son of God, who was erroneously revealed to them by their master, the devil, as the king of the Jews. Their number, nationality, and country are not known; any addition as to their number or names is contrary to the Bible's warning that we should not add or remove from the Word of God. What is known is that they were a priestly caste that uttered prophecies, explained omens, interpreted dreams, and practiced divination. These were such as were gathered by Nebuchadnezzar in the book of Daniel to interpret his dream.

> Then the king commanded to call the magicians, and the astrologers, and the sorcerers, and the Chaldeans for to shew the king his dream.
>
> Daniel 2:2

These wise men, the magi, as they are known in their East, like the ones King Nebuchadnezzar assembled above, were of practices forbidden in the Bible. There are about twelve of these practices mentioned and forbidden in the Bible: witchcraft, sorcery, soothsaying, divination, wizardry, Necromancy (divination by means of pretending communication with the dead), charm, prognostication (foretelling by indication or omen or signs), observing time, and astrology. These practices are carried out in connection with demons called familiar spirits. Three of such with the Bible passages that condemn the practice are illustrated below:

Astrology and star gazing—this involves reading stars by divination: Isaiah 47:13; Jeremiah 10:2; Daniel 1:20, 2:2, 10:4-7, 5:7-15

Magical arts: Exodus 7:11, 22; 8:7,18; Leviticus 19:26; Deuteronomy 18:10;

2 Chronicles 33:6; 2 Kings 17:17, 21:6, Isaiah 47:9, 12, Jeremiah 27:9; Daniel 1:20

Divination—the art of mystic insight or fortune telling: Numbers 22:7, 23:23; Deuteronomy 18:10-14, 2 Kings 17:17; 1 Samuel 6:2; Jeremiah 14:14, 27:9, 29:8, Ezekiel 12:24, 13:6-7, 21:22-29, Micah 3:7; Acts 16:16

According to the Bible, the penalty for the practice of any of these is destruction: Leviticus 19:3, 20:6; Deuteronomy 18:11; 1 Samuel 28, 2 Kings 21:6, 23:24, 1 Chronicles 10:13; 2 Chronicles 33:6; Isaiah 8:19, 19:3, 29:4; 1 Timothy 4:1-8; 2 Thessalonians 2:8-12; Matthew 24:24; Revelation 13, 16:13-16, 19:20

These wise men from the east that sought the newly born king of the Jews were of these Bible-forbidden trades. These wise men were far deeper into the world of spiritual darkness than the demonized slave girl Paul delivered in Acts 16:16. Like the demonized slave girl, who recognized Paul and his team as the servants of the most high God, "The same followed Paul and us, cried, saying, these men are the servants of the most high God..." These wise men, also with the same power, recognized the infant Jesus as the king of the Jews. I want you to understand that these wise men were of a higher level in the kingdom of darkness than the demonized slave girl. They were heathens and do not know or worship the God of Abraham, the Father of the newborn they set out to present gifts to. If Paul had encountered them, their story might have taken a different turn. The means with which the wise men discovered the newborn King—star-gazing—is completely satanic, so it could not have come from God. It is by this cultic power that they observed the birth of Jesus. They used this power as a way to finding the Way—Jesus Christ. I am stressing this point this much because most Christians, especially in the Sunday school, tend to see these wise men before their encounter with the infant Jesus as men of God, the same way some Christians today take people of other faiths, like Islam, as believers just for the fact they recognize the existence of one God. This is not true, because the Bible tells us that the devil does the same: "Thou believes that there is one God, you do well, but the devil also believed and trembled" (James 2:19). The devil was using them for a mission under a cover that they want to pay respect to the king of the Jews. On arriving in Jerusalem they proclaimed: "Where is he that is born king of the Jews? For we have seen his star in the east and have come to worship him" (Matthew 2:2).

The effect of this declaration was the reason the devil sent them: "When Herod the king had heard these things, he was troubled, and all Jerusalem with him" (Matthew 2:3).

The devil had apparently achieved his aim. The helpless infant Jesus had been revealed to a waiting enemy. Herod must finish Him for envy of his throne, and God's purpose would be thwarted. If the devil was sincere about leading these men to Jesus, why did he hide the star from them after leading them to Jerusalem, the home of Herod? Why did the star reappear after the damage was done, revealing the infant Jesus to Herod? Why did the star now lead them to Bethlehem, the right place, after it had "misled" them to Herod in Jerusalem? Why did the star disappear in Jerusalem, which resulted in their open enquiry about the birthplace of Jesus that got to Herod? This is how the Bible recorded the reappearing of the star:

> When they had heard the king, they departed; and lo, the star, which they saw in the east, went before them till it came and stood over where the young child was.
>
> Matthew 2:9

There are so many questions to ask. Why didn't the star come and stand over where the young child was born instead of taking them first to Herod? The Bible exclaimed, "lo," at the reappearing of the star, a remark to note. In all, the Way reigns supreme; the devil's plan came to nothing except to fulfill the prophecy of Jeremiah in chapter thirty-one verse fifteen and repeated in the Gospel according to Matthew.

> In Ramah was there a voice heard, lamentation, and weeping, and great mourning, Rachel weeping for her children, and would not be comforted because they are not.
>
> Matthew 2:8

The devil's plan to forestall the mission of the Christ had failed. His agents had forsaken his way. They have found the right Way. The devil's reaction was to appease himself with the blood of innocent children.

In a blind rage and callous determination to destroy Jesus before He established His authority, Herod wiped out a generation of infants that would have included Jesus, if not that God is always ahead of the devil and always ready to make a caricature of the devil's plans.

When these wise men from the east met the infant Jesus, the Bible recorded that God took them over from the devil and revealed the new Way to them.

> And when they were come into the house, they saw the young child with Mary His mother, and they fell down, and worshipped Him, and when they had opened their treasures, they presented unto Him gifts: gold, and frankincense, and myrrh.
>
> Matthew 2:11

The Bible tells us that we cannot serve God and mammon at the same time. If you were serving God, the moment you bow down to the devil, your name is removed from the Book of Life. We know that a name can be removed from the Book of Life, because David prayed God not to remove his name from the Book of Life.

We also know that at conversion, the devil is driven away from a person's life if the person remains faithful to the conversion. How furious the devil would have been at seeing these heathens fall and worship Jesus; this can only be imagined. The Bible recorded that they did three things, namely: they fell down on seeing the infant Jesus; they worshiped Jesus; they made offerings to Jesus. There are some great lessons to learn here. No matter your standing with God, no matter how dark your life in darkness may be, the moment you show the right attitude toward God through Jesus Christ, you are made a new creature.

That is a lesson to learn from these wise heathens from the east. First, at seeing the infant Jesus, they forgot their priestly personality and fell down before the infant. Humility! That is the lesson here. They worshiped Jesus, total surrender to God through devotion. They opened their bags and presented gifts to Jesus, thanksgiving with things that cost much.

I have always believed that accidents, either of fortune or misfortune, are always merited. The same way I believe that God's grace, though unmerited, is not a handout. We as mortals may not see why one receives a greater grace than the other and why some do not even receive it at all, even when they appear to us as worthy. I believe that God searches the hearts of men and sees what we cannot see. For the humility of these heathens, their devotion, and their gratitude, God released His grace upon them. Can any blessing be greater than having communication with God?

> And being warned of God in a dream, that they should not return to Herod, they departed into their own country another way.
>
> Matthew 2:12

Another Way! They have now discovered the right Way. The way they came was the dirty one. Amazing grace! It is even speculated in Christian history that these men found the churches of the East before the arrival of the Apostles. This new Way that was revealed to these men is Jesus Christ. He is the Way to the truth that sets free and leads to Life in God. He is the Way unto obedience to God. The formerly worldly wise men had become heavenly wise men and, in obedience, established themselves in the Way. Like unto Levi, Jesus is still calling, "Follow me," meaning follow the right Way.

The Way to the place where the glorified Christ had gone

The Way to the place where the Christ redeemed shall gather

The Way to the place where the faithful ones shall assemble

The Way to the place where there will be great joy and no sorrow

The Way to the place of everlasting glory.

That Way is Jesus.

The Holy Spirit

We first met the Holy Spirit—the Spirit of God, the Breath of God, the Spirit of Jesus—in the second verse of the first chapter of the Old Testament. He was moving over an earth that had lost form, become void, and was in darkness.

> And the earth was without form, and void: and darkness was upon the face of the deep. And the Spirit of God moved upon the face of the waters.
>
> Genesis 1:2

Man and Lucifer had utterly disappointed God. The earth had become chaotic and lost form, and darkness had covered the face of the waters that had flooded the then earth. Water from then has become and still is the habitation of the kingdom of Satan.

We also first met the Holy Spirit, the same Spirit of God in the New Testament, in the very first chapters of the entire four Gospels doing the same.

This is how the Gospels introduced the Holy Spirit in these first chapters:

> She was found with child of the Holy Ghost…for that
> which is conceived in her is of the Holy Ghost.
>
> Matthew 1:18, 20

> And the Angel answered and said unto her, the Holy
> Ghost shall come upon thee.
>
> Luke 1:35

In John, we read "And the Light shineth in darkness; and the darkness comprehended it not" (John 1:5).

In the beginning, God created a perfect world. The earth was as perfect as heaven. That was the world that then was according to the second epistle of Peter.

> …whereby the world that then was, being overflowed with
> water perished. But the heavens and earth which are now,
> by the same Word are kept in store.
>
> 2 Peter 3:6-7

Lucifer's rebellion brought chaos upon this original, perfect world, and the earth became void, without form anymore, and darkness covered the face of the flooded earth. But there was no peace for Lucifer, whose action had made God destroy His first, perfect world. The total darkness upon the face of the flooded earth was too hash for the former angel of the morning star and former head of heaven's choir. You know that Lucifer was the master of the heavenly choir before his expulsion from heaven: a case of falling from grace to grass. It is therefore understandable that the devil should envy the choir. Pastor Tunde Barkare once told us that a choir that does not pray becomes a prey to Satan. To make the situation worse for Satan, the Spirit of God kept him in captivity by constantly moving over the face of his habitation—the waters that had flooded the earth. This is how

Peter described the condition of Lucifer and the other angels that sinned with him, then inhabiting the dark flooded earth:

> For if God spared not the angels that sinned but cast them down to hell and delivered them into chains of darkness to be reserved unto judgment.
>
> 2 Peter 2:4

It was after the casting out of Lucifer and his fellow fallen angels into hell, as described by Peter, that the Holy Spirit came back and fertilized the earth for the present creation: "And the Spirit of God moved upon the face of the waters" (Genesis 1:2b).

After He had done the job of conceiving the new earth, Elohim (God in the plural form), the Father, the Son, and the Holy Ghost, said, *"Let there be light; and there was light"* (Genesis 1:3). All others followed this light, including man. In the creation of man, the true nature of the plural form of God was revealed.

"And God (Elohim) said, 'Let us make man in our image, after our likeness'" (Genesis 1:26).

At the completion of His creation, God established a perfect communion with man in the garden of Eden. We are sure of this relationship because the Bible tells us that upon disobedience, Adam hid himself from God when He came to fellowship with them.

> And they heard the voice of the Lord (Yaweh—here, God is in singular form) walking in the garden in the cool (physical condition that implies bodily presence) of the day, and Adam and his wife hid themselves from God.
>
> Genesis 3:6

Why do you think the Bible used Elohim, the plural form of God, in creation and Yaweh, the singular form of God, in this visit? Because this visit was by God the Father, but creation is by God the Father, God the Son, and God the Spirit, all three in one Godhead. Luckily, the creation narrative did not leave us ignorant of the other two persons of the Godhead, the incarnate Son and the Spirit. In Genesis too, we meet the incarnate God who, from the beginning, is the Word of God.

> And the Lord God commanded the man, saying, of every tree of the garden thou mayst freely eat: but of the tree of the knowledge of good and evil, thou shalt not eat of it: For in the day that thou eatest there of thou shalt surely die.
>
> Genesis 2:16-17

This is the Word of God given to man in Adam at creation, the same Word that later became the incarnate Son of God and the propitiation of the very sin that violated Him.

It is worthy of note that when the devil tempted humans concerning obedience to the Word of God, man fell because of greed and ambition to be as wise as God.

> And the serpent said unto her, ye shall not surely die: for God doth know that in the day ye eat thereof, then your eyes shall be opened, and ye shall be as gods, knowing good and evil.
>
> Genesis 3:4-5

See how the devil had perverted the Trinity of God to plural gods: "Ye shall be as gods."

There is a lesson here, a very important one. The devil became aware that Eve was not grounded in the Word of God. Read how she misrepresented the passage she quoted to the serpent:

> God have said, "Ye shall not eat of it, neither shall ye touch it lest ye die."
>
> Genesis 3:3b

This misrepresentation was the devil's assurance that he would succeed with her. Be careful how you use God's Word in your war against the devil. He knows it inside out, and any sign that you are not grounded in it encourages him to attack you. More especially, exercise great care over the versions of the Bible you quote from, because some Bible versions are translated for the devil's purpose. That is why we must endeavor to receive from the Holy Spirit the power of discernment. This gift of the Spirit will enable us to know which Bible versions or spiritual leaders are misleading us.

I am building this background to show that the Holy Spirit did not become the Gospel phenomenon from nowhere. He has been a partner from creation to re-creation and now from regeneration to sanctification of believers.

In Genesis, the devil tempted man, and he failed woefully. The man that was made in the image and likeness of God failed. In the Gospel, the devil tempted God in the image and flesh of water and blood of man, but He defeated the devil. Get the picture? In the Old Testament creation, God made man in His image and likeness, and the devil tempted man and succeeded. In the New Testament redemption, God made Himself in the image and likeness of man, and the devil tempted God and failed.

> Then Jesus said to him, "Get thee hence, Satan, for it is written, 'thou shalt worship the Lord thy God and him only shall thou serve.'"
>
> Matthew 4: 10

We first met the Holy Spirit in the first chapters of the New Testament Gospels, just as we met Him in the first chapter of the Old Testament. In the Old Testament, we met Him first fertilizing the earth for rebirth of life in the world after the fallen Lucifer had caused God to destroy it with flood (2 Peter 3:6-7).

In the New Testament, we first met Him fertilizing Mary, the blessed mother of Jesus, for the rebirth of a new Life into mankind after his fall caused by the same Lucifer and his agents.

In the Old Testament, we met the Holy Spirit a second time in unity with God the Father and the Word, the incarnate God, the Son that dwelled here with man: "Let us make man in our own image and likeness" (Genesis 1:26). Though the Bible did not tell us who the *our* and *us* in the creation passage are, we know that apart from the Son and the Holy Ghost, the rest with God are His messengers, which Lucifer was one of before this time. They cannot be trusted with the duties of the deity, because they are not sovereign. They are servants and could not have been consulted by God in creation. Though more knowledgeable than man, the angels are not more important to God than man. That a nanny is more knowledgeable than your infant baby does not make the nanny more important than your child, even though the child's needs and care are to a large extent entrusted to her. The angels are God's nanny equivalent for our sake and are entrusted with our cares, because we are God's children by adoption through Jesus. That is why Jesus loves us as His brothers and sisters. Do you love Him like your brother?

The "we" in the God of creation are the Father, the Son, and the Holy Ghost. In the Gospels, we meet this union at the baptism of Jesus as we did in creation. The assurance to the Christian that the *we* and *our* in creation are the Father, Son, and Holy Ghost is its replay at the baptism of Jesus.

And Jesus, when he was baptized, went up straightway out of the water and lo, the heavens were opened unto him and he saw the Spirit of God descending like a dove and lighting upon him. And lo, a voice from heaven saying: "This is my beloved Son, in whom I am well pleased."

Matthew 3: 16-17

And straightway, coming up out of the water, he saw the heavens opened and the spirit like a dove descending upon Him. And there came a voice from heaven saying, "Thou art my beloved Son, in whom I am well pleased."

Mark 1:10-11

In the Gospel of Dr. Luke, we see this union in two passages:

The Holy Ghost shall come upon thee, and the power of the Highest shall overshadow thee, therefore also, the Holy *thing* which shall be born of thee shall be called the Son of God.

Luke 1:35

Did you notice some strange word in this passage? I deliberately introduced Luke by his professional title as a medical doctor. He certainly cannot afford to be carefree in his use of words in such natural-science matter of animate and inanimate nouns. The angel called Jesus in Mary's womb "the holy thing." It is not Dr. Luke's word; it was the angel's. The angel, as we have said before, is a messenger of God. His duty is to deliver the message. Mary will be conceived by the Holy Ghost, he has been told. She will deliver God, He relayed. But that God would be born like a baby was more than he could comprehend, so he decided to call the outcome of this holy phenomenon a holy *thing*, because he could not comprehend that God would be born as a child.

In the Gospel of Luke, again we meet the union of God, as in the other Gospels, during the baptism of Jesus.

And the Holy Ghost descended in a bodily shape like a dove upon him, and a voice came from heaven which said, thou are my beloved Son in thee I am well pleased.

Luke 3:22

This introduction is necessary to make us familiar with the person of the Holy Ghost, the third Person of the same one God, before going into details about Him. We seem much more familiar with the Father and the Son. God is not complete without the Holy Spirit. And you cannot be a complete child of God until you know Him well enough. That is the reason Jesus commissioned His followers to go all over the world and baptize in the name of the three:

> Go ye therefore and teach, all nations baptizing them in the name of the Father, and of the Son and the Holy Ghost.
>
> Matthew 28:19

Note that the three are proper nouns and start with capital letters all through the Bible, a form generally reserved for names of persons.

Names of God for the Holy Spirit

The names of God, we find in His Word; the Bible serves as a roadmap to understanding the person of the Holy Spirit. Elohim is the first name of God we meet in the Bible and appears some 2,300 times in the Old Testament. Elohim is derived from the Hebrew word meaning strength or power. This name is an attribute of one item that exists in a plural form. This statement may seem an abstract expression if we do not bring it into perspective. For example, we say, "Give me a pant for the night's outing," for communication's sake. But in reality, we know that pant does not exist in the singular, but in the plural form. The correct thing to say will be, "Give me a pair of pants."

In Genesis 1:1, we see this plural one God: "In the beginning, Elohim (translated simply *God* in English) created the heavens and the earth"; this is the name of God of creation, One God, but plural in existence. "And Elohim said, 'Let us make man in our image and likeness.'" This is the first indication that God exists in the plural form. Through the course of the Bible, we discover the three Persons of God as the Father, the Son, and the Holy Ghost. How primitive we would have been if the Lord Yeshua (Yeweh) did not reveal these persons of God before His departure back to heaven.

> Baptizing them in the name of the Father, and of the Son, and of the Holy Ghost.
>
> Matthew 28:19

This is one of our assurances that God exists in three persons.

We must not let this revelation lead us into the slightest doubt about the monotheism of God. Even the devil, who came down from heaven, knows that there is one God.

> *Thou believest that there is one God: thou doest well: the devils also believe and tremble.*
>
> James 2:19

Please check your own Bible; mine says, "the devils." The knowledge that the devils are not Lucifer alone, but a number of other fallen angels, should make us desire the presence and protection of the Holy Spirit all the more.

Despite this final revelation, we have other pockets of information in the Bible relating to the existence of God (Elohim) in three personalities.

> I have not spoken in secret from the beginning: from the time that it was, there am I: and now the Lord God (Yaweh) and His Spirit, hath sent me.
>
> Isaiah 48:16

a deeper evangelism

We know who the speaker in this verse is. He mentioned Himself and His mission. *I am,* who was sent, as we read in the Gospels. So here, we see that the Father and the Holy Spirit sent the Son into the world. "The Lord (the Father) and His Spirit (the Holy Spirit) hath sent me (the Son)."

An interesting relationship is emerging. A general impression is that the Son proceeds from the Father, and the Spirit from the Son. The implication is that this view tends to create a hierarchy in the Godhead, which I think is not true. We have seen from the verse above that the Son was sent by the Father and the Holy Ghost. The Bible says it.

From the Bible also, we see that the Holy Ghost is sent by the Father with the Son.

> But when the comforter (the Holy Spirit) is come whom I (the Son) will send unto you from the Father, He shall testify of me.
>
> John 15:26

It is clear from the two passages that the "me" of Isaiah 48:16 above that the Son was sent by the Father and the Holy Spirit, and from "He" and "whom" of John 15:26 that the Holy Spirit is sent by the Father and the Son.

We see again that the Holy Spirit and the Son combined to offer Jesus as spotless sacrifice to the Father for our sins.

> How much more shall the blood of Christ [the Son], who through the eternal Spirit [the Holy Spirit] offered himself without spot to God [the Father], purge your conscience from dead works to serve the living God [Elohim]?
>
> Hebrews 9:14

Having established these three persons in God, the question the devil might lead us to ask is how we are sure that God is composed of *only* three persons. What if there are unmentioned persons in the "us" and "our" of Genesis chapter one? The answer, my brethren, is in the Bible. We are specifically informed in the first letter of John that the personality of God is in three persons: the Father, the Word, which is the incarnate Son, and the Holy Ghost.

> For there are *three* that bear records in heaven, the Father, the Word, and the Holy Ghost, and these three are one.
>
> 1 John 5: 7

Note that the Word is written as a proper noun, which means a person.

Can there be any clearer way of telling us that God is three in one? If I now call this divine phenomenon *trinity*, will you understand, or is our problem the name *trinity*? Call it anything, but the Bible clearly states that God is three persons in one: "… and these three are one."

Do not let the fact that the name Trinity does not exist in the Bible constitute a hindrance to your faith in the Holy Spirit. At least you have seen that the concept is scriptural. The Holy Spirit led the church fathers into calling the concept of three Persons in the one God of the Bible *Trinitias* in Latin, translated *Trinity* in English. Just as we do not have the name Bible in the scripture, the same church fathers called the Holy Book of Christianity *Biblia* in Latin, translated *Bible* in English. So also, they called the concept of three persons in one God *Trinity*. The Gospels never mention the Bible in all their pages, just as it did not mention the Trinity. Peter never read the Bible as so called; the same goes for all the apostles. Reject the name Trinity and the name Bible together, or accept both because the same Spirit gave the two names to the church fathers. It is immoral and hypocrisy to accept one and leave the other. Do not let anybody fool you; Trinity is a gospel concept and truth.

In fact, a practical way to visualize the Trinity, or three in one, is to consider water, one substance that exists in three forms or states. Like the general name of God, Elohim, water is expressed in the singular form though plural in existence. Water in the form of ice and vapor cannot be drank or used in washing. Water in the form of liquid and vapor cannot be used in cooling and preservation. Water in the form of liquid and ice cannot condense to rain. In all three forms, it remains with a constant identity—H_2O—water but different functions.

First Corinthians 12:4-6 reads,

> Now there are diversities of gifts, but the same Spirit (Holy Spirit) and there are diversities of administration but the same Lord (the Son) and there are diversities of operation but it is the same God (the Father) which walketh in all.

Please do not submit yourself to the devil as agent of confusion in the body of Jesus by rejecting the obvious because of mind set or ego.

A search of the Bible shows that the Holy Spirit is attributed with all the characteristics of God the Father and the Son. This is essential information in the execution of our commission as Pentecostal Evangelists. We have seen the attributes of the Son in line with the Father. It is also necessary that we examine the attributes of the Holy Spirit in line with the Father and the Son. This will give us the boldness to conclude before the cynical world that the three are one.

One attribute of God we shall beam a searchlight on is the intra God love. This is the attribute of God, the Father, the Son, and the Holy Spirit, that is the building block of the bridge that links humanity to God. We are so dirty that if not for love, God

RETURN TO Smith Wigglesworth

would not have anything to do with us. Sometimes in the past, I would tell God that if what I was praying for did not come through, I will stop praying in protest. Foolish me, I thought I was doing God a favor by disturbing Him with my prayers. Somehow, my premature mind, in ignorance, might have been right. He cares a lot because of His great love for us. We call it grace; that is correct, but we cannot explain it.

Concerning the love of the Holy Spirit, I am going to take you to a new dimension. The internal love in the Godhead fills the Bible. The Father calls Jesus His beloved Son in whom He is well pleased many times in the Bible. Jesus expressed the love that exists between them from the beginning. This brings us to the question, what is the mission of the Holy Ghost? We know the mission of the Son is to redeem man. So what is the mission of the Holy Ghost? Let us review again their interaction regarding our salvation.

1.   The Father and the Holy Spirit sent the Son to redeem us. (Isaiah 48:16)

2.   The Father and the Son sent the Holy Spirit to comfort and teach us and show us the way to God (Elohim). (John 15:26)

3.   The Holy Spirit and the Son offered Jesus, without spot to the Father for our redemption. (Hebrews 9:14)

A background knowledge that Jesus came into this world as a human with all the inherent limitations of the flesh, such as time and space, hunger and sleep, merriment and enjoyment, sadness, pain, and sorrow, and anger and punitive action will help us appreciate the fact that the success of His mission was possible through the enablement of the Holy Spirit.

So, while in the flesh, Jesus emptied Himself of all divinity but love and abided on earth like ordinary human. The distinction is that He was filled at all times with the Holy Spirit on merit. Listen to Paul's description of Him in flesh:

> For we have not an high priest which cannot be touched with the feeling of our infirmities; but was in all points tempted like as we are yet without sin.
>
> Hebrews 4:15

The point I am trying to make here is that Jesus, while here in flesh, surrendered himself to the empowerment of the Holy Ghost, and their love for each other and with the Father knew no bounds. Jesus made it very clear to His disciples that He had to leave this earth in order that the Holy Spirit should pay attention to them. The moment Jesus came into this world, the Holy Spirit concentrated on Him so much that John the Baptist acknowledged that he must begin to diminish now that Jesus has come. And he diminished so much that he had to ask at a time if Jesus was He who they expected or if they should look for another.

Have you been lucky to have experienced true love in a spouse, father, mother, sister, brother, son, or daughter? We know the meaning of true love. The absence or presence of it in any relationship determines the momentum of that relationship. Let us go into a genuine soul search and see how much genuine love we have for Jesus and our neighbors—not lip services or zeal, but naturally flowing love. I have heard and read of *agape* love. Is it religion or philosophy? There is only one love in a Christian's mind, and that is the love taught by Jesus. Do you think you love Jesus as He taught us to? How would you answer this question, which He asked Peter three times, if He were to ask you now?

"Simon, son of Jonas, lovest thou me more than these?" This is how Peter answered: "Yea, Lord, thou knowest that I love thee." Easy to answer, but Jesus knows that it's not an easy question; hence, He added, "feed my lamb."

Jesus put it to His followers that they can do greater things than they saw Him do, if and only if the conditions for the filling of the Holy Spirit is met by them. They met the conditions and did wonders. Therefore, the mission of the Holy Spirit is to relate with us the same way He did with Jesus and His immediate followers and those who followed them. But what is our relationship with Him today? Let us look at the conditions for the filling of the Holy Spirit and see how and why we are empty. Jesus listed out these conditions before His departure to heaven, but the greatest, He tells us, is love. The Holy Spirit loves Jesus so much that His measure of love in us is on a scale of our love for Jesus and, by extension, His people.

Soon again, Jesus asked Peter a second time, "Simon, son of Jonas, lovest thou me?" this time, without "more than these."

Peter answered again, "Lord thou knowest that I love thee," and Jesus returned, "Feed my sheep."

Then again, a third time, He asked, "Simon, son of Jonas, lovest thou me?" Peter got grieved because He had asked the same question three times, but he calmly replied again, "Lord thou knowest all things: thou knowest that I love thee." Again, Jesus commanded him, "Feed my sheep" (John 21:15-17).

What Jesus is emphasizing here is that a great measure of love for Him is required to attract the Holy Spirit into our lives. If your love current is not high enough, it will not carry the spiritual load of the Holy Spirit. So is your love current for Jesus high enough? The last answer from Peter satisfied Jesus: "Lord, you know all things." This convinced Jesus that Peter could make it. You cannot love Him enough if you are not convinced that He knows all things and that all things work together for your good in Him. The reason the Holy Spirit is distant from the church today is due to low love current for Jesus. And the reason for this low love current is that the church today, unlike the church of the first century, has not answered Jesus in sincerity as Peter did—"thou knowest all things." It is only when this is established in our mind that we can develop enough love current to carry the spiritual load of the Holy Spirit. Ask yourself, church, how many of us will be called by the seat of ungodly, corrupt, and unchristian government that will say, "Let me find out what Jesus wants me to do over this invitation" before rushing out to grab the material benefit of such a high-level invitation? How many of us will be kidnapped by anti-Christ terrorist groups and will ask our interest, be it family or government, not to negotiate our release with the devil but trust in Jesus with all our heart? How many of us will not beg, cry, and even denounce our faith in face of crucifixion as it came upon Peter, who, rather, demanded that he should be crucified head down to differentiate him from his master? How many of us will hear a gun shot in the premises of our church and will remember that Jesus is in charge and continue with our worship? Until we hold Him at such esteem, we cannot love Him enough, and the Holy Spirit will at best remain dormant in us instead of spurring us with His spiritual gifts.

Has the church become helpless because of our inability to love Jesus enough? God forbid. God's grace is more than sufficient to pull His church out of any helpless situation. But the church must do the needful by loving Jesus appropriately; otherwise, as the church stands today, we are ridiculed by all sorts of groups, religion, and governments. The government put out all kinds of legislations to deny us of the freedom and privileges won at the cost of the blood of past saints. The Muslims are beheading us for preaching Christ. The atheists are mocking and making public show of shame with our faith. The occults are mesmerizing us with their cultic power. And we are just there, shouting, "Holy Ghost fire, Holy Ghost fire," trying to switch on air conditioner under a condition of low electric current. The needful is that the church as individuals, local and universal groups and denominations must come back to her first love— Jesus. That is when the Holy Spirit will once again take over the leadership of the church.

The church is not helpless because she knows what to do, and He who has called us is faithful and just to forgive our past indifference and come to our defense.

But the church must first overcome confusion by the power of the Holy Spirit and get focused on Jesus, the author and finisher of our faith. The moment this is achieved, the Holy Spirit will quicken the church of today as He did to the apostolic and the early church. We can then have the power and authority to ask the fig tree to wither because it did not offer us fruit when we were hungry, and it will; we can ask the lame to walk, and he will; we can ask the blind to see, and he will see; we can ask the mountain to be removed into the sea, and it will. The Holy Spirit is eagerly waiting.

How Can the Church Overcome Confusion?

Confusion comes from the enemy, the devil, because he is afraid of what the church can do to him if the Holy Spirit comes back to the church in full force. So his primary interest is to create confusion in the church and divert attention and love from Jesus. Until the church sets aside its differences and comes together as a body, we shall continue to erroneously expose the church to the devil as a polygamous home. But Jesus cannot be the husband of a polygamous church. As long as the church remains in a state of polygamy, the Holy Spirit remains at a distance. In a polygamous home, the man of the home, the husband of the wives, suffers extreme denial of love because the "nucleus homes," mother and children, look for their own interest first. That is what is happening to the church today, but not according to the wish and desire of God. Pastor Tunde Bakare of Later Rain once imagined a situation where the denominations were disputing over their differences, and Jesus came to mediate, but they pushed Him aside. They have become consumed in their hot debate over doctrine that they did not recognize that the person they pushed aside was Jesus. This is the sad condition of the church today.

Now, if we agree the situation that has laid the church bare of the powers of the Holy Spirit was brought about by the devil, why do we still allow it to hold us down? Or are the weapons of our warfare, which served the early church perfectly well, not available to today's church? We can find all the weapons and army we need in the Person of the Holy Spirit if we devote our love to Jesus. That is what the message here is about. Lucifer, at his best, was an angel. He could not even then compete with Jesus, much less now that he is fallen. It is an insult, and a big one for that matter, for the church not to perform over the excuse that the devil has put a shackle on her wheels.

The Work of the Holy Spirit

The Holy Spirit cannot perform in isolation. His love for Jesus is beyond imagination, and He must see that love of Jesus in us and in the church; otherwise He will remain dormant in us. But if He sees the love of Jesus in us, I can assure you, brethren, the devil and his agents are in trouble. Jesus was sent into the world by the Father and the Holy Spirit (Isaiah 48:16) to reveal Elohim, the Godhead to mankind. We know from the Bible that His principal assignment is to destroy all the works of the devil, including confusion and obstruction to the truth.

> For this purpose the Son of God was manifested, that he might destroy the works of the devil.
> 1 John 3:8

The God of the Bible, Father of the church, His Son Jesus Christ, the Husband of the church, and the Holy Spirit, the Light of the church, is not a God of confusion, but a God of order, peace, and unity, and that is what He desires in the church.

> For God is not the author of confusion, but of peace, as in all churches..."
>
> 1 Corinthians 14:33

The church must arm herself with the knowledge that the Holy Spirit has the task of consolidating the victory of Jesus, and He is very willing to teach and protect us from the evil one as He did for the early church. Jesus tells us that the Holy Spirit shall receive of that which belongs to him, and the church does. He has given us over to the Holy Spirit. What He did while here, He has assured us we can do, and it's true, because the early church did. The early church was His as the present church is, and the same Holy Spirit that performed through them is still available to us.

> Howbeit when he, the Spirit of truth is come, he will guide you into all truth: for he shall not speak of himself, but whatsoever he shall hear, that shall he speak; and he will shew you things to come. He shall glorify me, for he shall receive of me and shall show it unto you.
>
> John 16:13-14

The church has delayed for too long and has suffered greatly. Let us go back to our first love, and all will come in place. No more, no less. Have you heard the saying that if you want to go quickly, you go alone, but if you want to go far, you go together? The church needs to get to Jesus quickly and must, therefore, go as individuals. The church needs to go far with Jesus and, therefore, must go as a congregation. The Holy Spirit will show us the things we otherwise cannot know about Jesus, but under condition. He must be sure of our love for Jesus. He cannot reveal the secret of Jesus to an enemy.

I agree that the Reformation that swept through the medieval Roman Catholic Church was a great achievement. To me, it was a revolution, not a revival. The devil got the final victory, because it brought about a denominated body of Christ. Denominations brought doctrinal corruption into the church. The Holy Spirit was not active in that movement, because the Reformation team did not anchor their struggle on the strength of the *full gospel*. Human intellect fought the devil and won, but human intellect has its limitations. The devil took advantage of that limitation and thwarted the gains of the Reformation. The church today has become worse for it. The ruin this glorious Reformation brought to the church is a result of lack of the deployment of all the provisions of the Holy Ghost as stipulated in the gospel, especially in the area of spiritual companionship with Him in our struggle and war against the devil. I am not exaggerating the revelation I received from Mr. Demos Shakarian's book, *The Happiest People on Earth*, but permit me to say that from this book, my fear of the devil's victory over the Reformation was confirmed. I thank God the church has come to terms again with the message of the full gospel and through the empowerment and gifts of the Holy Spirit, the Regeneration process has started in earnest.

The title of Mr. Shakarian's book *The Happiest People on Earth* synopsizes the entire message of the book. The gift of peace to the Christian is a function of his faith in God. Hebrews 11:1 defines faith thus "Now faith is the substance of things hoped for, the evidence of things not seen." It is only by faith that we can confess that we are strangers and pilgrims on this earth. Hebrew 1:13. That is the only time the turbulence of this world would cease to hamper our happiness. Unfortunately we still surrounded ourselves with the worries and cares of this world, especially when life becomes a bit rough. You have become the Christian Paul advocates if you rejoice evermore (1Thessalonians 5:16). I wondered how many of us that can equal our difficulties in this present life with what Paul went through as a Christian. If he commanded us to rejoice evermore, it means that he also rejoiced evermore. If this is true as I believe it is, then Paul was one of the happiest people that lived.

"Who are the happiest people on earth? Are they the ones with the most money? The most Friend? Beauty? Fame? Good health?" Mr. Shakarian asked. They are none of these, according to Demos Shakarian, but the ones who have found faith in God according to the full Gospel.

The intellectually based medieval Reformation is today receiving the full refinement of the Holy Spirit. All the provisions of the Gospel are now on the Christians worship program irrespective of denomination. This can be attributed to the Pentecostal evangelism pioneered by the likes of Smith Wigglesworth and sustained today by such Christian organizations as the Full Gospel Businessmen Fellowship. If this refinement of the medieval Reformation is sustained, we can with confidence say that the glorious days of the church is a matter of time.

The Holy Spirit is on duty, revealing Jesus and His redemptive work to us, directing us to Him for our Salvation, enabling us to surmount the obstacles of the evil one on our match to Jesus, encouraging us to bear fruits and giving us gifts for the edification of the church of Jesus Christ. He is a great personality in the Godhead and cannot be ignored by the church. No wonder Nicolaus Decius, in 1526, raised an appeal to Him in hymn:

> Spirit divine, attend our prayers
> And make this house thy home.
> Descend with all thy gracious powers;

O come, Great Spirit come!
Come as the light, to us reveal
Our emptiness and woe
And lead us in the paths of life
Where all the righteous go.
Come as the wind; sweep clean away,
What dead within us lies
And search and freshen all our soul
With living energies.
Come as the fire and purge our heart
Like sacrificial flame;
Let our whole soul as offering be
To our redeemer's name.

To our redeemer's name! We must have natural love for Jesus to enable the Spirit do His work in us.

We cannot short circuit God. The church today is still the church of Peter and Paul. The difference is that the church of their time brought forth the fruit of the Spirit in order that the gifts of the Spirit should become available to them and the church. The Holy Spirit is waiting for us to bring forth fruit so that He can pour out the gifts of the Spirit to the church. As much fruit (note in the singular) as we bear becomes the measure of the gift we receive. The fruit of the Spirit is listed as love, joy, peace, longsuffering, kindness, goodness, faithfulness, gentleness, and temperance (self- control). Nine of them (Galatians 5:22-23, NKJV).

The gifts of the Spirit are listed as word of wisdom, word of knowledge, faith, healing, work of miracle, prophecy, discerning of spirits, different kinds of tongues, and interpretation of tongues. Nine of them (1 Corinthians 12).

Let us arrange the two lists and see how we have fared in each pair because, in vain, we search for the gifts until we bear the fruit. God cannot entrust us with the gifts of the Spirit until we are qualified for them by bringing forth the fruit of the Spirit.

The Nine Fruits and the Nine Gifts

So many today seek the gifts without first acquiring the corresponding fruit in their life. We must manifest the virtues of the fruit if we want God to entrust us with His gifts.

Gifts of the Spirit 1 Corinthians 12	Fruit of the Spirit Galatians 5:22-23 (NKJV)
1. Word of Wisdom	1. Love
2. Word of Knowledge	2. Joy
3. Faith	3. Peace
4. Healings	4. Longsuffering
5. Working of Miracles	5. Kindness
6. Prophesy	6. Goodness
7. Discerning of Spirits	7. Faithfulness
8. Different Kinds of Tongues	8. Gentleness
9. Interpretation of Tongues	9. Self Control

This is how the fruit and gifts of the Spirit pair:

The Word of Wisdom is the first in the list of gifts of the Spirit, and *Love* is its counterpart fruit of the Spirit, also first in the list. Spiritual wisdom is a supernatural disclosure to our minds, the purpose and the way of God as applied to specific situations. The Old Testament says the fear of the Lord is the beginning of wisdom. The New Testament equivalent would read, "The Love of God is the beginning of wisdom. In the dispensation of the Law as in the Old Testament, relationship with God was by fear;

but in this period of grace, our relationship with Him is through Love. That is the relationship of a son with father."

> For ye have not received the spirit of bondage again to fear: but you have received the Spirit of adoption (to become brothers and sisters to Jesus) whereby we cry Abba, Father.
>
> Roman 8:15

Spirit of wisdom is the gateway into all the other gifts of the Spirit, so the condition must be right before we are entrusted with it. In the Old Testament, the Bible associated Solomon with wisdom. Unfortunately, and unlike his father, David, he did not have the prerequisite for this divine gift, which is love for God. The outcome of his wisdom was materialism and disappointment to God.

So the Bible makes it clear that the prerequisite for the Spirit of wisdom, which is the gateway into the entire gifts of the Spirit, is love for Jesus Christ; hence, love is made the gateway for the fruit of the Spirit.

How do we know that we have started bearing the fruit of the Spirit? In a nutshell, we know the love of Jesus has come back to the church when the gifts of the Spirit return to the church. No amount of prayers, no amount of fasting, no amount of devotion, no amount of worship, no amount of zeal, no amount of warfare, no amount of revival meetings, no amount of evangelism, no amount of righteousness can bring the full manifestation of the gifts of the Spirit until we meet the single requirement of love for Jesus. This may sound too loud and uncomplimentary, but it is Scriptural. This is what the Lord told the church at Ephesus.

> Nevertheless I have somewhat against thee. Because thou left thy first Love. Remember therefore from whence thou art fallen, and repent and do the first works: or else I will

come unto thee quickly, and will remove thy candle stick
of his place except thou repent.

Revelation 2:4-5

He that loveth father or mother more than me is not
worthy of me; and he that loveth son or daughter more
than me is not worthy of me. And he that taketh not his
cross and followeth me, is not worthy of me. He that
findeth his life shall lose it: and he that loseth his life for
my sake shall find it.

Matthew 10:37-39

This is the word of God describing the type of love for Jesus that
is missing in the present-day church, but that was the dynamism
of the apostolic and early church and the ministry of Wigglesworth, hence the abundance of the gifts of the Spirit.

Let us not make any mistakes about it; the gateway into the
fruit of the Spirit is love, and true love, for Christ. And the prerequisite for the gift of the Spirit is the fruit of the Spirit. Jesus
came into this world to teach us love, to show us love, and to give
us love in abundance.

Greater love hath no man than this that a man lay down
his life for his friend.

John 15:13

If we have to be logical and of a balanced mind, can we say of
anybody who has given us so much as He has? Take away salvation; look at the world today and see if the present civilization is
possible without the principles laid down by Jesus. Is it natural,
if we claim to know Him, that we should love anybody, anything,
whosoever, whatsoever, better than Him? Who do we have that
He has not given us? What do we have that He has not given
us? Is it our spouse, our children, our fathers and mothers? What

is it that we should love in preference to Him? But let us judge ourselves and the church today. Have we not loved ourselves more than we love Him? Yet we read in the Bible,

> Who shall separate us from the love of Christ? Shall tribulation or distress, or persecution or famine, or nakedness or peril, or sword...? Nay, in all these things we are more than conquerors through Him that loved us. For I am persuaded that neither death, nor life, nor angels, nor principalities nor powers, nor things present, nor things to come, nor height, nor depth, nor any other creature (wife, husband, mother, father, child) shall be able to separate us from the love of God which is in Christ Jesus our Lord.
>
> Romans 8:35-39

If we know God, we shall definitely know love, for He is love. Talking about love is like talking about God. No amount of paper in the world can contain the subject of love. Let's look at what the Bible, through the Holy Spirit, teaches us about love, and we may begin to see why the gate of the gifts of the Spirit is still locked to today's church.

First, we must peep into the love within the Godhead in order to appreciate the kind of love required of us to be able to receive the gift of the Spirit of word of wisdom.

The word our Lord used concerning His departure and the Holy Spirit coming upon the church is *expedient*, meaning that it is advantageous for practical, rather than moral, reasons that He goes in order that the Holy Spirit should begin to operate in us.

> Nevertheless, I tell you the truth, it is expedient for you that I go away: for if I go not away, the comforter will not come into you: but if I depart, I will send Him unto you.
>
> John 16:7

Remember that the Holy Spirit was resident in Jesus for about three years. That is what the Bible said.

> And I knew Him not, but He that sent me to baptize with water. The same said unto me, upon whom thou shall see the Spirit descending and remaining on Him the same is he which baptiseth with the Holy Ghost.
>
> John 1:33

The Holy Spirit did not only descend, but remained on Him! Later, John the Baptist acknowledged that he would begin to diminish and that Jesus would begin to increase, because he understood the love between and inseparability of Jesus and the Holy Spirit. As long as He remains in flesh in this world, the Holy Spirit has little or no business with any other flesh. A jealousness of deity, a divine consummation of love, you may call it. The instruction to John the Baptist on how to identify the Christ is that the Holy Spirit will not just descend on Him, but will abide, will remain, will reside in Him. This is what Jesus is telling us in John 16:7, that it is expedient for our sake that He, Jesus, must go in order that the Holy Spirit should come fully upon human flesh. Did you notice that Jesus had to pray to the Father before the Holy Spirit was released to abide with man? Check your Bible:

> And if you love me, keep my commandments. And I will pray the Father, and He shall give you another Comforter that He may abide with you forever.
>
> John 14:15-16

There is a condition before Jesus prayed for the gift of the Holy Spirit to come and abide with the church. He continued to emphasize this condition and the criteria for receiving and being filled with the Holy Spirit when He left. The emphasis is on love.

> If a man loves me, he will keep my word: and my Father will love him and we will come unto him and make our abode with him.
>
> John 14:23

> If you love me, keep my commandment.
>
> John 14:15

> He that hath my commandment, and keepeth them he it is that loveth me. And he that loveth me shall be loved of my father and I will love him and will manifest myself in him.
>
> John 14:21

> As the Father hath loved me, so have I loved you; continue ye in my love. If ye keep my commandment, ye shall abide in my love, even as I have kept my Father's commandment and abide in his love.
>
> John 15: 9-10

> For the Father Himself loveth you, because ye have loved me, and have believed that I came out from Him.
>
> John 16: 27

> A new commandment I give unto you, that ye love one another as I have loved you, that ye also love one another.
>
> John 13:3

This is the emphasis on love for God and fellow man according to our Lord Jesus Christ, found within two pages of the Bible.

> And Jesus answered him, "The first of all the commandments is 'Hear, O Israel; The Lord our God is

one Lord. And thou shall love the Lord thy God with all thy soul, and with all thy mind, and with all thy strength'; this is the first commandment. And the second is like namely this, 'Thou shall love thy neighbor as thyself.' There is none other commandment greater than these."

Mark 12:29-31

Many Christians see Jesus Christ as the *subject* of their desire and faith instead of the *object* of their desire and faith. You cannot love Jesus as is required of a Christian until you realize that He is first and foremost a living personality and not just the subject of the New Testament history. It is only when we become involuntarily conscious of the fact that we are constantly in His presence in a concrete term and not in a mere abstract form that we can begin to remove ourselves from what He does not want us to do and begin to do those that make Him happy. We must see Him as our first spouse and treat Him as such. That is when the true love He demands from us will begin to manifest.

The spiritual fruit of love is the precursor for and the key that opens the gate into spiritual gifts through the word of wisdom, without which we do not have access to the other gifts of the Spirit.

The Word of Knowledge means a supernatural revelation of information concerning a thing or things that ordinarily would have been unknown, resulting in a reaping of benefits, avoidance of calamity, or creating of opportunities. So, divine knowledge must also bring divine joy. If the spiritual fruit of joy is lacking in us, where then is the platform for receiving the gift of word of knowledge? Fortunately, the church has a lot to show in the area of this gift. The civilization that Christianity has brought to the world and advances into the universe in accomplishment of the first or solaric covenant of Genesis 1:14-15 is a testimony to this. The world has seen more knowledge in the two thousand years after Jesus was here than it saw millions of years before it. If you want to appreciate the joy that knowledge radiates, join ignorant people in a discussion on an issue like current affairs or technology or just any field.

In one commercial city in Nigeria, the very rich traders are mainly illiterate people. A booming trade there, in medical technology, is the "washing of blood." Any doctor who does not know how to wash blood is a quack or not properly trained. The practice is that the patient is put on a drip solution; his urinary waste is connected to a clear-color plastic container smeared with an invisible grain of coffee. Some dummy probes are attached from his body and connected to a computer. When the blood washing operation starts, an animated program is started on the computer. The patient is told that the computer has started washing his blood. The drip induces him to urinate more, and as the urine collects in the clear-color plastic, the small grain of coffee dissolves, and the content turns into a dark brown color. At the end, he is shown how much dirt was washed out from his blood. These are very rich people, and if you do not wash your blood at least once a year, you are considered very stingy and a lover of money more than your life. The day I heard this story, in company of my late "brother," Rev. Chima Ogbuagu, a classmate of Bill Gates's in Yale University, he asked me if I remembered what he told me about knowledge and ignorance. I remembered. He said, "If you think knowledge is expensive, try ignorance."

The Bible says of joy: "These things have I spoken unto you that my joy might remain in you, and that your joy might be full" (John 15:11).

That is the wish of our Lord, that our joy should be complete through knowledge of Him and of things for the present and the ones to come.

Remember Isaac Newton (1642-1727), the English mathematician and physicist? Listen to him. "I can take my telescope and look millions of miles into space; but I can go away to my room, and in prayer, get nearer to God and heaven than I can when assisted by all the telescopes of the world" (Methodist Companion). Isaac Newton derived the law of universal gravitation. This discovery, considered one of the greatest intellectual achievements of modern science, explains how an unseen force known as gravity affects all bodies in space and on earth. "Newton's works represent one of the greatest contributions to science ever made by an individual. Most notably, Newton derived the law of universal gravitation, invented the branch of mathematics called calculus, and performed experiments investigating the nature of light and color" (Encarta Encyclopedia).

The point I am trying to make here is that the word of knowledge has landed man on the moon, set man in fulfilling the solaric covenant of Genesis 1:14-19. These are products of the fruit of joy, which the church has retained from the time of the apostles, and it is marvelous in our eyes. These manifestations have, as promised by our Lord, made our joy full. He is still ready to do more, so long as we continue to ask, because the fruit of joy is already in the church.

> ...ask and ye shall receive (knowledge) that your joy may be full.
>
> John 16:14

Faith: Now faith is the substance of things hoped for, the evidence of things not seen. For by it the elders obtained a good report. Through faith we understand that the worlds were framed by the word of God...By faith Abel offered unto God a more excellent sacrifice than Cain ... and by it, he being dead Speaketh. By faith Enoch was translated that he should not see death ... But without faith, it is impossible to please Him; for he that cometh to God must

believe that He is, and that He is a rewarder of them that
diligently seek Him.

Hebrews 11:1-6

If you continue down the verses, you will meet the faith of Noah,
of Abraham, and of Sara. The interesting thing is that these
people, according to the Bible, lived and died in faith without
receiving the promise of Jesus concerning the Holy Spirit.

> But by this nature, they believed absolutely that they were
> strangers and pilgrims on this earth. These all died, in
> faith, not having received the promises, but having seen
> them afar of, and were persuaded of them, and embraced
> them and confessed that they were strangers and pilgrims
> on the earth. For they that say such things declare plainly
> that they seek a country.
>
> Hebrews 11:13-14

The counterpart to the gift of *faith* is the fruit of *peace*.

> Therefore being justified by Faith, we have Peace with God.
>
> Romans 5:1

What can give us a greater peace than the knowledge we are
strangers and pilgrims in this world? That is the only way to bury
all our sorrows, disappointments, anxieties, fears, and pains and
bear the fruit of peace that will allow the Holy Spirit a dwelling
place in us to perfect the gift of faith. The Bible describes the
peace of God as passing all understanding, because it is peace
that is derived from removing your mind from things and hap-
penings of this world.

Permit me to quote Selwyn Hughes from *Everyday with Jesus*,
about his personal experience with life. "The first half of my
Christian life was comparatively free from suffering. Then my

wife was struck with cancer. After several years, she died. Three weeks later, my father also died. Some years later, I myself was diagnosed with cancer and maturity-onset diabetes. And then, within the space of just ten months, I lost my two sons—my only children." Till this day, Selwyn Hughes, who went to be with the Lord in January 2006, is still selling his monthly devotional, *Everyday with Jesus.* How was he able to get over these pains and remain focused in Jesus through the long years afterward? I have been a faithful reader of *Everyday with Jesus* for decades now, and from its pages, I will say the answer is that Mr. Hughes found that peace of God that passes all human understanding by realizing that this world is not his home. So as a pilgrim, he saw all these painful life realities as nightmares that would pass away when he woke up in his permanent home in heaven, which to God's glory, became eternal reality to him. That is faith from the peace of God.

We have no faith because of our unbelief. But we know Jesus; we believe in Him as Christians. His disciples, before the coming of the Holy Spirit upon them, knew Him and believed in Him too, but they did not have that peace of the fruit of the Spirit; hence, their minds were fixed, even on the day of His departure, at the things of this world.

> When they therefore were come together, they asked of Him saying, Lord will thou at this time restore again the kingdom to Israel?
>
> Act 1:6

This they asked Him on the day of His departure to heaven. But He had earlier prophesied of their lack of faith, knowing that their minds were fixed on things of the earth, with its inherent lack of peace, without which, there is no faith. This was before the coming of the Holy Spirit upon them.

> Because of your unbelief: for verily I say unto you; if ye
> have faith as a grain of mustard seed, ye shall say unto
> this mountain, remove hence to yonder place: and it shall
> remove: and nothing shall be impossible unto you.
>
> Matthew 17:20

It seems the church has gone back to the pre-Pentecost era, hence the lack of faith the size of a mustard seed. No wonder we have been unable to remove the mountains of Aso Rock, of Iran, of Syria, of Sudan, of politics and governments, and all other mountains on our ways as Christians. We know the problem. Not that our God is not capable, but because we do not bear the fruit of peace, derived only from removing our minds from the things of this strange world, and declare in faith that we are citizens of heaven. This is the prerequisite for the gift of faith.

Healing: Spiritual and orthodox healing are both the handiwork of the Holy Spirit. I wish I was a medical doctor or a pharmacist; I would have elected the Holy Spirit the life president of the World Medical Association or the Pharmaceutical Association. In creation, the Holy Spirit became, and remains in subsequent incarnations, an anesthesiologist and surgeon. In the conception of Jesus, He became a pediatrician. The Hebrew women believe that only the Holy Spirit shall deliver her of her baby. No complicated or even Caesarian operation. In the healing of the blind man, Jesus, filled with the Holy Spirit, prepared a pharmaceutical of clay and spit and used it to heal the blind man.

> When he had this spoken, he spat on the ground, and
> made clay of the spittle, and He anointed the eyes of the
> blind man with the clay. And said unto him. Go wash in
> the pool of Siloam (which is by interpretation sent) He
> went his way therefore, and washed, and came seeing.
>
> John 9:6-7

This is the only healing in the Bible that Jesus performed with a pharmaceutical. It's to teach us that medical healing and pharmaceutical breakthroughs are scriptural. I have heard of a religious sect that does not go to hospital or accept medical treatment. The Lord knew about the coming of such doctrine in His name and set an example. The rest of His healings in the Bible are by His spoken word.

What is our part if we must receive the gift of the Spirit of healing? The counterpart fruit of the Spirit is *long suffering* or *patience*. Time, they said, is the healer of all emotional wounds. I am a witness and you too, I suppose. Patience is a desirable attribute for healing. The church today is sick, but there is hope, because the church has also done well in the area of the gift of healing, which testifies that she is not barren in the fruit of long suffering. There is obvious hope for the healing of the church in Jesus's name.

Working of Miracles: Miracle is a manifestation of divine authority resulting in an event that otherwise would have been impossible under natural laws of nature. Miracle is regarded as an act of God. The counterpart fruit of the Spirit to the gift of miracle is *kindness* or *compassion* (NKJV). I would like us to have a look at the list of Jesus's miracles in the Bible, and we shall not fail to see compassion behind them. In fact, the Bible records compassion as the reason for His many miracles. His first recorded miracle was making wine from water. If you ever try to imagine the embarrassment that was staring this new couple and their families in the face, if you knew what the Jewish society was like then and even now, you would not fail to see the kindness in this miracle, though before His time, to save this husband and wife who had just been initiated into God's ordinance of marriage from shame. And His last miracle of healing occurred when Peter cut off the ear of one of those who came to arrest Him. The young man was bleeding to death and in pain. Serves him right, doesn't it? But Jesus's compassion drove Him to restore the young man's ear. That is kindness, even to your enemy, and not just an enemy, but the one that has come to kill you. The church of today is lacking in kindness, the gateway to miracles. The evidence agrees. A situation where a miraculous deliverance of the common cold becomes a news item in CNN leaves so much to desire. The church is far behind in bearing the fruit of the Spirit of kindness, which is the counterpart to the gift of miracle. In fact, a miracle seems more like a mirage to the church of this generation.

The Bible tells us how we can bear the fruit of the Spirit of kindness so that we can receive the gift of miracle. The practice of kindness in the early church was in the form of charity. When the lame man at the beautiful gate of the Temple in Jerusalem, according to Acts of the Apostles, saw Peter and John coming, he perceived the aroma of charity in them; hence, he asked them for alms. Certainly, Peter and John were not as flamboyant as the Pharisees and the nobles streaming into the temple at that hour. Nevertheless, he asked of them. Peter and John did not give him gold or silver, neither did they shun him, but that which they had, the fruit of the Spirit in the form of kindness, they gave to him in abundance. The manifestation of it was the healing miracle we read in Act 3:6-7: "Then Peter said silver and gold have I none, but in the name of Jesus Christ of Nazareth, rise up and walk."

Peter did not just watch to see him get up, though he knew the man was healed. Rather, he stretched out his hand and helped him to get up. This is charity, kindness in motion: "And he took him by the right hand and lifted him up and immediately his feet and ankle bones received strength."

The church must understand the meaning of charity by carefully studying the book of 1 Corinthians 13. Paul made us know that charity is the backbone of the believer, because it is the essential for miracles, without which the power of the gospel message is in doubt. Without miracle, the ministry of Jesus would not have been easy. Paul declared that they did not come with words alone but with power also. Where is that power in today's church? We must look for it, and the place to find it is the place we have dumped charity. And we must look for where we have dumped charity in earnest study of Word of God, lest we pick up counterfeits, and there are many counterfeits, such as alms giving, donations, and such. The lame man at the beautiful gate had been receiving alms from birth, but on this encounter with Peter and John, he received charity, and his life changed. We can understand the position of charity by searching the Word of God. Let us start with 1 Corinthians 13.

1. Though I speak with the tongues of men and of angels and have not charity, I am become as sounding brass or a tinkling cymbal.

2. And though I have the gift of prophecy, and understanding all mysteries, and all knowledge, and though I have faith so that I could move mountain and have not charity I am nothing.

3. And though I bestow all my goods to feed the poor, and though I give my body to be burned and have not charity, it profiteth me nothing.

4. Charity suffereth long, and is kind, charity envieth not, charity vaunteth not itself; is not puffed up.

5. Doth not behave itself unseemingly, seeketh not her own, is not easily provoked, thinketh no evil.

6. Charity never faileth, but whether there be prophecies. They shall fail, whether there be tongues, they shall cease; whether there be knowledge, it shall vanish away.

7. And now abideth faith, hope, charity, these three, but the greatest of these is charity.

This is the word of God.

Let us analyze the verses above and make our own deductions as to what Paul is saying. First, let us keep at the back of our minds that the quantities we are considering along with charity in this passage are the other gifts of the Spirit. Let us start by asking what this charity is. In the list of the fruit of the Spirit, Paul listed love and kindness, but not charity directly (NKJV). Love and kindness both carry the attributes of charity, but by inspiration, Paul listed them separately in the fruit of the Spirit, and by inspiration, also told us that by kindness, he means charity and not love ("charity suffereth long, and is kind") in 1 Corinthians 13:14. Without any fear of oversight, we shall treat charity characteristically from the point of view of kindness or, more appropriately, as kindness in action or divine love expressed in material gifts. The Greek word used here for charity is the same *agape* used most times as divine love. If we look at this Greek word in the context of verse three of 1 Corinthians 13, we see that agape does not always translate literally as love. Giving my goods to feed the poor is kindness. Sacrificing my body as burnt offering for others is the highest love—agape. According to the passage, even after making these two offerings and I lack charity-agape, I am still wanting before God. A simple analysis of this passage will show that the Greek word *agape* has two distinct meanings—love and charity, depending on use. Thomas Brown (1605 – 1682), English physician and writer, in his famous quotation, wrote, "…'Charity begins at home,' is the voice of the world…" This directs our minds to the fact that charity, to the world, is love, because if you do not love your home, mother, father, child, and spouse, how can you love others? He gave charity a worldly meaning. Paul gave it a heavenly meaning and tells us that charity is kindness. It does not have to begin at home. In fact, it has no home. No matter how much love you show at home, it is not charity, but an obligation. Love can start at home but not charity and not kindness. That is why it is the greatest. It has no boundary. It is sovereign. Mother Theresa (1910-1997) began her ministry tending to the sick and dying on the streets of Calcutta in India and not in her hometown of Skopje or her home country of Macedonia. That is charity; it rarely starts at home. *Kindness* is the *practice of being or the tendency to be sympathetic and compassionate.* It rarely starts at home; neither does it have to.

The Christian love is called agape. It is explained as selfless love felt by Christians for their fellow human beings. Love itself is explained as a passionate or tender affection toward others. If it does not start at home, it is questionable. The church, therefore, should not let the definition of charity as given by the world delude her. The Bible is our only authority. It has told us that charity is kindness in action, and that is what we are taking it for. These stories by Jesus illustrate what Paul means by *charity*.

> But a certain Samaritan, as he journeyed…had compassion on him…And bound up his wound… and brought him to an inn, and took care of him. And on the morrow when he departed, he took out two pence, and gave them to the host, and said unto him, "Take care of him; and whatsoever thou spendest more…I will repay thee."
>
> Luke 10:33-35

We know the relationship between the Samaritans and the Jews. And we know that this charity is not near home at all. This is not love; there is no emotional relationship between the two. We are not even told that the wounded man recovered consciousness as to notice the Samaritan before he departed. This is charity. It is kindness in action.

> For I was an hungered, and ye gave me meat; I was thirsty, and ye gave me drink; I was a stranger, and ye took me in; naked and ye clothed me. I was sick and ye visited me: I was in prison, and ye came unto me.
> Matthew 25:35-36

This is charity toward a stranger. But even the wicked can do the same for his son or his loved one.

We cannot categorically say that charity is kindness. The Greek word the Bible used for kindness when transmitted through a physical medium is *philanthropia*. "And the barbarous people shewed us no little kindness (*philanthropia*) for they kindled a fire..." Acts 28:2. But when kindness manifests in the form of moral or spiritual excellence, the Bible adopts the Greek word *chrestotes*. "By pureness, by knowledge, by longsuffering, by kindness (*chrestotes*), by the Holy Ghost, by love unfeigned" (2 Corinthians 6:6). Charity may be related to but is not limited in scope to love or kindness, because it can never be in excess. The adverb *too* has no place in charity. We often hear the words, "You are too kind; you love people too much." These are everyday expressions of the world. For charity, not even the devil has expressed it in extreme or excess. That is why Paul concentrated on charity in extolling the precursor for miracles. Paul describes charity as the bond of perfection: "...and above all these things, put on charity which is the bond of perfectness" (Colossians 3:14). Neither love nor kindness represents charity before God. All three are distinct.

Love has boundaries, but not charity. God does not love everybody. In fact, He hates the evil doer. But His charity is toward all, both the righteous and the unrighteous. "...For He is kind to the unthankful and evil" (Luke 6:35). He gives the same air to all, the same rain to all, the same kindness to all, and the same prosperity to all, but not the same love, not the same joy, not the same peace. The Bible tells us to avoid evil ones, even in marriage. It says we should not be yoked together with unbelievers and has not turned back to ask us to love evil-doers. No, God does not even love them. But our charity should not have boundaries, because His charity does not have boundaries. That is why the Bible called charity the end of the commandment and love the first: "Now the end of the commandment is charity…" (1 Timothy 1:5).

There cannot be love, there cannot be kindness, without charity from a pure heart. There can be no gift of miracles without kindness. And without the gift of miracle, the church is as a sounding brass or a tinkling cymbal, though we speak in millions of tongues.

Though we have the gifts of prophecy and word of wisdom to understand the entire mystery of this world and the one beyond, and we have the word of knowledge to make the globe a village, to travel to the moon for vacation and make our joy full, though we have peace from faith in our belief that this world is not our home, without the power of miracle, due to lack of charity, all are of no reasonable benefit to the church of Jesus Christ on earth. Without power, the church remains neglected; the church remains unable to show the cynical world the power of Jesus. Is there any reason to go to hospital when there is no drug? What is the purpose of warning if the person being warned does not have the capacity to make amends? I understand that a religious sect called Faith Tabernacle does not accept medical treatment. Do such need to go for medical check-up or laboratory test? If prophecy is only for our information, without power to put it into benefit, what is its use? Paul is telling us that the church needs divine power, and the precursor to such power is charity.

Apostle John is known by Christians as the apostle of LOVE. But in extolling Guias, John chose his quality of *agape* in form of charity according to the King James Version, which is the oldest English translation. "Which have borne witness of thy charity before the church..." (3 John 1:6). Certainly, there must be a strong reason for the King James to translate *agape* in some passages as charity and in others as love. That is why as Christians we stand on faith to declare that the Bible is inspired by the Holy Spirit including it translation.

Unfortunately, the New King James Version, probably in an attempt to be like other modern translations, has changed charity with love in these passages. Charity according to the King James Version is the perfection and the end of the commandment. "Now the end of the Commandment is charity" (1 Timothy 1:5). What an important quality. Love is also a very important quality being the first and second. "Thou shalt love the Lord thy God with all thy heart...This is the first Commandment. And the second is like unto it. Thou shalt love thy neighbour as thyself" (Matthew 22: 37-39). If one opens the commandments and the other closes it, then it is clear that love and charity can not mean the same before God. It is obvious to me what the devil wants to achieve by erasing the word charity as a quality of the Christian from the Word of God. Charity has the attribute of being the precursor for miracles without which the church remains a "sounding brass" or a "tinkling cymbal." That is what the devil wants. A church without power to fight him. "Follow after charity and desire spiritual gifts" (1 Corinthians 14:1). If charity disappears from the Christian's vocabulary, where is the platform on which the Holy Spirit will stand to release the gift of miracle without which the church is powerless? Let us resist the devil and return to the proper terms as inspired by the Holy Ghost.

The major difference between charity and love can be found in 1 Corinthians 13:5. It says of charity, "...seeketh not her own..."

Charity does not choose. It is for foes and friends, believers and unbelievers. Charity is one quantity that can never be found in the devil's camp. Satan loves too. Yes, temporary as it may be, he loves his own. But he has no charity at all. The coefficient of love is emotion. That is why psychology classifies it into types, depending on the driving motive. But the driving force behind charity is compassion. Love does not necessarily require a visible material medium for its transmission. That is why you can still love someone who has transited into glory, someone who is no more physically present in this miserable world. That is why you still love Jesus, who you do not see with the naked physical eyes nor hear from or talk to in earthly vocabularies. On the contrary, visible material medium must exist for charity to manifest. That is why in my reasoning King James Bible translated agape in this chapter 13 of 1 Corinthians and in other passages like 1 Corinthians 8:1 correctly as charity. All the modern Christian books I have read, without exception, interpreted charity as love. And their authors are the authorities of modern Christian theology. The Holy Spirit says I should not accept that. From my vision, love shines in heaven as the firmaments, while charity shines as the stars. Charity is the greatest; that is why it is the end and the perfection of the commandment.

Ananias and Sapphira, his wife would not have died the way they did if they had not tended to abuse charity. They had before this time pretended to love Jesus and His congregation, and God ignored their falsehood. But when they tried to ridicule charity, they met their doom, because charity is the precursor to miracles, either of blessing or of wrath, the route to God's power. While love is the first and the beginning of God's commandment, charity is its end and perfection, so says the Word of God, and no earthly authority can change it.

Let me sum up with the message of John the beloved in chapter 3:17 of his first epistle. Love, the gateway into the gifts of the

Spirit, must dwell in the heart to open the bowl of compassion for charity to manifest. Charity is the evidence that the love of God dwells in a Christian. Miracle is the outcome.

Prophecy is a supernatural ability to accurately disclose the things of the future concerning the events of this world through the inspiration of the Holy Spirit for the purpose of bringing exhortation to the body of Christ. The counterpart fruit of the Spirit, or the precursor for prophecy, is goodness in the form of decency, generosity, and righteousness.

Discerning of Spirits: This implies the ability given to a child of God to determine the source, origin, and purpose of persons, thoughts, objects seen or unseen, images, visions, dreams, wishes, signs and wonders, powers and magic, and acts and manifestations that present themselves to a person in the course of life and means on this earth. The counterpart is given to us as faithfulness. This does not need any explanation except that I would like us to understand that faith is not the same as faithfulness, because faith is the gift of the Spirit if we bear the fruit of peace. If you think otherwise, write and close your letter to your Muslim boss, who knows you are a Christian, with "Yours in faith" and face his wrath. But write him the closing remark, "Yours faithfully," and no problem. If we are faithful, satanic spirits will come to us with great fear, and we cannot miss to identify them by their timidity. But without being faithful, you are like being tossed about by the wind, and all spirits come to you with impunity. An unfaithful wife cannot discern the father of her baby. The same way, an unfaithful believer cannot discern the spirits.

Different Kinds of Tongues demand that we should first bear the fruit of gentleness. Our speaking in tongues must be in a very orderly and gentlemanly manner. Our God is not an author of confusion and rowdiness.

Interpretation of Tongues demands that we should have self-control.

Let me repeat that we must first bear the fruit of the Spirit before we can receive the gifts of the Spirit. The church has been misled by the devil for too long in believing that once we become believers we should fold our hands and open our mouth for the Holy Spirit to spoon-feed us with milk and honey. Not so, because Peter said, "As new born babies, desire the sincere milk of the Word that ye may grow thereby"(1 Peter 2:2).

This is one of the most prominent directives to the new convert from the apostles. The devil has misconstrued this in the heart of the church, that we shall desire the meat instead of milk from conversion. We must first bring forth the fruit of the Spirit before we can begin to desire the gifts of the Spirit. And to bear the fruit, we must first desire the sincere milk of the Word of God. The devil laughs at us, and the Holy Spirit groans when we pursue the dart the devil has thrown in the wrong direction to mislead the church. The church is asking the Holy Spirit for the fruit of the Spirit; the church asks the Holy Spirit for the gifts of the Spirit. No, the Christian is not called into idleness of the mind but to service according to the will of God in Christ Jesus. This is the instruction of our Lord concerning the requirements in the believer to bear fruit (always in the singular).

> Every branch in me that beareth not fruit He taketh away;
> and every branch that beareth fruit, He pruneth it that it
> may bear forth more fruit.
>
> John 15:1

What the church of today may be misrepresenting as a promise that the Holy Spirit is bearing fruit in the believer may be the passage below, which, rather, is directing the believer to his or her responsibility and conditions for bearing fruit.

> Abide in me, and I in you. As the branch cannot bear fruit of itself, except it abide in the vine; no more can ye, except ye abide in me.
>
> John 15:4

The passage clearly says that bearing of fruit is not possible to the unbeliever but only available to those who meet the requirements by abiding in His teachings.

By the time the devil has fully established this false impression in us, God forbid, and creates in us a state of idea speculations concerning the work of the Holy Spirit in the believer, he will move to the next level, which may be to impress on the church that the Holy Ghost will begin to go to the dangerous locations of the world and convert unbelievers and save us from the risk of going to such areas for evangelism. And the church will agree, especially when there are seeming passages in the Bible to suggest that. I am not saying there is anything to suggest that, but anything is possible with an idle mind. This could be the next level if we do not start now to ask for what we need to do to please God instead of asking Him to spoon-feed us. Let us ignore the devil and see the Word of God through the guidance of the Holy Spirit for what it is. We are concerned here with the fruit of the Spirit and the gifts of the Spirit, both presented to us through the Spirit-inspired hands of Paul, listed to us as counterparts. Paul, on the fruit, said, "…but the fruit of the Spirit is (1) love, (2) joy, (3) peace, (4) patience, (5) kindness, (6) goodness, (7) faithfulness, (8) gentleness, and (9) self-control."

On the gifts of the Spirit, he said, "To one is given by the Spirit "(1) Word of Wisdom, (2) Word of Knowledge, (3) Faith, (4) Healing, and (5) Work of Miracle (6) prophecy (7) discerning of spirit (8) different kinds of tongues, and (9) interpretation of tongues."

From the opening phrases in the message of the fruit and the gift, it is quite clear that the fruit resides within and needs to be cultured, while the gifts are endowed. I am not saying that the Spirit has no interest in our bearing this fruit; He does. He needs this fruit in order that He should pour out His gifts; hence, He continuously fertilizes our spirit so as to be able to bear this fruit. But our willingness to accept the conditions is our prerogative and not the duty of the Holy Spirit.

The Greek word translated spiritual gifts in 1 Corinthians 12:1 is *pheumatikos*, literally meaning things of the Spirit. The same word is used in Romans 7:14 as an opposite of *sarkikos*, which literally means natural or carnal things. The Greek word translated fruit in Galatians 5:22 is *karpos*. Strong's Greek dictionary suggests that it has its base meaning from *a* plucked fruit. Therefore Paul gave us a list of nine things and called them fruit and gave us another list of nine entries and called them gifts. The fruit is in the singular, *karpos*, and the gifts are in the plural, yet both are nine in number. The Spirit is looking forward to our fruit, by which we shall be known.

> For the tree is known by his fruit.
>
> Matthew 12: 33b

The Christian is also known by his fruit. The Holy Spirit is as ready and willing as ever to endow the church with gifts of the Spirit. The moment the church bears the right fruit, the gifts shall begin to rain healings, miracles, you name it. The Holy Spirit is not going to give us the characters by which we are known. That would be partiality. He will give gifts according to our characters.

Paul wrote to the church that he did not desire a gift from them except that receiving from them would increase their fruit-bearing capacity and consequently their gifts from the Holy Spirit:

> Not because I desire a gift from you, but I desire fruit that may abound to your account.
>
> Philippians 4:17

Is it not clear from many Bible passages that the fruit is the precursor for the gift? The church can come back to its power-filled condition of old if we can look for and begin to bear the necessary fruit of the Spirit for the entrustment of the gifts of the Spirit. The will is ours; the enablement is the Holy Ghost. The proper thing the church should pray for is the empowerment of the Holy Spirit to bear the right fruit. The moment we bear the proper fruit, the corresponding gift is automatic. Jesus has already prayed for that on our behalf.

The church must come out from the Rock of Ages it is hiding in and begin to bear fruit by abiding in the Master.

"Rock of Ages, cleft for me. Let me hide myself in thee," is an ancient hymn by Augustus Montaque Toplady, but it is not the instruction of the Master. Rather, He tells us that we are the light of the world.

> Ye are the light of the world. A city that is set on an hill cannot be hid.
>
> Matthew 5:14

We cannot continue to hide under the cover that the Holy Spirit is going to produce the fruit of the Spirit in us. If this is true, the Bible would have told us, but rather, the Master again says that His church is the salt of the earth. He did not tell us that we shall be salted by the Holy Spirit if we lose our savor but that we shall become good for nothing.

Ye are the salt of the earth; but if the salt have lost his savor, wherewith shall it be salted? It is thenceforth good for nothing, but to be cast out and to be trodden under foot of man.

Matthew 5:13

How is it difficult for the church to see that the fruit of the Spirit is composed of ordinary dictionary words of worldly vocabularies of earthly quantities: love, joy, peace, patience, kindness, goodness, faithfulness, gentleness, and self-control, while the gifts of the Spirit are scriptural and cannot be explained from ordinary dictionary definition without putting them into context with the Word of God? They are heavenly entities and outside of the reach of mankind without the anointing of God.

If character molding is the prerogative of the Holy Spirit, then the moment we become Christians, who or what we are becomes the responsibility of the Holy Spirit. That is what the devil teaches, but that is not what Jesus taught in the parable of the seed sower in Matthew 13:3-8. He mentioned four conditions and categories of the environment the seeds fell upon.

1. The ones that fell by the way side,
2. The ones that fell on the stony places,
3. The ones that fell among thorns,
4. And the ones that fell on the good soil.

Of the four groups, only the one that fell on the good soil brought forth fruit, some one hundred fold, some sixty fold, and some thirty fold. If the Holy Spirit begins to bear fruit in Christians from the moment of conversion, then the second and third groups that did not bring forth fruit and the discrepancy in the fourth

a deeper evangelism

group's fruit-bearing capacity should be blamed on the Holy Spirit. That is the doctrine the devil has introduced to the church from the back door by putting the responsibility of bearing fruit and character molding on the shoulders of the Holy Spirit.

The Lord makes it clear once again in the parable of talents that the gift of the Holy Spirit is according to our individual fruit-bearing capability.

> And unto one he gave five talents, to another two and to another one; to every man according to his several ability..."
>
> Matthew 25:15

An interesting relationship between the two parables is that the Lord draws the same conclusion from both. In the parable of the sower in Matthew 13, the conclusion is found in verse 12: "For whosoever hath, to him shall be given, and he shall have more abundance; but whosoever hath not, from him shall be taken away even that he hath." In the parable of the talents of Matthew 25, the same conclusion is found in verse 29. "For unto every one that hath shall be given and he shall have abundance; but from him that hath not shall be taken away even that which he hath." Maybe you have not noticed that the Lord concluded the two parables on the same note, almost word for word. The determination to bear fruit is the major difference between today's church and the early church. The Holy Spirit is the giver but not the selector. As He gives abundantly to he who has, so also He takes away the little he who has none is bragging with.

Another deadly impression of this belief that the Holy Spirit bears fruit for the believer is that it associates the Holy Spirit with a character of the devil. Please pardon my boldness. Jesus has invited us to paradise, and by the help of the Holy Spirit, we shall be there. But we must first accept the invitation and put on the required garment and the right attitude. If we don't, no way. For the devil, he has not invited anybody; he comes and conscripts with or without your will. There is no standard, no qualifications, willing or unwilling, he just comes. He wants us to believe the Holy Spirit is like him, cheating and struggling for souls with him. But this is not true. How do we conceive in our hearts the Holy Spirit can be partial, letting one bear fruit and denying the other, under the same circumstance of conversion? No, what makes the difference in converts is the fruit they bear of love, joy, peace, patience, kindness, goodness, faithfulness, gentleness, and self-control, or none. The presence or lack of these components of the fruit of the Spirit determines what gifts and the magnitude of them He bestows on us. The Holy Spirit is not like the devil, looking for souls to conscript. No, He is sacred and holy and operates only in pious environments.

What do you think Jesus meant by the sin against the Holy Spirit in Mark 3 and Matthew 12?

> Wherefore I say unto you, all manner of sin and blasphemy shall be forgiven unto men: but the blasphemy against the Holy Ghost shall not be forgiven unto men. And whosoever, speaketh a word against the Son of man it shall be forgiven him, but whosoever speaketh against the Holy Ghost, it shall not be forgiven him, neither in this world, neither in the world to come.
>
> Matthew 12:31-32

Jesus is telling them here that they were not accusing Him of a relationship with the devil but instead their accusation is against the Holy Ghost that is at work in Him.

Why is the precious blood of Jesus not willing to save one from the sin of speaking against the Holy Spirit? This is a very essential subject for every true believer, because we speak about the Holy Spirit in all we say and do most times. Let us always be guided not ever to speak against Him, either in error, in omission, or in commission. How can we achieve this? By speaking according to the teachings of the Word of God and rejecting all human indoctrinations that are contrary to the character of the Holy Spirit, even in jokes. The Holy Ghost does not reside in the air or operate in vacuum. He resides in Christians and operates through them. We must be careful about what we say against another, especially when there is a claim of duty under the anointing of the Spirit.

But the Pharisees spoke against Jesus in the passage under reference. How come it becomes a blasphemy against the Holy Spirit?

> But when the Pharisees heard it. They said, "This fellow doth not cast out devil, but by Beelzebub the prince of the devil."
>
> Matthew 12:24

The question above brings us back to the issue of fruit and gifts of the Spirit. The Bible tells us that Jesus came into this world in human flesh. We have discussed that earlier. He surrendered himself to the full influence of the flesh. He molded His character under the same worldly pressure of the demands and desires of the flesh as you and me. He molded His character under the same satanic temptations we face. The work He did was by the power of the Holy Spirit, not by His power as mere flesh. That is what He acknowledges in the passage above. He is telling them that they are not insulting or abusing Him, because He was just flesh like them and could not do any such as they have seen on His own, but by the power of the Holy Spirit operating in Him and who He will also send down to operate in the world through those who will acquire His character when He goes. It is this power, the Holy Spirit, that these Pharisees, who called themselves the custodians of God's law, attributed to devil, not because they do not know the truth but because of envy and fear of the Romans.

> If we let Him alone, all men will believe on Him, and the Romans shall come and take away both our place and nation.
>
> John 11: 48

This was the reason the Pharisees decided to call the manifestation of power of God evil: envy and fear. The lesson for the church here is that the Holy Spirit abhors any comparison or reference with the devil in method, character, similarity, or in any form. Unlike the devil, He will not come until you are willing to freely open the door of your heart for Him to enter. And He will not give us gifts until we begin to bring forth fruit in the Spirit of Jesus.

The Pharisees had all along noticed the sincerity of Jesus. They had just observed an undeniable and powerful miracle that was clear evidence of the power of God. For the sake of love, Jesus had rescued many from sufferings and oppressions inflicted upon them by the devil. For the sake of a firm mind set against accepting Jesus as the Messiah, the Pharisees rejected and perversely twisted the obvious truth before their very eyes in order to turn the crowd against Jesus. They openly credited the work of the most ultimate good to the most ultimate evil.

There are still many of these Pharisees in our midst today, but we are a city on the hill, the light of the world. By our fruit, we shall be known, even by the Holy Spirit.

Please note that while the gift of the Spirit is toward the church (as individual, as family, as local church, or as Catholic or universal church) the fruit of the Spirit is the product of righteousness brought forth by a total surrender of our lives to the redemptive power of the passion of Jesus through the enablement of the Holy Spirit, who teaches and guides us. He does not give the fruit; rather, it is a landing platform for the release of His gifts of the Spirit. I have heard people pray for the gift of the fruit of the Spirit and, of course, the Spirit groans, and the devil laughs. It is like seeking a loan from the bank and asking the bank manager for collateral. I am not saying the Holy Ghost does not have any input in making our fruit-bearing possible. No, He has, and quite a lot.

1. He teaches us things about God and ourselves and brings all that Jesus came for to our remembrance. "But the comforter which is the Holy Ghost, whom the father will send in my name, He shall teach you all things and bring all things to your remembrance whatever I have said unto you" (John 14:26). To learn and accept His teaching is our prerogative. Remember that you can take a horse to the river, but you cannot force it to drink.

2. The Holy Spirit shall teach us all we need to know concerning the way, the truth, and the life. "...even the Spirit of truth, which proceedeth from the Father, he shall testify of me" (John 15:26). He cannot force us to accept the truth or follow the way, but until we accept and follow and enter into life, He will not release His gifts to us.

3. He shall guide us into the entire truth of the mission of Jesus, and most importantly, into things to come—prophecy. "Howbeit when He, the Spirit of truth, is come, He will guide you into all truth: for He shall not speak of Himself, but whatever He shall hear, that shall He speak: and will shew you things to come" (John 16:13). My interpretation of this passage is that

the Holy Spirit is calling, come back to your first love so that my guidance and counseling can become effective in your life; so that your prophecies can become accurate; so that you can have a clear picture of the end time. Listen to the conflicts of interpretation of the end time and the prophecies of the church's super pastors and super ministers, and you will see how far the Holy Spirit's guidance into the truth and into things to come is reflecting on the church.

4. He will bring to our knowledge and conscience the foolishness of our sins; hence, the need for repentance. "And when he is come, he will reprove the world of sin and of righteousness, and of judgment" (John 16:8). When last did you hear the word sin mentioned in its crude name from the pulpits? Adultery has become having affair; homosexual is now called same-sex. The church seems to have told the Holy Spirit that these words are too harsh and can wait. And the Holy Spirit has also told the church that His gifts are too precious and will also wait. Can we continue to wait and remain a caricature of the world—a church without power? The church must wake up to its responsibility so that the gifts of Spirit can come back. Granted, we are pardoned by God's grace, but we must not take His mercy for granted.

5. He is in continuous prayers for us.

Likewise, the Spirit also helpeth our infirmities: for we know not what we should pray for: but the Spirit itself maketh intercession for us with groaning which cannot be uttered. And he that searcheth the heart knoweth what is the mind of the Spirit, because He maketh intercession for the saints according to the will of God.

Romans 8:26-27

According to the will of God? How far away is the will of today's church from the will of God? I have always said to my evangelical audience that there is nothing you can give to God that He cannot get without you except one thing: your will. He does not need to ask for anything, because everything belongs to Him except your will, which He has given you absolute freedom to exercise as you desire until you spiritually will it to Him. We must consciously, determinedly, and spiritually, as in the legal term, *will* our wills to Him if we must receive His precious gifts. The early church did, and that is the power ministry of that church we read today. What will the future church say about the church of our generation? Did we give to God the only thing He needed from us, our will, or did we harden our hearts against Him? The legal profession borrowed the term *will* from the church and has remained faithful to it. The legal will you make now, when you are alive, determines who takes over your material possession when you die. The *spiritual will* you make now determines who takes over your soul when you die: God or Satan. When altar calls are made, the essence is for you to will your will to God, and when you have done that, do not look back, for you have made the best will that can be, witnessed by the servant of God who made the call.

When the will of the church synchronizes with the will of God, the outcome is command and from the Holy Spirit. The word *command* has a military origin, I suppose; it does not carry any force of its own but operates on an assumption of totally established obedience. That is why a commander cannot issue command to enemy troops, no matter how superior. The power of a commander's command is determined by established obedience or loyalty and not his physical power or rank at the time he is giving the command. When we become God's troop, the Holy Ghost will begin to command us on the strength of established obedience and loyalty to God. This is the will, the allegiance He demands from us, which He cannot take unless we give and cannot give unless we surrender to His command. The early church surrendered her will to His command, and He became their commander-in-chief.

> As they ministered to the Lord and fasted, the Holy Ghost said separate me Barnabas and Saul for the work whereunto I have called them.
>
> Act 13:2

The Holy Spirit commanded, and it was obeyed.

When shall the Holy Spirit come back to the church as her commander-in-chief? Even in nature, it is a bitter thing not to have a commander, such as someone without a legitimate spouse, a child without parents, a man without a discipline; name them. My dear, it is a terrible thing to live without a commander. The church today is suffering from not having the Holy Spirit, as it should, as her commander.

My beloved in Christ, the problem of the church today is that we do not know the Holy Spirit enough. We have not submitted to His teachings as we ought to. He cannot give power He cannot control. We are anxious for His gifts but not willing to bear the fruit to satisfy His hunger. The church must wake up, lest what happened to the fig tree of Matthew 21:19 happens to her.

The Flesh and Familiar Spirits

To fully comprehend the negative influence of flesh, we must first investigate its origin and be able to visualize what man was before this evil came into existence. This will help us to have a good understanding of what a man becomes when he puts the flesh into captivity and what he is when he allows it to rule him. Let us take a look at some Bible passages that will be of help in this regard:

> In the beginning, God created the heavens and the earth.
> Genesis 1:1

This is the beginning of God's Word. He created a perfect earth that could have remained as peaceful as heaven if Lucifer did not rebel and come into the earth and cause havoc. The Bible could have been an all-sweet story of God's relationship with His perfect creation. We know this from 2 Peter, which tells us that this perfect creation was destroyed with flood. The next verse in

Genesis gives us a picture of what happened after Lucifer polluted the earth:

> And the earth was without form and void; and darkness was upon the face of the deep...
>
> Genesis 1:2

After the Holy Spirit had cleaned up the mess Lucifer and his fellow fallen angels had brought upon the earth, God perfected another beautiful creation in seven days.

By this creation was man, whom God formed from clay and put His own breath into. What we call Holy Spirit in English translation is called *Ruwach* in Old Testament Hebrew and *Pnuma* in New Testament Greek, literally meaning *breath* or *breeze*. We can, for certain, call the Holy Spirit the Breath of God. This being true, we can say that what God put into man for life after forming him from clay was the Holy Spirit.

> And the Lord God formed man of the dust of the ground and breathed into his nostrils the breath of life and man became a living soul.
>
> Genesis 2:7

The lessons here are:

1. The body of man was formed from clay.

2. Life entered into man in the form of the Holy Spirit.

3. And man became a living soul. This is the difference between man and all the other creatures that did not become a living being through the Breath of God.

This was the perfect being God created from a body of clay, a life of the Holy Spirit, a living soul called man. "And man became a living soul."

There was no aging body and no probably blood as we know it now in association with human flesh of this perfect man. The Bible tells us that this living soul called man did not know the meaning of good, because there was no evil. Everything was perfect.

> But of the tree of the knowledge of good and evil, thou shall not eat of it.
>
> Genesis 2: 17

Man's duty was simply to take care of the garden of Eden for fellowship with God. In this heaven-on-earth garden, the Bible tells us that God comes in physical form to interact with Adam and Eve. Other creatures were also in communion with man; the Bible tells us that Eve had a conversation with a serpent, who, from the tone of that conversation, must have been very familiar with Eve and Adam. Certainly, Lucifer and the other fallen angels could not come into this garden, because it was an extension of God's home from which they had been banished. But there was need for Lucifer to reach man and hit him down and destroy his relationship with God. So he had to reach him through a being that was familiar to the garden. The serpent was willing and delivered the devil's arsenal into the garden of God. This is the origin of the devil's engagement of familiar spirits in reaching man. It was the first medium of the devil's attack on the living soul called man, composed of a body made from clay and life made possible by the Breath of God, or the Holy Spirit. This attack so well hit its target that the consequence has become the ugly situation of the natural man, because right there and then, the living soul of man died. The living soul became a dead soul, because the Holy Spirit, the source of life to man, left him. Man has to live by his own breath, which has an expiring date. This is contrary to God's original design for man when He put His breath in him. If man had not fallen and lost God's breath, there would not have been death. This everlasting life is what Jesus has redeemed for man, I mean, believers, even after the believers physical body may be dead. While on the earth, the body of man is left to survive on the breath or spirit of man, to become venerable to all sorts of influence, especially now that it has become aware of the power of evil against good. This is how the power and influence of the flesh came into being.

Let us take a much closer look at the picture again. God has made all in perfection. Man was to live in fellowship with God forever. There was no evil, because there was no good. Everything was in unity with God. This is the picture Paul is showing to us in his messages of no more works but faith for the Christian, because he has returned to a life of not knowing good and evil. He lives, whether here on earth or in paradise when earthly life is over, by the Breath of God as it was before the fall and evil flesh.

With this knowledge of good and bad, man became able to see his nakedness despite the glorious aura God had clothed him with from creation; hence, Adam and Eve hid themselves at the coming of God, because they saw themselves as naked even when they had made a covering with fig leaves. This was the beginning of the sin of the flesh. It was not there in creation. It is not the body God made from clay or its organs that took over the functions of maintaining natural life in man after the Breath of God or the Holy Spirit had left the fallen man. The Bible is very clear on the fact that God created a perfect man. Flesh is the radiation man received from Lucifer when he rejected God's instruction in obedience to the devil. The medium was the serpent, a familiar object to Eve. Flesh, like other visible or invisible spirits, is not the physical biological human body. It comes in so many forms, such as thought and behavior, but always in an invisible form, though its manifestations are usually in physical, concrete forms such as murder, cheating, adultery, stealing, drinking, eating, and so on. The human hand has no intention of its own to steal until the flesh commands it to do so. The human hand or leg or any other human body part is therefore not the flesh. At most, they can be regarded as agents of the flesh, but not the flesh.

The other names the Bible called the evil flesh are "our old man" (Romans 6:6) and "corruptible seed" (1 Peter 1:23). Biological flesh, on the other hand, is the material in the human body that covers the bone. That is what Adam referred to when he rejoiced in the bone of his bone and the flesh of his flesh. That is not the flesh of our interest here. The flesh we are talking about has no specified location in our body. Flesh is used in the Bible, especially by Apostle Paul, in a spiritual sense, always implying an attachment to the devil, with an inherent capacity for evil. Its attributes include arrogance and being overbearing, boastful, proud, loud, and lustful. It usually presents its intentions in the form of suggestion in a self-righteous manner to proffer solutions to pain, hunger, loneliness, sorrows, and fear. It can surface in many forms and characters; it can quote the Bible, it can be a preacher or a Sunday school teacher, it can be in the choir, make large donations in the church, and can be generally provokingly evangelical. Its main purpose is to thwart God's will for man. Remember the Lord's prayer: "Let your will be done on earth…" Why is the will of God not being done on earth in many lives many years after our Lord taught us this prayer? The flesh. At any time you say, "Let Your will be done" as in the Lord's prayer, you are invariably saying, let flesh retire in my life. That prayer is answered any time flesh retires in a single life.

Having seen the source and nature of the flesh, it is now time for us to see how it is running our lives, ruining our relationship with God, and taking us farther away from the Holy Spirit. We

shall also see the need to go back to the perfect man God created. This is only possible through a new birth in Jesus Christ
by crucifying the Old man, the man that disobeyed God and
received the radiation of Satan and remained separated from the
Holy Spirit.

The Bible says that Jesus Christ became flesh. Yes, flesh in
purpose, not in essence. He came into this world, not through
the process of evil flesh, for He was of a virgin birth free from
the original sin we all inherited from our first parents, Adam
and Eve. We need to realize that we are products of sin and
therefore dwell naturally in sin. There is no way we can live in
this world in the form that displeased God and expect to meet
His requirements. The more we tend to be good, the more the
knowledge of evil poisons our minds. That is why Paul tells us
that no amount of work can save without first destroying the old
man and becoming a new creature in Jesus Christ. He is the only
one who can return the Breath of God into the living soul of
man. The body is not the flesh or the spirit that is in opposition
with the true Spirit that comes only from knowing Jesus. The
same way the object the devil is using to mesmerize us is in itself
not an evil spirit, but what the devil has injected into it to pass
to us is the evil. In fact, the flesh is also out to destroy the body
as well. Check and see if there is anything the flesh presents to
the body that is not detrimental to it: alcohol, cigarettes, fornication, gluttony, entertainment, and so on. The flesh has no limit
to its demands for the body. The flesh will persuade the body to
take in excess the very basic requirements for the body's upkeep
in order to impair the body and anger the Holy Spirit whose
habitation the human body is suppose to be. So the flesh is also
in enmity with the body as it is with the soul.

The flesh is a spirit, but an evil one, like his twin, the familiar spirit that we shall meet later in this chapter. All spirits that
are not of Jesus are evil and at war with the Holy Spirit. The

flesh is an enemy of the soul, because the moment man lost the Breath of God as his source of life, the human breath took over as man's source of life here on earth. Because the man dies, his soul, which lives forever, becomes the main object of interest for the devil. The flesh and familiar spirits are his media. The familiar spirit he sends to us through agents, but the flesh, he deposited on man when he caused him to fall. So your body is not the evil flesh, though most of its atrocities are accomplished through the body, to its own detriment. Not according to the will of the body, because the living soul tells of consequences and the punishment the body suffers when it allows itself to be used by the flesh to glorify the devil. The flesh does not gratify the body; on the contrary, the flesh sacrifices the body on the altar of Satan. The body is helpless, because it depends on the devil-defeated human breath for survival. The message of the Bible is that we must return to the Breath of God as the source of life so that the flesh can no longer enslave the body through its dependence on a defeated man's breath. There is nothing God put in the human body at creation that is not pleasant. What the flesh does is to commandeer body functions and use them for its purpose, which at all times are evil. When Jesus asked us to cut off any part of our body that has become consciously or unconsciously obedient to the flesh, it does not mean that the part is evil from origin but that it has become a willing tool through corruption by evil flesh to serve Satan. A eunuch that does not have the Breath of God as his source of life may still be obedient to flesh of sexual lust, though he lacks the required bodily part for the function. So removing the infested part does not stop the flesh from warring, but denies it the instrument of implementation. This is advice of Jesus to the wicked world, but to His church, He promises the return of the Breath of God, which sends the flesh back to chains and allows the body to function in absolute obedience to God as it was at the beginning of creation.

The flesh and familiar spirits are the horrible warriors the devil engages as his weapons fashioned against man, and they prosper in man's weakness. The serpent, being a familiar creature in the garden of God in Eden, brought the devil's message of disobedience to God into the garden. Man acquired the power of knowledge of good and evil by receiving and complying with this message. Familiar spirits are still doing the same today.

The evil flesh entered into man in the form of greed and lust when man became disobedient to God. Adam and Eve had been living in this garden for some while and had not seen themselves as naked. But after acquiring the power of knowledge of good and bad, the spirit of evil flesh took them over, and lust (self or ego) and greed manifested: lust, as they saw themselves naked; ego, as they refused to appear before God in selfish recognition of their inadequate dressing; and greed, as they saw the forbidden fruit as very appetizing and very pleasing to the eyes. This is the ungodly grip the flesh has on humanity still today.

Unfortunately, what seems to dominate the pulpits of today's church is donation and money instead of sin, holiness, power, Jesus, and Holy Spirit. The result is that the church gets richer materially by the day and poorer spiritually by the minute, and the devils rejoice at the steady stream of humans into captivity.

The passages below are a few of the cardinal issues the Bible put before us concerning how we are to conduct our ways in regard to life of purity in the Holy Spirit and of sin in evil flesh.

> Walk in the Spirit, and ye shall not fulfill the lust of the flesh. For the flesh lusteth against the Spirit, and the Spirit against the flesh and these are contrary to the other, so that ye cannot do the things that ye would…For they that are after the flesh do mind the things of the flesh, but they that are after the Spirit the things of the Spirit, for to be

carnally minded is dead; but to be spiritually minded is life
and peace.

> Romans 8:5-6

For if ye live after the flesh, ye shall die; but if ye through
the Spirit do mortify the deeds of the body, ye shall live.
For as many as are led by the spirit of God, they are the
sons of God.

> Romans 8:13-14

For what the law could not do in that it was weak through
the flesh, God did by sending His own son in the likeness
of sinful flesh, on account of sin.

> Romans 8:3

From the passages above, we make the following deductions:

1. We are asked to walk following the guidance of the Spirit so that we shall not be led by the evil flesh and be found in the camp of disobedience to God.

2. We are told there is a continuous intrusion or lust for power of control by the spirit of the devil against the true Spirit of God in controlling the life of the Christian.

3. These two, the Spirit of God and the spirit of the devil, are opposite, but definitely not equal.

4. Anybody that follows the directives of the spirit of the devil does the things the devil likes.

5. Anybody that follows the directives of the Spirit of God does the things God likes.

6. To believe the devil that we are pleasing or entertaining the body by using it according to the directives of

the spirit of the devil brings death both to the body
and the soul.

7. But to live in accordance with the directives of the
Spirit of God is to be alive both in body here on earth
and also preserve the soul for eternity with God.

8. We are told that the law was unable to curb the atrocities of the body under the influence of the spirit of the
devil, because the law itself, as a product of the knowledge of good and evil, is not strong enough to check
the excesses of its own very origin.

9. Finally, we are told that God sent His own Son, who,
though he came in the likeness of sinful man, lived
above the influence of the spirit of the devil (the flesh)
and did what the law and blood of lamb could not do:
the return to a life in which man again becomes a living
soul by the Breath of God.

I would like to interchange the word *flesh* with *spirit of the devil*
or *sinful man*. To me, this gives a better understanding of what
the Bible means by *flesh*. We first met the word *flesh* in the Bible
in the sense we are considering it here in Genesis 6:3:

> And the Lord said my spirit shall not always strive with
> man, for that he also is flesh. Yet his days shall be one
> hundred and twenty years.

God did not pass this judgment on the flesh of man at the beginning when Adam called Eve " flesh of my flesh" in Genesis 2:23.
The flesh then was pure and did strive with God as He main-
tained regular physical visits to them in the Garden. "And they
heard the voice of the Lord walking in the cool of the day." If
it was a spiritual visit, that weather report "in the cool of the
day" would not have been necessary. The flesh under reference in
Genesis 6:3 above is different from the one God was visiting in

the physical. It has received the devil's baptism and could no longer always strive with God. It has becomes the devil's property until born again in Christ. That is why I prefer to call it spirit of the devil.

Let us take the operational phrases in this passage one after the other, and the meaning of *flesh* will begin to crystallize further in our mind.

"My spirit shall not always strive with man." If God had said that His Spirit shall not strive with man in a definite term, we may not have had people like Noah, Enoch, Abraham, Israel, Moses, the prophets, or John the Baptist, men that God's Spirit strived with before the coming of Jesus Christ, and the gospel message would have been a great difficulty to spread, because there would not have been prophetic references to the Christ. But in His kind nature, He used the phrase *shall not always strive*. More also because He knows that man shall return to Him through Jesus Christ, who will conquer death, release man from the bondage of flesh, and return him to a life of the Breath of God. To reject Jesus is to miss the opportunity of this privilege made available by God's statement above.

"Yet his days shall be a hundred and twenty years." God put the days of man in number instead of His provision at creation that man should live without end of days like Him, since man's source of live was His Breath.

In verse five of the same chapter, we read:

> And God saw that the wickedness of man was great in the earth and that every imagination of the thoughts of his heart was only evil continually.
>
> Genesis 6:5

These are the passages the church of today and Christians like to ignore. Until we come to the reality of our position with God, we can never be able to appreciate the gift of God in Jesus Christ. If we put the above passages together, we shall agree that the original, perfect creation of God in man was not evil flesh that is in opposition to the Spirit. Before the fall, man was a living soul, sustained by the Breath of God (Genesis 2:7). After the fall, man lost the privilege of a life sustained by the Breath of God and become sustained by *blood, water, and breath of man,* all of which are powered by human body organs that have an expiration date.

> And there are three that bear witness *in earth, the spirit and the water and the blood and the three agree in one.*
>
> 1 John 5:8

From a literal translation of the Hebrew word *ruwach*, we can take the Holy Spirit to literally mean *Breath of God* and the human spirit as the *breath of man.* After the fall, man became aware of good and evil, and God therefore gave him the right to choose. The beauty and pleasantness of Eve, which Adam had called bone of his bone and flesh of his flesh, became to him an object of lust when he became aware of good and evil; hence, he realized that Eve was naked. Among the consequences of man's fall is that God withdrew His Breath and replaced it with human breath, circulated by blood and water, a form of life sustenance God provided for non-humans at creation so that at the expiration of the number of days given unto man, his shall die like other creatures. Even the Son of God, Jesus Christ, came into the world in the form of life sustained by human breath.

> This is He that came by water and blood, even Jesus Christ; and it is the Spirit that beareth witness because the Spirit is true.
>
> 1 John 5:6

God Himself told us what He meant by *flesh* in verse five: the very imagination of the thoughts of the heart of man and the wickedness of man; "...every imagination of the thoughts of his heart was only evil continually." This new character man acquired after his fall made God regret creating him:

> And it repented the Lord that He had made man on the earth, and it grieved Him at His heart.
>
> Genesis 6:6

We therefore must be aware that until one puts off the flesh or the spirit of evil and puts on the Spirit of God through Jesus Christ, one remains a creature of regret to God. Oh! I wonder how many of us would delight in the presence of a child we regret giving birth to. Our wish for such a child is that he or she were dead. Death is God's wage for sin as written in Romans 6:23. If the Christian is a son of God according to Romans 8:15, the same should be his or her position for an unrepentant child. God's wish for humanity is that all should embrace the glory of His Son. Our wish for a bad son or daughter is to turn a new leaf in the positive. The frustration and anger we feel when we cannot get a bad son or daughter to repent of his or her criminal ways is same God feels when we refused to repent from our sins. As long as you remain in your sinful nature, as long as you are led by the flesh, the spirit of evil, you are a source of regret to God and, of course, dead, because His wish is a reality: "...if ye live after the flesh ye shall die."

a deeper evangelism

What Is Living After the Flesh?

Living in flesh is:

1. Surrendering the body to do the wishes and desires of the devil in obedience to the commands of his spirit embodied in us as flesh through the manipulation of our minds, which brings destruction to both body and soul.

2. Obedience to dissimulated familiar spirits in an effort to become wise and knowledgeable like God. Genesis 3:5: "And the serpent said unto the woman ye shall not surely die: for God doth know that in the day ye eat thereof, then your eyes shall be opened, and ye shall be as gods, knowing good and evil." I have earlier explained why such spirits, as the serpent onto Eve, are called "familiar." First let us understand that the serpent was one of the familiar creatures in the garden of God in Eden. The devil cannot come there himself, because he had been expelled from heaven and the presence of God, which Eden, by extension, represented. So he had to use a creature that had free access and was also familiar to Eve and Adam as the medium for the assignment of bringing man into enmity with God. The serpent was like any other creature in the garden, walking on legs, but after this wicked act, God cursed it to crawl on its belly. "And the Lord said unto the serpent, "Because thou hast done this, thou are cursed above all cattle, and above every beast of the field, upon thy belly shalt thou go, and dust shalt thou eat all the days of thy life" (Genesis 3:14). While the devil's spirit has residence in our body in the form of thought and imaginations and manifests as deeds of our body, which the apostle Paul asked us to mortify, his use of familiar spirit remains as at the time of the

serpent. He cannot come into the church because we know him; he cannot come to the house because we know him; he cannot come to the office because we know him. He therefore comes in the person or object that is familiar to us, such as father, mother, spouse, son, daughter, friend, family member, church member, supposed man of God, supposed prophet, moon, star, pet, entertainment, or ancestors.

The flesh and familiar spirits are the two principal media with which the devil enslaves man by keeping him away from God's rescue mission in Jesus.

We must first realize that most activities that constitute living in the flesh are not, on their own, evil. They become evil due to the purpose the devil intends their applications to achieve with regard to time, manner, quantity, and quality. Every activity of the flesh hurts the body and therefore could not have been the desire or a freewill action of the body; rather, because of the weakness of the operating system of the fallen man, his body becomes susceptible to the manipulation of the spirit of the devil, either through the flesh or familiar spirits. Let's take them one after the other.

The satisfying of our sensitive appetites cannot be sin in themselves; otherwise, the only time we may be without sin is during fasting and under vow of abstention. In fact, abstention is not generally encouraged, because it is one of the most pungent weapons of the devil. If denying the body essential pleasure such as food, recreation, socializing, rest, dressing styles, and enjoyment is mortification of the deeds of the body, their demand on the Christian is very minimal compared with the denials devil worshipers are subjected to. So denying the body essential pleasure cannot in any way translate to mortification of the body. As we go further, we shall see that what the spirit of the devil does either in the form of flesh or familiar spirit is to dissimulate the principles of God concerning natural, legitimate activities by turning them into vile indulgence.

These vilenesses are the outcome of dissimilation when the devil, in the likeness of evil flesh, succeeds in poisoning the productive and constructive thinking of the mind and manipulates the body to carry out such constructive ideas of the mind in a way that is detrimental to both the body and the soul. For example, the productive and constructive idea of living in a good house is nothing wrong; the spirit of God tells us how to decently go about it, through hard work in transparent and honest venture. The spirit of the devil tells us to stop wasting time and pick up a gun and go for robbery, even if it results in murder. Assuming you go it the way of the Spirit of God, you got your dream house and still have mortified the body but have given her a dream house. If you go it the way of the spirit of the devil, you have gratified the body by providing her a dream house. The means here determine whether the action of acquiring a dream house is for or against God by walking or not after the flesh.

Let us take the case of one Miss Jones in shedding more light onto this illustration:

> The doctor walked to the waiting Miss Jones and announced to her, "Mrs. Jones, I have good news for you."
>
> She corrected him, "Miss Jones, please."
>
> The doctor replied, "I am very sorry, Miss Jones, I have a very bad news for you; you are pregnant."
>
> To the same Miss Jones, the same news that was to be good news became bad just because of the circumstance. The same pregnancy we pray to God for has become a curse to Miss Jones because the circumstance of it is outside the mandate of the Spirit of God.

I am creating this picture so we can see that the war against the flesh in the form of spirit of the devil is not what we can fight with human flesh and blood. The flesh is not visible, not physical as we think, but mighty in pulling down and dissimulating our God-given desires.

The desire for prosperity has nothing wrong with it. But events before and after the prosperity determine whether we have mortified the body or gratified the flesh. If we became prosperous through the direction of the Spirit of God, which is devoid of violence, murder, cheating, robbery, lying, false witness, covetousness, whoredom, wantonness, and all such, we are not after the flesh but after the Spirit of God. If, after acquiring wealth, we get involved in drunkenness, gluttony, sexual immorality, suppression of truth, covetousness, pride, wastefulness, and disrespect and tend to live above the law, we are after the flesh. If, however, we acquired our wealth through decent, hard work and use it in a decent and God-pleasing manner, we are after the Spirit of God. So wealth can become a life in the flesh or one in the Spirit, depending on how we acquired it and how we use it. We can, therefore, safely say that flesh hides itself in the innocent, everyday quantities of our desire.

We can see that the flesh is responsible for all the malicious manifestations of man, his enmity with and disobedience to God and godliness. The flesh derives its energy from self-centeredness. We have tended to class selfishness with flesh or even consider it a component of flesh. Nothing can be more misleading. The devil is the master of flesh, and just as God is love, so is the devil egocentrism. It is the root of all evil. It is the most devouring idol.

The flesh, in Scripture, symbolically means human nature in its condition after the fall of man due to obedience to Satan in disobedience to God out of greed and a desire to become knowledgeable like gods (Genesis 6:3). It includes the totality of man, spirit, soul, and body. That is why Apostle Paul tells us that we all died in Adam. All of man's powers, his intellect, his will, his emotions, his desires, and his intents all are under the influence of the spirit of Satan, expressed symbolically in the Scripture as flesh.

The Bible tells us that to be in Christ Jesus is to crucify this flesh. I have seen some believers flogging their body or wearing rags or putting on pensive appearance in the name of crucifying the flesh. No, the flesh is not your physical body. In fact, some have tended fasting as a means of dealing with the body. In one occasion, I had to share my understanding of fasting with a group I felt was not using this blessed expression of a period in total consummation in the presence of the Divinity in the way of the Word of God. I told them that fasting is translated from the Hebrew word *tsom*, a practice originally associated with emergency or distress that causes people to lose their appetites due to anguish or fear. It is a condition that compares with a situation where a loved one has been knocked down by a hit-and-run driver. Even to the most insensitive, lunch must wait. Not as an expression of sorrow, but because the incident on the ground has pushed the thought of food out of the mind. From this understanding, the Christian believes, according to the teaching of Jesus, that a bigger-than-life problem demands fasting. So anytime you go into fasting, do not think you are dealing with the body in order to tame the flesh. No, the concept should be to direct your attention to God over a problem such that appetite for food is pushed behind. I told them that for me, in my normal prayers, I ask for God's hand to solve my problems. When after a while I am not getting the response I desire, I go into fasting. In fasting, I do not ask for His hand anymore but His face. When I find His face, I see His disapproval of me and the reason my prayers are unanswered. I come back to normal prayers after amending my ways to conform to His desire. Some of them agreed with me.

I believe that this is one of the ways Peter and Paul of the Bible found and remained in favor with God and had a power-packed ministry to the end. This I also believe is one of the ways Rev. Wigglesworth continued to receive the support of the Holy Spirit and became a proof to the Christian community of our generation that the era of miracles was not and will never be over.

As a matter of fact, any time you are fasting and missing your meal, you have not entered into proper fasting. So suffering the body is not the way to mortify its deeds or crucify the flesh. The flesh is a spirit, and we cannot fight it by punishing the material body. Our weapons of warfare against the flesh certainly cannot be physical.

The flesh is never out of innovative approaches. In recent times, it has skillfully camouflaged itself in a phenomenon called Christian entertainment. A Christian is identified in the Bible as someone who has come to see his past life, or his *old man,* in utter rebellion to God due to forces beyond his ability and, therefore, has come to Jesus Christ in true repentance through faith in the finished work of the cross. Walking after the Spirit of God in complete rejection of walking after the flesh has become paramount to him in obedience to the Lord's call that His followers must deny themselves, pick up their cross, even if it means suffering and death, and forsake all, mother, father, son, and spouse, and follow Him. Furthermore, the apostles of Jesus, under the power of the Spirit of Jesus, tell the Christian that he should crucify his old man, the flesh, its wants, goals, tastes, desires, and preferences, and become totally and completely focused on the Lord Jesus Christ, who has become the author and finisher of his faith. The Christian is to abandon his former lifestyle that had held him into a life of idolatry of self or worship of counterfeit gods known as the gods of this world.

Unfortunately, the Christian today has been filled with so many lies and distractions that it makes him no less than an idol worshiper. One of such idols is entertainment. The entertainers have been called "my idol" by many Christians in an unconscious truth. They include football players, musicians, actors and actresses, wrestlers, magicians, pastors, and so on. Today, if you are not an entertaining pastor, your church is empty. God save the church. Unfortunately, the word *entertainment* literally means *to divert* and *to amuse*. Our idols, including pastors, are true to name, meaning those who divert us from God and amuse us. As if this alone is not enough, entertainment also gratifies the lust of the flesh, which the Bible has commanded the Christian to crucify.

I have used the word entertainment as a general term. I will plead your discretion in deciding which entertainment and recreation are suitable for the Christian in accordance with Biblical standard. Choice of entertainment and recreation is very much an individual issue. I have my inclinations, like others. Apart from some few like magic display and pornography, entertainment or recreation has no evil of its own. The problem most times is what the performers portray. Below are clips of some lyrics published by Rob Mackenzie in *Bands, Boppers and Believers*.

> Shake hands with the devil. Don't be frightened; I won't hurt you. I don't want yourself or your gold. I am not after anything that you don't want to give me. I just want your body and your soul.

These are the lyrics of a song made popular by Kris Kristofferson in his album *Shake Hands with the Devil*.

This and the likes of it are what the church of Jesus Christ spend their hard-earned and God-given resources to "enjoy" as entertainment. It is a very sad reflection that the church of Jesus Christ has, within these last few centuries, completely succumbed to the fleshy spirit of romantic sentimentality in the form of entertainment. In other words, we have been assimilated to the world's middle-class views. A victory the church fathers won with their blood, bringing the message of salvation to us, seems to have been lost to the entertainment arena of this world. The man who sang such melodies as "Love Me Devil in Disguise" and other such lyrics, the man who got swallowed up by his own unusual success, the man whose body contained fourteen different drugs when he was found dead, face down on his bathroom floor in August 1977, became a hero and a model to the Christian community of this generation in its obsession for entertainment and to belong, to the extent that when the news of Elvis Presley's death reached the world, millions of Christians who had never met him in person wept openly. How many such Christians wept the first time they heard the news of their salvation through the passion of Jesus? Yet we claim to love Him more than any other thing. If we wept for Elvis as a lost soul, I would pass no judgment; maybe that is in line with our belief, but that was not the case. Jimmy Swaggart pointed out in his article "The Death of Elvis Presley" that even if Elvis talked about Christ, there was no significant change in his life to indicate a following of Christ. So we did not weep because we have lost a faithful, but because we have lost an entertainer in drugs, drinks, illicit sex, profanity, and dirty jokes.

If you ask many senior-adult Christian today who the Beatles were, he will tell you in great detail. Such is their fame among the leaders of the today's church. One example was when the stage of the Cavern Club, where they had often performed before their fame, was cut into pieces and sold piece by piece. The club owner announced that it was the most sought-after wood in the world. The Beatles made a staggering wealth from the pockets of Christians. John Lennon alone left a staggering $275 million when he died. Not bad at all for one who referred to himself as an instinctive socialist, for one who believed in the abolition of all money, police, and government. Nothing wrong with patronizing talent, but this was nothing but pure idolatry, and not just idolatry, but the worship of an enemy of Jesus. In *A Spaniard in the Works*, John Lennon described Jesus as a "garlic-eating, stinking, little, yellow, greasy, fascist bastard" and concluded with a categorical statement: "Christianity will go; it will vanish and shrink, I needn't argue about that. I am right, and I will be proven right. We're more popular than Jesus now." Many Christians bought that album, and the devil raked in some $23 million from the pockets of Christians in the name of entertainment.

Entertainment is the most powerful evangelical tool in the ministry of the devil. It is an avenue for him to receive praises and worship from Christians. We are currently witnessing occult explosive throughout the world through entertainment.

Remember *Chris De Burgh: Live in South Africa*. A large cross is seen above the stage. To the left of that cross is an inverted red cross, a clearly satanic symbol. The final lyrics of the sound track read:

> At the dead of the night, the whistle blows; she's running still. Far away is some recess; the Lord and the devil are now playing chess. The devil still cheats and wins more souls. As for the lord, well, He's just doing his best.

Can any message ever be more touching negatively and from the cursed mouth of the devil? Is the Lord's best enough to win you, or will the devil's pack of cheats and tricks sway you?

Black Sabbath made so much money from today's church leaders out of selling Satan. The cross of Jesus Christ was placed upside down on the cover of their first album. Their introductory show to the British press featured the mock sword sacrifice of a semi-nude girl. Another of their album, *Sabbath Bloody Sabbath*, shows a nude, satanic ritual with the number 666 across the back

RETURN TO **Smith Wigglesworth**

of the bed. The person on the bed is being strangled by a snake. Often in their concerts, they gave a satanic salute, the same salute Anton La Vey presented on the back of his satanic bible, and the audience, many of whom are today's church leaders, responded. Other songs of the group include "Wizard," "Children of the Grave," "Voodoo," and "Lord of This World." Some outstanding vocals in these albums are "But you choose evil ways instead of love; you made me master of the world where you exist; the soul I took from you was not even missed."

These albums adorned the homes of today's church leaders and may still be there. I have thrown away mine and have confessed and pleaded for forgiveness. This was and is the sin we put upon our heads in the name of entertainment. Many of today's church leaders have made covenants with lust and idolatry without knowing it through entertainment. We must search our homes and our minds and renounce all such unintended covenants.

Michel Jackson was a Jehovah's Witness, but when you take a deep look at his works of entertainment, you cannot miss the cultic influence it portrays. This is what *Newsweek* magazine, page 54 of January 10, 1983, quoted from "Bands, Boppers, and Believers" by Rob Mackenzic wrote about Jackson's hit singles, such as "Billie Jean," "Beat it," "Wanna Be Startin' Something," and "Thriller": "Each one is quirky, strange, and deeply personal, with offbeat lyrics that hint at Michael's own secret world of dreams and demons." How many of today's church leaders can count themselves free from companionship with Michael Jackson in his world of dreams and demons at one time or another in their lives? How many have truly confessed and renounced such companionship?

What about Bob Marley, the so-called king of Reggae, or Elton John, whose house is described by his lyricist, Bernie Taupin, as a "home laden with trinkets and books relating to Satanism and witchcraft"?

185   a deeper evangelism

Many Christians would buy for themselves and their family clothes with images of their idols, but not the one with Jesus. Have we renounced our association with them and their belief? We unknowingly entered into this association through entertainment. These are some of the problems that have clogged the wheels of the church on its journey back to Smith Wigglesworth and the apostles.

"Thank God, I am not even interested in worldly entertainment; I only take interest in Christian entertainment," I can hear you say. My brothers and sisters, Christian entertainment, if not moderated by the Spirit, becomes the same flesh we battle. The life of the Christian is characterized by self-denial. This is supposed to reflect in all our engagements. Some questions to answer before you can justify the type of entertainment you are interested in are: Is the so-called Christian entertainment conjuring up negative thoughts in you, such as anger, envy, lust, exaltation, competition, romance, and so on? Is the so-called Christian entertainment presenting God or His Son, Jesus Christ, or the Holy Spirit as an object of amusement instead of a subject of salvation? Is the so-called Christian entertainment creating a domineering impression of the entertainer in your mind? These are some questions you must answer urgently and truthfully before deciding what qualifies for Christian entertainment. Some so-called Christian entertainment can become hindrances to your walk with the Spirit. And if you are not walking with the Spirit, you are in the flesh and therefore cannot please God.

You tell me also that many have received Jesus by being attracted by entertainment offered by churches and ask, why are such churches growing more rapidly than those not offering entertainment? My brothers and sisters in Christ, let us examine who is being presented and who is being received at such entertainment-oriented churches. Paul tells us in 2 Corinthians 11:4 of another Jesus. Is it not another Jesus being received in such congregations, which, instead of being told to deny themselves and follow Jesus, are told to indulge, who instead of being told to take up their cross and suffer for Jesus if need be, are told to catch fun, who are told that their old lifestyle can be managed along with their new life instead of being told that their old lifestyle was abomination to God and must be dropped. This is how Apostle Peter described these new-generation entertainment churches, their pastors, their congregations, and those who receive the Jesus they present.

> But there were false prophets also among the people, even as there shall be false teachers among you.
>
> 2 Peter 2

What do we gain spiritually from entertainment? Laughter? My Bible listed the desired fruits of the Spirit as *love, joy, peace, long-suffering, kindness, goodness, faithfulness, gentleness, and temperance* (self control)— (Galatians 5:22-23). I did not see laughter, which is mentioned only on two occasions in the entire New Testament.

1. When they mocked Jesus as reported in Matthew 9:24, Mark 5:40, and Luke 8:53: "And they laughed Him to Scorn."

2. From the very mouth of the Lord: "Woe to you that laugh now, for ye shall mourn and weep" (Luke 6:25b). I am not in any way condemning all activities that give us happiness that often overflow into laughter. My massage is that laughter is not an essential spiritual requirement that a Christian should look for it at any cost. Any source of laughter that tends to hinder our spiritual growth must be abandoned even if such is coming from the pulpit.

So my dear "man of God," when your congregation is filled with laughter instead of the Holy Spirit, when you have become an entertainer instead of a minister, when you inspire ecstasy among your listeners instead of solemnity, "Man of God," watch it. Laughter is neither a symbol of joy nor a sign of happiness on its own; sometimes it is not a product of peace but a result of some sort of involuntary nervous agitation. It is not even emotional, as weeping. That is why it could be induced by ordinary propagation of the nervous system with common laboratory gas called nitrous oxide (N_2O), known as laughing gas.

Jesus responded to *all* who had encounter with Him, the righteous and the unrighteous, the wise and the foolish, the ignorant and the educated, the rich and the poor, the authority and the servant, except one person who intended Him for entertainment—Herod. He was the only person Jesus did not have a word for, because he was delighted at the idea that Jesus was coming to give him a good time in entertainment through supernatural performances when Pilate directed Jesus to him for trial. The best way to attract God's silence is to look up to Him in entertainment. Do not let anyone take away your salvation and the joy of hearing from God by offering you entertainment instead of the truth, that truth that sets free. Entertainment is an illusion, and only illusions propagate laugher. Reality and truth bring joy, happiness, peace, and weeping! "Jesus wept" is not just found in the Bible but has the remarkable attribute of being the shortest verse in the Bible, making it catchy. "Jesus laughed" is not found in the Bible.

What really do we look out for in entertainment? Romance, blissful expressions, jesters, animalistic competition, strained muscles, brutality, sorrow, revenge, lust for power and affection? That is for the world, so in Christian entertainment, is it crime and law, evil and punishment, good and reward?

Yet for the knowledge of good and evil, man found himself in the ugly, fleshy condition, for which, Christ came into the world and, through a hideous death, set man free; I mean set *Christians* free. Should the Christian continue in the appreciation and worship of good and evil and render the passion of Christ pointless? Has the Christian gone back to the law of good and evil, for which Paul said: "But if ye be led of the spirit, ye are not under the Law" (Galatians 5:18)?

Who owns good and evil of this world but the law? Who owns judgment, reward, and punishment of this world but the law? If the Christian is entertained by good and evil as determined by the world's standard of judgment, is he still led by the Spirit, which has made him free from the law? Or is he entertained by the good and evil, judgment, reward, and punishment as in heaven, which he only knows of by faith?

Why did Paul have to say that if ye are led by the Spirit, ye are not under the *law* instead of under the *flesh*? Because the law is a product of the flesh, and the flesh a product of the knowledge of good and evil.

> For God doth know that in the day ye eat thereof, then your eyes shall be opened and ye shall be as gods knowing good and evil.
>
> Genesis 3:5

Since the law is a product of the flesh and flesh came by man's desire to be like God and know good and evil, the law then must be true to type. It is bound to be self-centered. It must aggravate man for the aggrandizement of itself. It manifested after Adam and Eve disobeyed God in the garden of God called Eden under the direction of serpent sent by the devil. If Christian entertainment is all about the knowledge of good and evil for the purpose of judgment, reward, and punishment in contrast to the worldly entertainment of romance, brutality, beastly competition, flexing of muscles, and so on, then it is all about justification of the law of sin and death, which denies the law of Spirit of life in Christ Jesus.

It is this desire to be like gods that brought the knowledge of good and evil into the world. The consequence was that God cut man off from the source of life, lest he live forever and escape the real judgment. It is the origin of man's lack of faith in God and rule by the flesh. It should rather form the basis for the Christian entertainment instead of judgment, punishment, and reward. We must draw a line between vile entertainment of the world and Christian worship and edification entertainments so that we can confidently join Paul in saying, "For the law of the spirit of life in Christ Jesus hath made me free from the law of sin and death" (Romans 8:2).

The most the law can bring to us is discipline, which is acting in conformity with the norms of a given society. You cannot beat the world in pretending to be disciplined; neither can you rival the satanic worshiper in the act of discipline. The law is not omnipresent, neither is it omniscient. It is not everywhere at the same time; neither does it know everything. If the worldly steals and his laws do not catch him, he is free from judgment and punishment of the world, though not of God. Not so with the Christian. He is convicted of all sins there and then, because the Spirit he worships is everywhere at every time and knows all. The Christian is therefore not called to a life of discipline but to a life of self-control. In a life of discipline, you feign an attitude you may not mean so that the world will not condemn you. In a life of self-control, you reject what you should not be associated with in order to please God.

This is how the Bible puts it: "Do not love the world, nor the things in the world" (1John 2:15). That is a direct instruction to live a life of self-control. All the world offers is dissimulation of self-control in the name of discipline.

> For all that are in the world, the lust of the flesh and the lust of the eyes and the pride of life is not of the Father: but of the world.
>
> 1 John 2:5-6

What a shame that we have tended to change God for our purpose and delight. What a shame that we have become Herod inwardly, looking up to Jesus for entertainment instead of as the Author and Finisher of our faith as directed by the Bible, which is or should be our only guide. We must account for every single soul we mislead. The Bible records that believers have a place in the kingdom of God, but that those who win souls for the kingdom have a special honor and place. "And they that be wise shall shine as the brightness of the firmament; and they that turn many to righteousness as the stars forever and ever" (Daniel 12:3). By transposition, we can say, without any fear of contradiction, that infamy awaits those who turn any soul away from the kingdom of God.

We have not been told not to enjoy and amuse ourselves, but to do so within the context of walking in the Spirit. We have not been told not to live in beautiful houses; we have not been told not to drive nice cars. But we have been told that our desires should not hinge on the superlative. If you desire to build the most beautiful house in your locality, within a short time, another that is more beautiful than yours must come up. Because your desire and mindset is to have the most beautiful house around, you have to build another more beautiful than the current most beautiful. By the time you finish the next most beautiful, another more beautiful one comes up. And you will continue to build the most beautiful house, to your doom. But if your desire is to build a beautiful house, and by the grace of God you have it completed, those one million other houses that became more beautiful than it cannot in any way remove the beauty of it. Your house remains a beautiful house to the glory of God, irrespective of how many others are more beautiful than yours. That is what John is telling us in the passage above. The Christian must not be in competition like the people of the world, not even in church donations. We must not be in competition in anything. Competition is the way of the world. Ananias and his wife exhibited worldly, unscrupulous wisdom in the house of God, and the Holy Spirit caused them to perish.

I must caution that the church has been misled by ignorance—but especially from new-generation entertainment pulpits—into believing that being led by the Spirit means that the Christian's day-to-day applications, desires, engagements, character manifestations, rejections, and acceptance are controlled by the Holy Spirit, thereby dismissing everything with the phrase, "As the spirit directs." Nothing can be more damaging than this belief. This is what the devil has held the church down with, the master-has-become-the-slave kind of mentality. What is the difference between such mindset and that of the unbeliever who tells you not to bother to come and preach to him, that if it is the desire of God that he should be saved, he will without you disturbing him, because God can do it without you? The way he sounds to you is the same way those who believe the Holy Spirit should live their lives for them sound to me. Much as we know that his statement is correct—because with God, nothing is impossible—it is not the Bible truth. That the individual who is in Jesus Christ should not walk after the flesh is a big demand on him and demands a lot of self-control. That is when the Holy Spirit provides the necessary friction that makes his walk in the Spirit palatable. We walk in this physical world, not because of the earth's gravitational pull, but because we know how to walk and have the legs to walk and the strength and desire to move the legs accordingly on a surface that offers the desired friction. The gravity of the earth provides the necessary counter force to bring down our lifted legs and makes our walking involuntary. If at any time in a believer's life the Holy Spirit becomes accountable for his conduct, how come Paul became mindful that he needed to tame his body and bring it to subjection? This is what he said in 1 Corinthians 9:27: "But I keep under my body, and bring it to subjection: lest be any means, when I have preached to others, I myself should by a castaway."

When I started this book, I had just some few pages in mind for my church magazine, *The Christian Messenger*. But the Holy Spirit directed me to write a book and not just an article for my church magazine. I had to adjust my activities and attitude to a pattern that is conducive to developing a book in the name of the Most High. The moment I achieved that, the Holy Spirit came down in full force and continued to guide me to the end. I have never been to a formal theological school or been ordained a preacher, but have been from my youth a private Bible scholar. If I did not start, the Holy Spirit would not have started this work for me. The Ethiopian eunuch along the road to Gaza from Jerusalem, where he had come to worship, was struggling to understand the Word of God according to the prophet Esaias, a great effort that God felt should not go unrewarded; hence, the Holy Spirit, through an angel, sent help to him in the person of Philip. That is how the Spirit leads and assists the believer. He must deserve help, not just desire help.

The pulpits that present the Holy Spirit as Santa Claus know better from their own everyday efforts to remain on the path of the Spirit. If the idea of presenting the Holy Spirit, as do all in the life of the believer, is to win people to Jesus Christ, then it is not a worthy one, because the Gospel demands that we tell the truth no matter the consequence. Moreover, the teaching

a deeper evangelism

soon brings disappointment, if not total rejection, of the Gospel message when the new convert did not observe the Holy Spirit taking away cigarettes and alcohol from this mouth or lust and sexual craving from his life.

I was a victim of this erroneous belief. Those of us who were born and brought up in practical Christian homes and schools rarely can draw a definite line between when we were nominal Christians and when we became born-again. The demarcation is usually more on when we emptied ourselves of habits and vices picked up from associations while growing up. For me, I eventually mastered the act of stopping cigarette smoking but not the act of stopping starting again. I had believed that the Holy Spirit would one day do that for me automatically. I continued to pray and fast, hoping that I would wake up one day and the thought of cigarettes would never enter into my mind again. It was only when I confronted myself with the fact that I had to stop starting again by bearing forth the fruit of self-control that my attempt to stop smoking became successful. That was when the Holy Spirit came in, when He noticed that I deserved help. This is the true message of the Gospel. We must make sacrifices that cost us something in time, resources, and effort in order to attract the Holy Spirit into our situation.

Have you asked someone in the course of evangelism whether he or she is in Christ? If the answer is yes, do not mislead her by telling her that the Spirit will keep her from walking after the flesh; rather, remind her of her obligation not to walk after the flesh. It is a call to self-control. Self-control cannot be given to you by another; that is why the demand on the life of the Christian is *self-control* and not *Holy Spirit control*. It *must* come from self. This is one of many reasons to make you know that the fruit of the Spirit that includes self-control must come from you as a precursor for the gifts of the Spirit. We have discussed this issue, under the topic "Holy Spirit." If a believer is prevented from walking after the flesh by the Holy Spirit and not himself, why ask a believer or yourself the question, "Are you or Am I walking after the flesh?" This question is not necessary if the Holy Spirit is in absolute control of the will of the believer, nor is this passage relevant:

> All scripture is given by inspiration of God, and is profitable for doctrine, for reproof, for correction, for instruction in righteousness.
>
> 2 Timothy 3:16

Why do you have to reprove a believer who is not likely to walk after the flesh because the Holy Spirit directs his actions? Why does Paul have to instruct the believer not to walk in the flesh if he is auto-piloted by the Holy Spirit?

> Do not walk according to the flesh, but according to the spirit.
>
> Romans 8:4

Does a believer have a choice if the Holy Spirit is in control of all his activities? It does not matter how much we try to rationalize this message of the Holy Spirit taking over the life and character of the believer; the truth is that it is misleading. The Christian *must* be told that much has been given to him—the blood of Jesus—and much is expected of him: love, joy, peace, long-suffering, kindness, faithfulness, goodness, gentleness, and self-control. This is the only way the present church can return to the church of Peter, the church of Paul, and the ministry of Smith Wigglesworth. The contradiction we face every day in this issue is not from the Bible but a product of our effort to excuse our inadequacies in the Holy Spirit. Otherwise, how can we say that the believer walks according to the guidance of the

Spirit and yet hold believers accountable for their ways of life? Or do we mean that the believer should. How can we explain that the Holy Spirit shall guide one believer to a life of righteousness and another to a life of uncertainty and another to a life of unrighteousness? Or do we say that there is no unrighteousness in all converts? What about the parable of the sower? Four categories of people were mentioned. One category did not believe at all. The other three believed but under different circumstances. One of the three groups that believed became fruitful, but not equally. Is the Holy Spirit selective among believers? Why do some believers have to be like Billy Graham and some like me? Why are not all like Smith Wigglesworth? The Holy Spirit is neither selective nor biased; He gives according to our abilities and efforts, seen only by Him. It is the responsibility of evangelists to make believers and new converts understand that their relationship with the Holy Spirit is a personal thing. There is no uniform or standard measure of the Spirit rule over every believer. The dose for every believer is in his or her own hand. The further away you stay from the flesh, the nearer you are to the Holy Spirit. If you have been waiting for the Holy Spirit to come and bring you out of the grip of the flesh without your effort, you may wait until it is too late. Now is the time to do the right thing. You must decide, you must begin, you must bear fruit, and the Holy Spirit will know you by the fruit you bear and will give you gifts accordingly.

If you have followed me to this point, you will agree that there is hardly any sin that does not have its root from flesh. The flesh, as we have seen, has its own origin from the desire of man in Adam and Eve to be like God and have the knowledge of good and evil in disobedience to God, instigated by the devil through a familiar spirit in the person of the serpent. If all of us sinned through the sin of Adam, and if God called this *flesh* (Genesis 6:3), then flesh is the mother of all sins. It is sin that is driven by self. Adam desired to be like God, knowing good and evil. This is the height of self-aggrandizement. His refusal to show up when God came looking for him and Eve because they were not dressed the way they desired, being only covered with fig leaves that did not befit their personality in their imagination, is the height of pride.

> And the eyes of them both were opened, and they knew that they were naked and they sewed fig leaves together and made themselves aprons. And they heard the voice of the Lord God walking in the garden in the cool of the day and Adam and his wife hid themselves from the presence of the Lord God among the trees of the garden. And the Lord God called unto Adam and said unto him where are thou? And he said I heard thy voice in the garden and I was afraid, because I was naked and I hid myself.
>
> Genesis 3:7-10

A long passage, I agree, but I want you to see for yourself the gravity of the sin of flesh, which we as offspring of Adam inherited from birth.

"Wherefore, as by one man sin entered into the world, and death by sin, and so death passed upon all men for that all have sinned" (Romans 5:12).

So every human born into this world except Jesus, whose birth was by the power of the Holy Spirit, is guilty of the sin of flesh. That is why the Bible says that all must be born again, in a manner different from the birth through the curse of Adam, if he must have a personal relationship with God. For in Adam, we all sin and come short of the glory of God. How do we know for sure that it is the sin of the flesh that demands us to be born again? The Bible says so.

And the Lord said my spirit shall not always strive with man, for that he also is flesh.

Genesis 6:3

For the sin of flesh committed by Adam when we were still in his loins, God condemned man and separated Himself from him. Because of His mercy and love for man, God sent His only begotten Son to reconcile man with Him so that man can once again live forever.

For God so loved the world that he gave His only begotten son that whosoever believeth in Him should not perish but have everlasting life.

John 3:16

For the sin of flesh committed by Adam, inherited by you and me, Jesus came unto this world, died on the cross in humiliation, and paid the price for us to live by the Breath of God again as it was in the Garden of Eden before the fall.

Before we met Jesus, we lived with this sin, in complete alienation from God. Now that we have met Him, we are free from this sin unless we go back to it, in which case, Adam is no more responsible for our second fall. This second fall is the sin the Bible calls *apostasy*, and says it has no forgiveness.

And it is impossible for those who were once enlightened, and have tested of the heavenly gifts, and were made partakers of the Holy Ghost. And have tested the good word of God, and the powers of the world to come. If they shall fall away, to renew them again unto repentance; seeing they crucify to themselves the Son of God afresh, and put Him to open shame.

Hebrews 6:4-6

As a matter of fact, Adam is no more responsible for the sin of flesh in any man, because the Gospel of Jesus has reached all ears. That is the number-one priority of the Holy Spirit, and He has accomplished it. A Muslim boy in northern Nigeria received a copy of the New Testament Bible from a group of Gideons that came to preach Christ in his school. On his way back home, he became worried over what to do with this "small book," because if his Muslim father found it in his possession, he will be killed. But he believed what those who gave him the book told him. Getting to the front of their house, he impulsively flung the Bible on top of their roof and asked God to bring it into their house if what they told him about Him is true. The evening became windy, and the family, father and brothers, including our little friend, were sitting in the veranda of their house. A little book fell down in front of their house. The father asked one of the sons to pick up "that book that fell from the sky." The senior boy rushed out and picked up the small book, looked at it, and screamed, "Christian book!" and let go of it. The father asked him to bring it to him. He looked at it with amazement. "A brand new Christian Bible, direct from heaven above, to me and my family. What does this mean?" The old man marveled in confusion and went into his room with the small book. He locked himself in and began to read it, believing that God threw it to him from heaven for a purpose. That was how he and his family were saved. God had done what the little boy asked Him to do! This is the extent the Holy Spirit goes to bring the knowledge of Jesus to people of different religions and races. Whether or not we accept the message of the Gospel is our responsibility. Whether we allow the Spirit of Jesus to lead us by rejecting the way of the flesh is our responsibility and not that of the Holy Spirit. He has brought the good news to us at a very high cost. How can we ignore so great a Salvation? How can we let anything separate us from the love of God in Jesus Christ? How

a deeper evangelism

can we allow the flesh, whose havoc in Adam and in our past life, separated us from the love and power of God? No, we must resolve to reject the flesh in whichever form he comes, pride, covetousness, whoredom, sexual immorality, wantonness, gluttony, drunkenness, entertainment, tradition, or social demand. What is it that can disrupt the relationship we have with God in Jesus Christ?

> Shall tribulation, or distress, or persecution, or famine, or nakedness, or perils, or sword…Nay, in all these things we are more than conquerors through Him that loved us.
>
> Romans 6:35, 37

These are few hints to help us keep away from walking after the flesh:

1. Focus your mind always on heavenly things in rare faith that you are a stranger and a pilgrim in this world. "Dearly beloved, I beseech you as strangers and pilgrims; abstain from fleshly lust, which war against the soul" (1 Peter 2:11). Do not let your mind dwell on the events and matters of this world any longer than is necessary to perform your civil, moral, or religious duties.

2. Try not to ask God questions as why things are going on the way they are in this world. Don't ever think that you can make it better for God.

3. No matter your present situations, always, in faith, hope for the best at the end. You have an assurance that you are more than a conqueror.

4. Remember always that all things work together for your good in Christ Jesus. It says "all things," not "some things." It says "together," not "in parts." The part you are touching now may not appear good, but wait until

they come together. If you gave a blind man an aircraft, he would never be able to appreciate its beauty because he would never be able to feel it all together at the same time. Some part feels good, some bad, according to what he is touching, but together, the aircraft looks beautiful. At all times, hope that whenever your situation comes together, it must be for good, irrespective of the part you are currently touching.

5. Constantly fix your mind on the greatness of the eternal joy in heaven that awaits you and how miserable it will be if you, because of worldly riches and pleasures, miss it. In this regard, at any time a fleshly pleasure raises up its head, fortify your determination to reject it with the knowledge that it has the capacity of denying you everlasting pleasure in heaven.

6. You must highlight your shortcomings and design how to handle each. First, remember that the Holy Spirit is assisting you to overcome them but will not overcome them for you without your persistent determination and total commitment to shun evil in any form. Always keep a window of vision of how disappointed the Holy Spirit will be if you succumb to evil temptations, thereby rendering His assistance ineffective and inadequate. Will He still be willing to assist you the next time?

7. Bring to memory those you know who are enjoying higher, sweeter, and more dignified pleasures in this life than you because they are living in accordance with the Word of God.

8. Do not ever think like the unbeliever, who says that if God wants him to repent, let Him use His power by relying on the Holy Spirit to stop you if He does not like what you are doing or want to do. The way He

might stop you is to take away your life or good health. You will not wish that.

9. Avoid ribald, filthy discussions and romantic songs and scenes and sensuous snares, too much sleep and idleness, items that draw too much attention to you, worldly popularity, fame and man's applause, and unprofitable and sinful company.

10. Look up the Bible passages that describe the hopelessness of a life in flesh and the reward of life in God. Such as:

God setteth the solitary in families. He bringeth out those which are bound with chain but the rebellious dwell in a dry land.

Psalm 68:6

11. At any time you feel reluctant to pray, compel yourself to go on your knees and confess your rebelliousness and take permission from God to cancel the purpose for which the devil wanted to stop you from praying.

12. Equip yourself with the Word of God according to Scripture that you will use to counter the voice of flesh when he begins to entice you with the apparent pleasure and pleasantness of the things you have rejected. Remember your companions in worldly indulgence that were not as lucky as you, but died in their sins. Those pleasures you people used to ravage together are still there, waiting for new victims and returnees, which you must not be one of. Remember that it could be your own time now, and if so, how wonderful that you died as a true child of God.

13. Compare your health and risk level and unnecessary expenditure concerning you now that you have rejected life in flesh and at the time you were a slave to it, like

when you were smoking or like when you were a drunk-ard. Like when you drive around in the night looking for fun. Like when you lived a life of promiscuity. "Ye ask and receive not, because ye ask amiss, that ye may consume it upon your lust" (James 4:3).

14. Continuously look at your new self in the mirror and behold your new look in a new life in Jesus Christ. Check your pocket and the things you could do and have done with money since you stopped the wasteful-ness of life in flesh.

15. Finally, ask yourself this question: If gratifying the flesh so adversely affects my carnal environment as clearly as I have observed, how much damage is it doing to my spiritual environment? This question should keep you alert and ready to fight back any time the enemy comes with his many tricks. "Submit yourselves to God. Resist the devil, and he will flee from you" (James 4:7).

Open and keep permanently open a window in your mind with a message of pity for those who are pretending to be living well in the name of wealth obtained from evil and ungodly sources: pol-iticians who got and are getting rich by stealing what they have been given to share, businessmen who got and are getting rich by cheating in any form or by occult means, workers who got and are getting rich by corrupt means, policemen who became rich by selling justice to the highest bidder. Memorize Psalm 37:1-7 to fortify your defense against such for you and your family.

> Fret not thyself because of evildoers, neither be thou envious against the workers of iniquity. For they shall soon be cut down like the grass, and wither as the green herb. Trust in the Lord and do good. So shalt thou dwell in the land and verily thou shalt be fed.
>
> Psalm 37:1-3

Familiar Spirit: It is impossible to discuss and understand the operations of the flesh without a look at the medium through which it came into the world.

The term *familiar* refers to a relational aspect of association that carries an impression of knowing or recognizing. Lucifer and his fellow fallen angels had been expelled from the presence of God. Man and other creatures, including the serpent, had been created and put in a garden God made and visited. By extension, Lucifer and his followers cannot come there and freely associate with God or man, who is made in the image and likeness of God. But Lucifer needs to reach man and destroy his relationship with God. His only chance was to use a creature that is familiar with man and that has unlimited access to the garden. The serpent was available. Like the other creatures of the garden, the serpent was walking on legs before it was cursed to crawl on its belly by God.

The serpent agreed with Lucifer to convince man to disobey God. That was the origin of familiar spirit. The serpent became the first. Ever since then, the devil has used objects and people that are familiar or close to us in his war against God through the humans He created for His worship and pleasure. For the same reason that he had to use a familiar agent in Genesis, he uses familiar agents to reach pious places and persons that naturally will not tolerate his presence, such as holy churches and persons with natural tendency to fear God but may not have become grounded in the Word of God. Also, because he is not omnipresent, that is, he cannot be in different places at the same time, he uses objects and people that are familiar to us to get his message of destruction across to us. Like his first mission, the mission of the familiar spirit is to deceive and bring man into enmity with God.

These are what the Encarta Dictionaries says about the word *familiar*. It is an adjective meaning:

1. Well known, commonly seen or heard, and easily recognized.

2. With a thorough knowledge and good understanding of something.

3. In or characteristics of a close personal relation with somebody.

4. Unduly friendly or intimate in a way that is seen as presumptuous or impertinent.

5. Relating to or involving a family.

According to Encarta Dictionaries, it has its origin in the Latin word *familiaris,* via 13th century French. Paranormally, it represents a spirit-helping witch or a supernatural being often taking the form of a cat or other animals that supposedly acts as a witch's assistant.

I find this brief introduction of the spirit called familiar necessary so that we can see how the flesh came into this world and why we must keep him at arm's length. Even David, the mighty man of God, at most of his unguided moments became victim of flesh. Let us look at this example:

David had, within a short period toward the end of his reign, defeated a combination of Ammonites and Syrians and recorded a resounding victory over the Syrians and Philistines, slaying the three giants and bringing to an end the mention of giants in the Bible. The flesh took control of him again. This time not sexual lust, but self-glory. He directed Joab to conduct a census of the men of Israel. This is the way the Bible recorded this order to count the people:

> And Satan stood up against Israel and provoked David to
> number Israel. And David said to Joab and to the rulers
> of the people, "Go, number Israel from Beersheba even
> to Dan and bring the number of them to me that I may
> know it."
>
> 1 Chronicles 21:1-2

Dear brothers and sisters, is there anything bad about a ruler
conducting a census to know the number of his people? Certainly nothing is wrong with that, just as nothing is wrong with
all of flesh's objects of operation on their own. What is usually
wrong is the motive behind the desires, or the circumstance of
it. Like the case of Miss Jones we read earlier, when the doctor
thought her married, the result was good news, but when he
realized that she was not married, the same result became bad
news. Why was God so angry with David over numbering his
subjects? Because David's desire was not to know the number
of the people so as to make adequate provisions for them, but
to gratify himself in the sin of self satisfaction and pride in the
sense that he has enough men to fight and defeat any neighboring nation. The devil had blinded his mind from realizing that
his past victories had not been as a result of the number of men
in his camp, but by the hand of God. This is flesh in action. The
outcome was catastrophic. Seventy thousand men of Israel died.

> So the Lord sent pestilence upon Israel and there fell of
> Israel seventy thousand men.
>
> 1 Chronicles 21:14

God took away these seventy thousand men because David had
begun to see them as his strength. What God took away was not
the life of these men but the illusion that had become David's
source of pride. This is another danger of flesh. It could cost you

your loved one, it could cost you your wealth, it could cost you your own life, and it could cost you your health. Is there anything you are depending on as your strength other than God? Is there anything that is your object of admiration more than God, including yourself? Search, and if you find any, this is the time to destroy it before it destroys you or your loved ones.

The Helping God Spirit

The earliest manifestation of the helping God spirit in the midst of followers of Jesus, according to the book of Acts of the Apostles, came a few days after our Lord had ascended. His disciples, on returning from the Mount of Olivet, assembled at the upper room of John Mark's mother's house, waiting for the promised comforter. The tension and expectation in this room of one hundred twenty people, who had just returned from an event beyond their wildest imagination, and the vagaries of the last forty days can only be imagined.

We first met the manifestation of this helping God spirit in the Bible when Sarai offered to help God fulfill His promise to her husband Abraham, who was then called Abram.

> Now Sarai Abram's wife bore him no children; and she had a handmaid, an Egyptian, whose name was Hager. And Sarai said to Abram; Behold now the Lord hath restrained me from bearing; I pray thee, go in unto my

> maid; it may be that I may obtain children by her. And
> Abram hearkened to the voice of Sarai.
>
> Genesis 16:1-2

This single act of trying to help God has brought unimaginable hardship to the world, Israel in particular, till this day. It is the root cause of the problems facing the world today. It is the cause of Africa's backwardness, especially countries like Nigeria, where the struggle for political supremacy between the children of the promise and that of the slave girl has left desolation. It is the cause of the problems and genocide in Sudan. It was the cause of the air suicide bombing of the World Trade Towers on September 11, 2001. It is the single biggest threat to the world today.

In the Old Testament again, an attempt to help God prevent His ark of the covenant from falling off the cart was resented by God Himself. During the occasion of bringing the ark of God to Jerusalem by King David, at the threshing floor of Nachon, Uzzah tried to help God by preventing His ark from falling when the oxen shook. The Bible recorded that God got angry against Uzzah and smote him there and then for his error of thinking that he could help God (2 Samuel 6:6-7).

The ark of the covenant, mentioned throughout the Old Testament, symbolized the agreement of faith made between God and the Israelites at Mount Sinai. The ark contained the Decalogue (the Ten Commandments given by God to Moses), Aaron's rod, and a pot of manna. The ark represented God's presence to the Israelites, who carried it with them while wandering through the desert and into battle.

This was how God responded to such serious offences before the coming of His Son.

The coming of Christ has given us the opportunity to realize and repent of our offences instead of instant death. That is why, I believe, God allowed Peter to reach his full apostolic height despite his repeated impulsive attempts to help God, especially the one under consideration below.

The disciples of Jesus, including His mother and brothers, Jude and James in particular, as mentioned in Acts, had just returned after seeing Jesus off to heaven. The mystery of His resurrection and ascension still overwhelmed and bewildered them. Full of guilt over their various degrees of lack of proper knowledge of who He was before now, they continued to stare at each other in perplexity.

Sometimes it becomes desirable to ask God for sanctified creative imagination into some Bible stories in order to appreciate them better. This is one such time. Imagine the state of the eleven apostles before this crowd of one hundred twenty people with full knowledge that everybody there knew they had deserted Him at His arrest. *Thank God we are not like Judas Iscariot, who, if he had seen what we saw at last, may have repented and believed.* This, in my imagination, is part of the reflections that might be going on in their minds. But the case of Judas Iscariot is more than mere venial sin. He wanted to help God bring about the fulfillment of his promise concerning the restoration of the Jewish kingdom back to Israel. How disappointed he was when he saw that Jesus did not intend to destroy the Romans and become the king of Israel. Could God's plan for restoration of mankind through Jesus have prevailed without human interference, without Judas helping? This is the question you must ask yourself any time your action tends toward helping God. My humble answer is obviously yes. What led Judas to the crime of betraying his master was an inordinate zeal to help God by thinking that he could fast forward His purpose in Jesus. Let's be careful with our tendencies to become the one who made it happen, especially in things of God, lest we fall into the same trap as Judas Iscariot.

Let's go back to the upper-chamber room of Mark's mother's house.

Imagine how His brothers were feeling before this gathering, knowing that all knew they did not believe Him until now that they had seen.

Imagine Peter's state of mind in the midst of this crowd with the knowledge that everybody there knew he denied Him. A burden certainly must be on him to make the first move. It was therefore a relief to break the deafening silence, especially with a statement that conveyed some high degree of authority. Remember that Peter and the rest were still ordinary. The Holy Spirit had not come upon them yet at this time. So it was easy for the devil to enter into Peter's thought and began to manipulate it: "Peter, you are the leader, no doubt; do something about the replacement of Judas. It is even in the Scripture that another should take his office. 'Let his habitation be desolate and let no man dwell therein: and his office as bishop let another take.' By this, you will help your master fulfill this scripture." This is what the devil probably was telling Peter, and he unfortunately swallowed the idea hook, line, and sinker. The devil had achieved an apparent victory. Meanwhile, Jesus was preparing Saul of Tarsus for the replacement of Judas for the obvious reasons, as revealed in Acts and the Epistles. Without realizing that his action amounted to trying to help God, Peter conducted an election for the replacement of Judas. Mundane humans, by simple majority selected an apostle for Jesus in the person of Mathias. Some have justified this election with the argument that they prayed that God should make His choice. Can that be called a choice? An environment that limited the choice to one or the other? One person must emerge the winner, but it is no certitude that he was God's choice for that office. In fact the emergence of Paul in the apostolic arena indicates that if Peter's poll options had included a third in the form of "none of these two," it would have been God's choice. So the devil must have rejoiced, but Jesus is and has been and will always be steps ahead of the devil. "Shut up, Satan, you have made no score; when the time comes for me to choose my apostle, the human-made one will give way." Jesus must have told the devil. No wonder Mathias was not mentioned again in the Bible after his election, but the God-chosen apostle of Jesus was everywhere and justified his position as the replacement for Judas. If you are still in doubt of Peter's error in conducting this trying-to-help-God election, look at the calling of the apostles of Jesus from the first to the last according to the Gospel and see if any was by election other than direct call by Jesus. The call of Paul is like the call of the others, a direct call by Jesus. Please note the difference between the apostles of Jesus, which remain twelve to eternity and which Paul is one of, according to prophecy, and the apostles of the Gospel of Jesus that included Barnabas (Acts 14:14) and today's apostles. The former were called directly and physically by Jesus, the latter by the church and/or the anointing of the Holy Ghost. Imagine how difficult it would have been to evangelize to the gentile world; maybe the gospel may not have reached me. Imagine how much information and knowledge would not have been available to the church if Mathias's election had annulled the call of Paul.

> Paul, an apostle (not of man, neither by man, but by Jesus Christ and God the father…)"
>
> Galatians 1:1

This is how Paul described his apostleship. Could Mathias or any other apostle apart from the other eleven make the same claim? A great moment in the history of the church was the moment of Paul's commission for the work of the gospel. The history of the entire world was reoriented that moment, and the modern civilization that has swept the world was born. That was when the church apparently became open to everyone without distinction, thanks also to Peter's encounter with Cornelius.

In recent times, we have been trying to help God make His world more palatable and easier to understand by translating the Bible in simpler and more general language. In this regard, we seem to forget that the understanding of the Bible is the prerogative of the Holy Ghost. We have sometimes, in this attempt to simplify the Bible, caused the Holy Ghost to groan due to misrepresentation of the message of the Scripture. Take for example Romans 8:15, "...for we have not received the spirit of bondage again to fear; but ye have received the Spirit of adoption." Many translations, like the New International Version, in their effort to help God by making His Word more palatable, have changed the word *adoption* in the passage above to *sonship*. They argue that *adoption* sounds derogatory.

Hear this story and see the misrepresentation that has been imputed to this passage by changing *adoption* with *sonship*.

An adopted little girl was always being taunted by her playmates. They would always hurtfully tease her with the notion that she was not a bona fide child of her parents. In her agony, she one day summoned up courage and called them together. She told them that she was special. That she was the only one among them whose parents saw, liked, and chose, that they were all imposed on their parents. She put it to them that should their parents have seen them prior to their birth, a good number of them would have been rejected. That is the significance of the word *adoption* in this passage. The Bible tells us that we are a chosen generation. We are not an imposition on God. That is the message in that *adoption*. We did not choose God; rather, He chose us. We have corrupted that message in an attempt to help God. There are so many other examples. Maybe you have not noticed. This is how we represent God when we try to help Him. There are many such in NIV and other new translations. Try and discover them yourself and judge. That is what the Bible asks us to do. These new translations, in an attempt to help God by making His word easier to read, have deliberately or otherwise *omitted* the following verses of the New Testament Bible:

1.   Mathew 17:21: Howbeit this kind goeth not out but by prayer and fasting.

2.   Mathew 18:11 For the son of man came to save that which was lost.

3.   Mark 7:16: If any man has ears to hear, let him hear.

4.   Mark 9:44, 46: Where their worm dieth not, and the fire is not quenched.

5.   Mark 11: 26: But if ye do not forgive, neither will your Father which is in heaven forgive your trespasses.

6.   Mark 15:28: And the scripture was fulfilled which saith and he was numbered with the transgressors.

7.   Luke 17:36: Two men shall be in the field; the one shall be taken and the other left.

8.   Luke 23: 36: And the soldiers also mocked him, coming to him, and offering him vinegar.

9.   John 5:4: For an angel went down at a certain season into the pool, and troubled the water: whosoever then first after the troubling of the water stepped in was made whole of whatsoever disease he had.

10. Acts 8:37: And Philip said, if thou believest with all thine heart, thou mayest. And he answered and said, "I believe that Jesus Christ is the son of God."

11. Act 15:34: Notwithstanding it pleased Silas to abide there still.

12. Acts 24:7: But the chief captain Lysias came upon us, and with great violence took him away out of our hands…

13. Acts 28:29: And when he had said these words, the Jews departed and had great reasoning among themselves.

14. Romans 16:24: The grace of our Lord Jesus Christ be with you all. Amen.

15. 1 John 5:7: For there are three that bear record in heaven, the Father, the Word, and the Holy Ghost: and these three are one.

Many more in the Old Testament, such as Job 32:20, concern giving flattering titles to man. These passages are either omitted or corrupted in many of these new "helping God" translations. It reminds me of an article I read in a Methodist journal a long time ago. The audit report stated in one of the invoices, "Amending the Lord's Prayer," and a cost, was indicated. Imagine that during the collection of the apostolic documents in the first century AD, an invoice that bore such was found. Till now, the debate as to what extent the Lord's Prayer was amended would still be on. In the case of the report in the Methodist journal, the statement was queried by the audit team, and it was explained as the cost of fixing back some letters that were about to fall out of the Lord's Prayer engraved on the wall of the church. This is the kind of misleading information we leave behind when we try to help God by changing a word in His Book. The subtlety of these new Bible versions is also capable of misleading even the very elect. This is what Dr. C. Peter Wager, a professor of church growth and a recognized leading authority in the field of evangelism and spiritual warfare, wrote on page 126 of his book, *Blazing the Way*: "The New King James Version, which I am using almost exclusively, lets us down here. The New International Version is more accurate, so I will use it: 'When Silas and Timothy came from Macedonia, Paul devoted himself exclusively to preaching…'" I have checked that passage (Acts 18:5) in the Greek translation, and it agrees with the English translations that say, "And when Silas and Timotheus were come from Macedonia, Paul was pressed in spirit, and testified to the Jews that Jesus was Christ." I found out that the NIV is not even accurate, not to talk of being *more* accurate. Dr. Wager found support for his argument that Paul abandoned his self-support of tent making because these guys swelled his pocket with donations from Macedonia. That is what prosperity-religion Bibles say, according to purpose.

Has the church not fought and won the battle for the devil when her leaders gave the impression that the accuracy of the Bible is version dependent? It took one hundred and twenty people in the upper room chamber of Mark's mother house to establish the gospel of Jesus in the whole world. Today's congregations are in thousands. If just one becomes willing to go back to the principles and fundamentals of Christianity, I can assure you that the devil and his agents inside and outside the church will be on the run. The Word of God in its pure form is the place to start. The Word of God in its pure form cannot be found in Bible translations for commercial purpose anchored on intellectualism. But on one inspired by the Holy Ghost and anchored on Revelation. If you have been able to read a Bible translation in any native language, undertaken years ago by uneducated primitive interpreters (unfortunately you are likely not to have, but mark it as a research topic), you will understand what I mean. The major challenge of the church today is her lack of faith in the accuracy of the Word of God brought about by the emergence of fit-for- purpose versions. It is unfortunate that some leaders of the church of today lack faith in the Word of God due to perceived translation inaccuracies and show support for versions that even deny the authenticity of some passages of the original Greek script by patronizing them. Or do you not know that the New International Version and other versions reject some passages of the original Greek script, especially portions that give support to the Trinity and the Deity of Jesus such as 1 John 5:7, "For there are three that bear record in heaven. The Father, the Word and the Holy Ghost, and these three agree in one." The inability of today's church leaders to reject and protect their flock from heresy is a major shackle on the wheel of the church towards power ministry. Christianity is not academics where you need proof for acceptance. It is not religion where you have to see before you believe. It is spiritual where you believe by faith before you see.

The difference between Christianity and religion is that in religion, adherents look for their gods, protect their gods from perceived human enemies, and help their gods in so many other ways, such as killing those that may harm or have harmed their gods, shielding their gods from public comments, providing food, shelter, drinks, or blood, etc., for their gods. In Christianity, the opposite is the case. God is our Father through Jesus Christ. As a perfect Father, He looks out for us to make sure we are in sight. When we tried to hide from Him in disobedience, He called us back, so much as to send His only begotten Son in our human flesh to gather us to Him at the great cost of the cross. We must take advantage of this privilege of having a Father that wants us at *all cost* and return the church to God's Word. He does not need our help but obedience.

At a point, Peter drew his sword to help Jesus escape from those who had come to arrest Him for the cross. How little did Peter know that he was working against God by that supposed act of help?

"God helps those who help themselves" is a popular saying. The problem is that sometimes we are unable to draw the line between helping ourselves and trying to help God.

How little did Peter know that it would be the blood that would flow at Calvary, the blood that had been anointed in River Jordan for atonement that would do the gathering of the lost back to the Father, and not the human Jesus he drew his sword to protect?

One major area the church, especially the new-generation churches, are in an unholy competition to help God is in the area of dismantling the doctrines handed down to the church by the apostolic or church fathers (Note: the church fathers are not the Roman Catholic fathers).

Surprisingly, politicians still refer to themselves as servants of the people; God knows how far that claim is true. But the leaders of the church do not see themselves any more as servants of God as they were called when the apostolic doctrine dominated the church. They now refer to themselves and make us call them "Man of God." By transposition, God will call them "My men," creating the impression that God has special men and women in the world helping Him to fight His battle against the evil one. This is a glory bestowed on man by man. Not even James and Jude, blood brothers of our Lord Jesus, made any special relationship claim but regarded themselves simply as servants of Jesus.

These doctrines that are the targets of these "church owners" came to us from people who were closer to God than we are, closer to the events of Jesus's ministry on earth than we shall ever be, possibly were at Jerusalem at His crucifixion, and certainly heard directly from the apostles like St. Linus, mentioned in the Bible (2 Timothy 4:21) as disciple of Paul, and Polycarp, known by the early church as a disciple of John, and Clement, mentioned by Paul in Philippians 4:3. These doctrines and creeds have stood the test of Christian experience down the centuries. Only the selfish desire of some have led them to cast suspicion on them so that they can advance some reasons why they left their former assembly to start their own, while the main reason is actually to establish their own empire for the glory of man.

Someone truly said that he who has God and everything else has no more than he who has God only. I also add that he who has everything else but no God has nothing at all. But you cannot have God until you are truly born again. You must become childlike to have God, childlike in followership and in obedience.

My Bible tells me that I cannot enter into the presence of God except like a child. We have, in our effort to help God, restructured the true glory of God, which exists in the form of childlike humility, into youthful exuberance. A childlike humility can be established by comparing the reaction of a five-year-old child with that of an adult under the same circumstance. You took your five-year-old child to a shop. At the counter, she asked, "Daddy can I take some chocolate?" You answered no. She continued to pester you to know why you said no. She became very uncomfortable, not because she did not have the chocolate, but because she could not understand why you should say no, more so without reason. She was disturbed because she knows that money for chocolate cannot be your problem and therefore is not the issue. If you had said "No, it is not good for your teeth," she may have relaxed, but not with just a no like that. If, however, you change your mind and say, "Okay, take," she will rush for it. Not so, fifteen years later, when maybe in the university. You take her to the same shop, and at the same counter, she asks, "Daddy, can I take chocolate?" And you answer no. That is the last you will hear of it. It is your money. *When I start getting mine, I can buy myself what I want*, she would tell herself, even regretting asking. No thought as to why you said no. Even if you changed your mind and asked her to take some, her response would surprise you. "No, Daddy, thank you. I don't want it anymore." At five, she was very concerned as why you said no and became worried. This is unconscious humility, and it is childlike and only found in them. Her later, adult response is what I would like to call unconscious arrogance or youth-like pride. Her ego is at stake.

We have replaced childlike humility in the heavenly glory, which means approval by God as handed down to the church by the apostolic fathers with fame conferred by our fellow humans. The humblest and most childlike pleasure, or the specific plea- sure of the inferior, is no more than the pleasure of a beast when praised by men, the pleasure of a child when praised by his or her father or mother, the pleasure of a student when praised by his or her professor, the pleasure of a creature when praised by his creator. This is the glory the soul enjoys when he (remember that soul has no sex) receives praise or approval from God as having pleased Him. This is the fame of the man who has been redeemed.

The glory most of us seek today is the glory of approval of humans, derived from our self-centered desires for fame and wealth in the name of helping God by teaching the supposed correct gospel message that denies the root of the message of the true gospel as handed down by the apostolic fathers. The end result is banishment for both teacher and learner from the presence of He who is everywhere, erasing from the knowledge of He who knows all.

In many Christian communities, one thing has become com- mon to three sets of people: posters. Any poster you see any- where belongs to one of these three: the dead, the politician, or the pastor. In the case of the first, it does not look for earthly fame, the glory or approval by man for itself, but is used by the worldly, its owner, to look for it. In the case of the second and the third, the politician and the pastor, it is national and interna- tional fame at all cost; hence, posters everywhere, reachable even when such places are out of target, and adverts placed illegally on TV channels. The latter has become very common with so many so-called men of God today and, surprisingly, by some respected ministries, that one begins to doubt their genuineness. These are typical cases of seeking glory through fame conferred by human.

Seeking glory or fame or luminosity through God's notice and approval, transient as it may appear, is the language of the entire New Testament. Seeking glory by trying to help God in order to acquire fame and luminosity through man's approval, rewarding as it may appear, is ungodly. The gospel message of Paul in 1 Corinthians 8:3 is that those who *love* God shall be known by Him. That you know Him does not matter, because even the demons know Him. What matters is whether and how He knows you. He knows you as a worthy servant if you love Him, not if you help Him, because He does not need your help. His ways are not yours. The Bible tells us of two tracks—the broad track that leads to destruction and the narrow one that leads to life. Every Christian is on the right track, but not all are going in the right direction. It is time to pause and make sure you are moving in the right direction.

My Bible says in Matthew 19:24 that it is easier for a camel to pass through the eye of a needle than for a rich man (fame by world standards) to enter into the kingdom of God. This statement appears an exaggeration until we put it into the right perspective. "The eye of the needle" according to Dake's Annotaed Reference Bible by Finis Jennings Dake, was a small, circular gate on the Jerusalem City main gate. When a merchant came back from business after the city gate was locked, he had two options, either to unload his camel and take home his wares through this small hole, leaving the camel outside the city wall to the mercy of agents of darkness and the wild, or unload the camel and take across his wares and his camel through the same hole. For him and his wares, it was easy, but for the camel, it was nearly impossible. A camel that was able to pass through this ordeal was regarded as courageous. Inside the city, the master carried his wares on his head or shoulder, and this camel that had passed through the eye of the needle walked home unburdened. People cheered it as a courageous camel as it walked home unburdened.

The master was joyous that his camel was going home with him despite the suffering of getting across the small hole on the gate called "the eye of the needle" or "the needle's eye." The camel walked home gloriously, receiving the praise of his master and others. Most camels did not make it across and were left to their fate on the other side of the wall. Rarely were any found alive the next morning.

The inability of some camels to pass through this hole is what our Lord compares with what is facing anybody, be they a politician, a pastor, a business man, or a public worker, who seeks fame through the glory or praises of man. It is praise from the wrong side of the wall. Passing through the eye of the needle is difficult enough for the camel, but the Lord says that to enter into the kingdom of God is more difficult for the worldly. Anything that is more difficult than the camel passing through the eye of the needle must be considered impossible.

In the Book of Job 32:21, we read, "Let me not, I pray you accept any man's person, neither let me give flattering titles unto man." (This is not found in a number of Bible versions like NIV.)

Poor Job, his heart must be bleeding for the church and humanity. Flattering titles have become the order of the day in the House of God. All kinds of titles, celestial, ecumenical, ecclesiastical, traditional, etc., have become the confirmation of man's approval, or glory or fame, and luminosity. In the ecclesiastical, there is satanic competition for "holy" titles, just to show that one is closer to God than others or more qualified to help God, especially in the area of removing or modifying the Christian doctrines handed down to us by the apostolic or church fathers (please note, not the Roman Catholic fathers).

First of all, I must establish my personal, unshakable claim that these doctrines as handed to us are dominical. I also believe that they cannot be separated from the teachings of Jesus Christ or His disciples. If you do not believe them, your presence in the church is very unfortunate and tragic. If you believe them, come out of your spiritual prudery and accept them, for they are there, whether or not you accept them or whether you have rejected them to further propagate your selfish interest or preserve your ego, which you suppose may be hurt by your coming back to the truth. These doctrines do not create any new absolute situation. They simply bring the gospel message home so that we shall live by it in a food-like manner, where it will no longer be easy for us to ignore it. These doctrines and creeds make the Christian become like a man who has lived in many places and therefore is most unlikely to be deceived by the mistake of his local community.

In some of the new churches, even the ancient hymns and canticles have become their victims. Their leaders, in trying to become original in what originated some two thousand years ago, have become blind, pulling down even the very foundation of the church. The Gospel tells us, "Whether ye eat or drink or whatsoever you do, do all to the glory of God" (1Corinthians 10:31). Unfortunately, we have turned all we do, eat, or drink, even in the church, to the glory of man, including the holy sacraments.

I thank God that He has not allowed the devil to raise up a new enemy in this regard for His church. But the same old enemy that Paul and the other apostles defeated and the Gospel came to us unpolluted. Read what Paul says about such:

> For he had greatly withstood our works.
>
> 2 Timothy 4:15b

By special grace, my generation, like Paul's, will overcome, and history will record that the wilderness manna of the gospel, the creeds and Christian doctrines handed down to us from the time

RETURN TO Smith Wigglesworth

of the beginning of the church, suffered attacks in the hands of new church founders seeking the glory of man instead of God's.

I am certain that these new church founders who are pulling down the apostolic institutions have concealed from the itching ears of their congregation the fact that these apostolic writings, which include the doctrines, creeds, and date tables, are older than the Gospel itself, as the Book of New Testament Bible. In your judgment, do you think the apostolic fathers were inspired by God to assemble the New Testament but not inspired to write down doctrines and creeds, which they stuck to in conformity, for the selection of the New Testament canon? This is the weight CS Lewis, in a sermon titled *Why I am Not a Pacifist*, gave to the apostolic writings in his defense of nations drafting Christians into their armies.

> Nor, I think, do we find a word about pacifism in the apostolic writings, which are older than the Gospel and represents, if anything does, the original Christendom, whereof the Gospels themselves are a product.

How I wish that C.S Lewis was alive to see the pulling down of these foundations of the Gospel. Maybe this writing would not have been necessary, because he would have made such as are doing this ashamed with words. The Rule of Faith, the Holy Canon, was established through the second, third, and fourth centuries. The test of canonicity was guided by whether a collection or book had been written by the apostles or was written with the authority of the apostles. How erroneous are those who ignore the apostolic doctrines that were the foundation for the New Testament Gospels. Ignatius, the bishop of the church at Antioch, who was martyred about AD 110, according to Christian tradition, followed the apostles and was ordained by Paul. He was one of the apostolic fathers who put down the doctrines

2 2 5   a deeper evangelism

and creeds. He was among those who assembled the New Testament Gospel. But read what he wrote: "I do not issue you with commands like Peter or Paul, for I am not an apostle." This is the man whose works you are told to reject as not conforming with the apostolic Gospel by those who did not see or hear from the Gospel writers but, unlike St. Ignatius, would like to issue you with commandments like Peter and Paul because they have assumed apostolic authority through glory conferred on them by human. Those whose only interest in establishing their own churches is personal aggrandizement. This is a generalization that does not include all new church founders. Some are definitely from pure desire to give their best to God, a desire they could not attend inside a traditional church set up. To differentiate the former from the latter, we need to close our itching ears and open our spiritual ones. We need to take away our eyes from entertainment and fix them on devotion and see how these people directing our Christian lives are conforming to the image of the Son of God. We have to begin to ask for reasons why they are rejecting the apostolic doctrines; we have to know why donations, tithe, and the claim of speaking in tongues have become more important than the doctrine of the Lordship of Jesus Christ. We need to know who is being advertised in their posters, themselves or Jesus Christ, and if Jesus, which: a familiar spirit or Jesus Christ of the Bible? Or have you not seen that their posters and handbills lack proper mention of Jesus, maybe because they have filled all available space with their images and glamour to the exclusion of the Master. When they speak in "tongues," we need to ask ourselves whose glory they are pursuing, theirs, other gods', or God of Jesus Christ's.

Those who are fortunate to have spoken in tongues, as St. Paul did, as I also have, to His glory, will understand the essence of this holy phenomenon and will be able to differentiate it from the hysterical, sometimes-staged phenomenon that dominates the entertainment theatres that go in the name of church today. Do not be afraid to examine anybody who claims authority over your walk to eternity. It is your greatest possession. The Bible tells us that spiritual things are discerned spiritually. Moreover, if you are a spiritual being, you must judge all things, because you will be judged of none. We must rise up against the fraud and injustice that has taken over the body of Christ. To them, the Gospel of our Lord has been turned into a jester; Christianity has been reduced to religion, to mere psychology, just as divine love –agape—is mere lust to the atheist. There is no real fear of God in these people. Their stage performance has brought misery and mockery to the body of Christ. Their speaking-in-tongues stage performance, which is merely speaking gibberish, not languages any person hears, has led people to regard this holy phenomenon as a kind of hysteria or an involuntary discharge of nervous excitement built up with time. Let us not believe the ethics of these ambitious church owners in accepting that Christianity, as one of the few world's religions with theology, should have the culture of arousing and satisfying our imagination. No, sir, Christianity is for the redemption of our soul and not for the benefit of our imaginations and desires. It is not about selecting the topics we shall like to know and rejecting the ones that do not suit our purpose. It must be the same theology, in full, as established by St. Paul about two thousand years ago.

I read in an edition of *Everyday With Jesus* how Billy Graham was accused of setting the church back a hundred years by the new church owners. When Billy Graham heard it, he responded that he had failed if he only succeeded in taking the church a hundred years back, that his goal was to take the church two thousand years back. If we are to succeed in taking the church to two thousand years ago, if we must continue from where people like Billy Graham stopped, we must open our spiritual eyes; we must open our spiritual ears. We must tell those leading us astray to repent and come back to their first love. Let us take the position of one of the faith's heroes, a converted atheist, C. S. Lewis, in tackling issues concerning our belief. "I believe in Christianity as I believe that the sun has risen, not only because I see it, but also because by it, I see everything else," wrote C. S. Lewis in his sermon *Is Christianity Poetry?* We must see all things with the light of Christianity.

The Christian is not called to a life of self but to a life of membership of the body of Christ. This membership must be in agreement always. If misunderstanding raises its head anywhere, as it did in the early church, it must be silenced, as did the apostles in Acts of the Apostle chapter six. The essence of that record is to give us an early warning that misunderstanding must come, but let it not bring disunity in the body of Christ. The word *membership* is of Christian origin, with its root in St Paul's theology. According to C.S Lewis, the word membership has its root from a Greek word that can be translated as organ. It means an individual, a family, or a church or domination, but it must be in agreement with one body. The absence of one member must be felt by the entire body. Therefore, if any person, family, or group separates from the church and the church remains unhurt, remains not lacking in performance, that missing person or group had not in the first place been members of the church at all. Do not let anybody make you irrelevant in the body of Christ by being an agent of unjustified separation. You may think you are merely changing from one body of Christ to another. No, there is only one body, and you must justify why you left your first call before you are readmitted. Forget that you have been given overblown recognition and office in your new place of worship; the essential question is, are you in the body of Christ? Our Lord and master, Christ, assures us that members are good enough to participate in the functions of the church and are spiritually endowed, that the church needs their contributions in an atmosphere of spiritual equality. Search your spiritual environment and see how the attitude and performances of the operators are in conformity with the service of God.

How much have we tended toward apostasy in our attempt to help God correct our perceived errors of the church fathers? Have we become ministers for nothing or have we forgotten that the term *minister* in the Christian concept means to serve or help another in the name of Jesus Christ, through His example and by the power of the Holy Spirit?

> Not that we are sufficient of ourselves to think anything as of ourselves: but our sufficiency is of God who also hath made us able ministers of the New Testament: not of the letter, but of the spirit, for the letter killeth, but the spirit giveth life.
>
> 2 Corinthians 3:5-6

By this principle, and the theology of priesthood of all believers, we are all ministers, though not all are ordained and set apart to take care of sacraments, preach sermons, and be devoted to the spiritual care of members of local churches.

Have we so soon forgotten the word *patristic*, meaning *that which comes from the leaders of the early church between the last of the apostles of Jesus and the council of Chalcedon* (according to *Catholic Encyclopedia-Fathers of the Church*)? These leaders are known as the "church fathers" or the patristic writers, if I may remind you. These leaders were not Roman Catholics, but built much of the foundation for today's theology, worship, and Christian creeds and church practices. Are we sincere in rejecting them or are we pursuing some personal interest? This is what the Bible says concerning those engineering division in the body of Christ or destroying the foundation of the Gospel.

Woe onto the pastors that destroy and scatter the sheep of my pasture.

Jeremiah 23:1

"Many pastors have destroyed my vineyard, they have trodden my portion under foot, they have made my pleasant portion a desolate wilderness."

Jeremiah 12:10

Search yourselves, my brothers and sisters. Hell is real. You have no business being there. No one has invited you to hell, not even the devil himself; otherwise, show me the invitation. You are only going there as a gatecrasher. But you have been invited to be with Jesus in heaven. The church fathers have handed down the invitation to us, received directly from Jesus and preserved for all generations. "Follow me; Come all ye that labor" (Matthew 8:22, 11:28). And many other such invitations to heaven that abound in the Bible. It's only by honoring this invitation in faithful obedience, according to the conditions laid down in His Word, that we can be in heaven with Him. Neither can we make it by our own imaginations, nor by how much entertainment we offered or enjoyed from church altars that have become theatres; neither by seed Faith or tithing, as we have been erroneously taught, but by true faith in Him.

What are seed faith and such other apostate doctrines we have replaced the patristic doctrines with? Seed faith is to entrust money or goods to a ministry so we can receive God's special material benefit or favor in return. That is what they told us. Certainly, a financial surrendering will give you financial gain, but "seed faith" is neither a biblical idea nor a biblical term. Let us stop the drift into apostasy in the name of helping God.

A woman lawyer once told me her experience in her new worship place. She said that she was going to church on a certain

Sunday and met an accident scene. A young girl was bleeding to death. With the help of others, she took the bleeding girl to a hospital. The doctor demanded payment before he could start any form of treatment. This is common with Nigerian hospitals. So she used her tithe to make a deposit. At the end of service, she told the story to her pastor, who became very angry with her for being "reckless" with God's money. The woman said that the pastor told her she was worse than an infidel if she could have the heart to spend money she had marked for God on anything else. I asked her what she said in her defense, and she said that she was too shocked to say anything and just went home. I again asked her what the pastor did when he saw her the next time, and she said that they had not met again since then, but that he called and asked her to come for deliverance, and she told him she had already entered his name for prayers in her fellowship meeting. "That means that you don't go to church anymore?" I asked her.

"No, I have gone back to my family church, Assembly of God," she answered.

Thank God for this woman, who had the ability to recognize that the greatest attribute of God, which is love, is missing in the heart of the leader of her so-called new worship place and probably in the entire assembly. Situations like this and worse are not uncommon in many new churches owned by individuals or groups. Teaching the attributes of God can wait, but to make sure that you help God collect all His levies and taxes must be paramount. This has become the replacement theology for the patristic doctrines.

The earliest church creeds and hymns express belief in the risen Jesus, just as the one preserved in 1 Corinthians 15:3-7 by Paul:

> For I delivered unto you first of all that which I also received, how
>> that Christ died for our sins according to scripture;

And that he was buried and that he rose again the third day according to scripture:

And that he was seen of Cephas, then of the twelve:

After that, he was seen of above five hundred brethren at once; of whom the greater part remain unto this present, but some are fallen asleep.

After that, he was seen of James: then of all the apostles.

The antiquity of this creed (the portions in italics) has been located to less than ten years after the Lord's death and resurrection, originating from the Jerusalem apostolic. Paul repeated this creed in his letter to the Corinthians to show us the importance of creeds. If it was not canonized here, it would not have made the creed any less important.

We cannot help God in any way. Test and see, if you are led by the Holy Spirit, whether any of the doctrines and creeds of the apostolic fathers contradicts the Word of God.

Trained in the scholasticism of the medieval Roman Catholic Church, 14th-century theologian John Wycliffe became disillusioned with ecclesiastical abuses. He challenged the church's spiritual authority and sponsored the translation of the Christian Scripture into English.

Granted, Reformation failed to restore the proper theology of eschatology, which was one of the main teachings of the apostles, and of course the concluding message of the New Testament in Revelation and tragically brought about denominational divide in the body of Christ, but we must accept that Martin Luther and the rest did an incredible job, especially in what is called soteriology, the theology of Salvation through faith alone. They returned to the Scripture. Many of them willingly died, being burned at the stake in their commitment to restore the authority of the Bible. They accomplished much, especially in soteriology, but failed to set out eschatology. The church continued to embrace a medieval eschatology called amillennia, a term used by those who deny a literal millennium of Jesus Christ's second coming to physically take over His kingdom, which is the meeting point of Judaism and Christianity.

This oversight on the part of the Reformation has become the momentum of the selfish "church" founders. Their congregation is enticed with the message that the kingdom of God is here now, and that God will give them all they need here and now. Eschatology (the theology of the end-time) means to them that Jesus rules in our heart. The denial of literal eschatology was one of the reasons that brought darkness into the medieval Roman Catholic Church. Origen, a very pious and persuasive prominent church father, a great figure of the third century church, in a possibly genuine effort to preserve the truth of the Gospel, introduced the theory of inspiration, which allegorized the Scripture to extremes, emphasizing that not everybody can read and interpret the Bible.

From about AD 325, the Roman Empire under Constantine declared the Christian religion legal. The story of how Nero and other Emperors before him attempted to destroy the church is a common history.

> For the first 300 years, the Christian Church in Roman Empire was subjected to violent attacks and persecutions, which reached their climax under Emperor Diocletian. Men, women, and children were arraigned before governors and magistrates, and on simple confession "I am a Christian" were cruelly put to death,

writes Geoffrey Hanks in his book *Great Events in the Story of the Church*. The Emperor after Constantine made Christianity the state religion. The pulpit became state funded and managed. Imagine the Pope, whose prerogative it has become to interpret the Scripture, imagine the Pope, who had become like the prime minister to the Empire, imagine the Pope, whose office is funded by the loot of the state, preaching that Jesus is coming soon to rid the world of its evil rulers, of which the Emperor is the chief. That would not only be politically wrong but an embarrassment.

The Roman Catholic Church began to lose the Gospel message of eschatology to please the state. The very essence of the Gospel started to be missing from the pulpit. St. Paul said: "If in this life only we have hope in Christ; we are of all men most miserable" (1 Corinthians 15:13).

He is saying that we should be ready to accept what comes our way here, because our hope is not only in this present world, but in the kingdom of Jesus. Such passages began to fade out. The moment such important messages as quoted above became lost, the Roman Catholic Church lost the Gospel truth and trend. There was no more fear of the future. God is here now. It is prosperity and pleasure on earth that to them had become the kingdom of God. Poverty and pain is the kingdom of hell and therefore not their portion. Messages like, "This year is your breakthrough year," as still continues in these new enterprises that answer churches, replaced the Gospel message of salvation. Heaven and hell became two illusionary extreme, hence purgatory. Jesus and His Father and the Holy Spirit became too difficult to please, so His mother, Mary, being a woman, they reasoned, could be manipulated to take them to heaven, so long as they could afford and were willing to pay indulgence money. Indulgence is the money one pays in the Roman Catholic Church to have one's relation released from purgatory to heaven. These are all products of the medieval Amillennial eschatology.

What has then become of those tough words of our Lord as written in the Gospel, such as, "Sell all you have and give to the poor and follow me"? Peter did, John did, Matthew did, Paul did, and all the disciples did. The apostolic fathers did, because they were certain about his return to rule—the message of eschatology, hence their millennial approach to the Gospel. The medieval Roman Catholic Church could not have held this concept due to its political position.

Amillennial perspective, apart from the protection it offered the medieval rulers, also provided the Roman Empire, the then owner of the Roman Catholic Church, an opportunity and avenue to deny the Jews their position both in the church and in the kingdom of God. It was an opportunity for the empire to shift the blame of killing Jesus from the Roman authority, represented by Pilate, to the Jews. Amillennial perspective was the precursor for the "replacement theology" that denies Israel's role in God's plan, but rather places the church as replacing Israel in God's program for mankind. This concept led to the tragedy of the Holocaust. The guilt of the murder of six million Jews in the concentration camps included the pulpits, where anti-Semitism was pouring out for the sake of promoting Amillennialism.

This is how Dennis Prager reported the extent of anti-Semitism emanating from the pulpits of that time.

> Christianity did not create the Holocaust, indeed Nazism was anti-Christian, but made it conceivable. Hitler and the Nazi found in the Medieval Catholic anti-Jewish legislation a model for their own, and they read and reprinted Martin Luther's virulently anti-Semitic writings. It is instructive that Holocaust was unleashed by only major countries in Europe having approximately equal numbers of Catholic and Protestants: both traditions were saturated with Jew-hatred.

What did Luther write against the Jews that is referred to here and reprinted and circulated by the Nazi? Many things, but in a particular track entitled, "Concerning the Jews and Their Lives," he wrote as reported by Dennis Prager in *Why the Jews.*

a deeper evangelism

Firstly, their synagogues or churches should be set on fire. And whatever does not burn up should be covered or spread over with dirt so that no one may ever be able to see a cinder or stone of it. And this ought to be done for the honor of God and of Christianity in order that God may see that we are Christians… (This is how humans help God).

Secondly, their homes should be broken down and destroyed.

Thirdly, they should be deprived of their prayer books and the Talmud.

Fourthly, their rabbis must be forbidden under the threat of death to teach anymore…

Fifthly, passports and travelling privileges should be absolutely forbidden to Jews. Let them stay at home.

Sixthly, they ought to be stopped from usury. For this reason, as said before, everything they posses, they stole and robbed us through their usury, for they have no other means of support.

Seventhly, let the young and strong Jews and Jewesses be given the flail, the axe, the hoe, the spade, the distaff, and spindle, and let them earn their bread by the sweat of their noses as is enjoined upon Adam's children. We ought to drive the lazy bones out of our system. If, however, we are afraid that they might harm us personally, or our wives, children, servants, castles, et cetera…then let us apply the same cleverness as the other nations such as France, Spain, Bohemia, et cetera…and settle with them for that which they have extorted from us, and after having it divided up fairly, let us drive them out of our country for all time.

To sum up, dear princes and notable who have Jews in your domain, if this advice of mine does not suit you, then find a better one so that you and we may all be free from this inseparable Jewish burden…the Jews.

This was the kind of sermon that filled the air from the pulpits of the medieval churches, both Roman Catholic and Protestants.

Two days after writing this track, Martin Luther died, but Hitler had received baptisms of Jew hatred from the pulpit and therefore continued from where Luther stopped in helping God eliminate "His enemies," the Jews that killed His son.

Amillennialists do not believe in a literal Millennium. To them the millennium thousand years is simply an expression. Many amillennialists believe that during this millennium period, the church will continue to evangelize and grow until the world is sufficiently ready for Christ's coming. The Second Coming will be a natural culmination of the process of world evangelization rather than a revolutionary event that brings sudden and dramatic change. Ammillennialism teaches that the kingdom of God will not be physically established on earth throughout the millennium, but rather that Jesus is presently reigning from heaven.

They believe that conditions in this world will continue to deteriorate until the time of the second coming of Christ. My main concern is their view that because Israel rejected her Messiah, the Church has inherited the promises that were originally given to Israel. This means that Israel no longer has any special place in the plan of God. According to them, the Old Testament millennial kingdom promises have been fulfilled by the church in a spiritualized rather than literal way. The amillennial position is that the millennial kingdom will never appear in any literal way. Instead, it is already being fulfilled through the Church Age in a spiritual sense. The Church has become "spiritual Israel" which has inherited all of God's unfulfilled promises to Israel, quoting from Romans 2:28, 29; Philippians 3:3; Galatians 6:16.

Return To Smith Wigglesworth, however, is not about theological ideology but spiritual growth of the Church, though I am of a firm belief that Christians should be familiar with the elements of the end-time. A tremendous amount of material is devoted to this subject in both Old and New Testament. Some scholars claim that as much as 25 percent of the Bible is devoted to end-time massage. This being so suggests its importance. The better we understand the end-time massage, the more we are motivated to serve the Lord with greater faith. But of note in our relationship with amillennalist ideology is Patrick Allen Boyd's thesis at Dallas Theological Seminary in 1977 that says, "None of the Church Fathers advocate amillennalism in the first century." This is very important information to me because I attach so much relevance to the opinions of this first century Church Fathers who heard from and learned at the feet of the Apostles. Some even might have seen Jesus before He returned to heaven.

Up to the time I was in secondary school in the 1970s, the most derogatory name you could call anybody was "Jew man." This was a product of Amillennialism. If you are one of its adherents, the origin is not in your pastor's teaching of prosperity now and here on earth, but on anti-Semitism handed down to the church, not by the church fathers, but the medieval church, both Roman Catholic and Protestant. The implication of association or fellowship with Amillennial principle is that you are unknowingly dismissing or explaining away the millennium and your salvation. You are inferring that God is not faithful to His Word, which is unfortunate. He is none of the other gods. The Muslims worship Allah, whom they present as being unknowable and capricious. The heathens worship different gods, whom they bribe at will to change the course of events regularly to their favor. The God of the Bible, the God of Abraham, Isaac, and Jacob, the God we worship, delights in keeping His Word, which He says must not return to Him void, nor shall He renege on His covenants. He made one with Israel, and He will keep it. He made another with the church of Christ, and He will keep both. To deny one is to impugn the character of God, so be careful where you put your faith. You may be denying the coming rule of Christ and your salvation without knowing it. Do not be consumed by the thought of how much you are going to donate to God when your prosperity comes. He does not need your help, just your obedience. Question the teachings you are receiving in your present worship place. The Bible says, "Prove all things; hold fast that which is good" (1 Thessalonians 5:21).

Do not be found in the congregation of hypocrites.

Be not deceived; evil communication corrupts good manners.
1 Corinthians 15: 13

Let us examine some of the apostolic doctrines the new age church founders are presenting as their reason for apathy. Please bear me witness that I have not at any point suggested that you should sit tight in a denominational church that has become a mere political system, killing your initiative and energy and making members mere denominational tools instead of soldiers for Christ, or worse, causing them to become more worldly minded than those in the world.

We shall start with the most celebrated and abused of these doctrines—Christmas. It is important to me that you understand the difference between the Catholic church and the Roman Catholic Church, because it will help you appreciate the doctrines and creeds of the Catholic church, which you are one of if you are in good standing before God in Christ Jesus, and the Roman Catholic church, which you may be one of also if you are in Christ. This does not mean two bodies of Christ. The Roman Catholic Church is within the Catholic Church, just as are the Anglican, Methodist, Redeemed Christian, Presbyterian, and Baptist churches and other denominations. *Catholic* is a Greek word (*katholikos*) meaning *universal,* derived from *katholou, in general.* The church was first called Catholic in a letter of St. Ignatius of Antioch to Smyrnaens in AD 110, before the coming of the Roman Catholic Church in the fourth century AD. In fact, the proper nomenclature for the denominations should be Baptist Catholic Church, Presbyterian Catholic Church, Anglican Catholic Church, Methodist Catholic Church, and so on. Most of the doctrines and creeds of the Protestant churches originated from the time before the Roman Catholic. Certain names listed in the chronology of Roman Catholic Popes could not have been, because there was no Roman Catholic Church at their time. For example, Peter was never a Roman Catholic. St. Linus was not a Roman Catholic. I mention St. Linus in particular, because he is listed second after Peter and also because I am going to trace the origin of Christmas to him. Saint Linus lived and died in the first century AD. The Roman Catholic Church claims he was the second Pope after Peter, AD 67-79. From Saint Irenaeus, we know that he was the person mentioned in 2 Timothy 4:21 and that he was also the bishop of Rome when Saint Polycarp was the bishop of Smyrna, now Izmir in Turkey, and Saint Ignatius the Bishop of Antioch. These names are important in relation to our study here. These were all apostolic or church fathers that were immediate successors to the apostles of Jesus. They met and learned at the feet of the apostles. During the reign of the Roman emperor Trajan, St. Ignatius was condemned to be devoured by wild beasts. On his way from his base in Antioch to Rome to honor his execution, he wrote seven letters, five to churches in the Asia Minor communities of Ephesus, Magnesia, Trellis, Philadelphia, and Smyrna, and the other two to Rome and Saint Polycarp.

I want you to understand that these church fathers were not Roman Catholics; otherwise, the emperor would not have been after them. I also want you to understand that the Bishop of Rome then, St. Linus, was not more important than the Bishop of Jerusalem or Antioch or any other. If there was any order of seniority, it should be the Bishop of Jerusalem and Antioch, where Christianity started and where it got its name respectively, before Rome. Let me remind you that at the period of time Roman Catholic history claims St. Linus began his papacy, Paul was still alive and in Rome. If Linus was the Pope with the powers and authority of that office according to Roman Catholic doctrine, then St. Paul did not only serve the early church under Pope Linus, but also should have submitted his epistles to him for papal approval. Incredible! On the contrary, we see from the Bible, in verse twenty-one of the second pastoral epistle of Paul to Timothy, that St. Linus was one of those who ministered to Paul in Rome up to the time the Roman Catholic Church claims he was Pope. The book of 2 Timothy was written in AD 68, after Peter's death. Christian history tells us that John the beloved died around AD 98, over thirty years after St. Linus and others had become popes and heads of the church, according to Roman Catholic history. Is it not strange that John did not mention, even in a flash, his "spiritual head," the pope, in his epistles and apocalypse, written some twenty years after Roman Catholicism claims Linus and others had been popes? John received messages for the Church in Revelation but none for the pope. Strange isn't it? Come to think of it, how could John, the only surviving apostle toward the end of the first century, have thought it expedient to write an epistle to the elect lady and her children and another to Gaius without a mention of the pope? Thank God for His omniscient nature, because if this epistle was addressed to the Elect without lady, we would have erroneously ascribed it to a pope that wasn't then.

St. Linus and the others were the apostolic or church fathers that set out the doctrines and creeds upon which the selection of the New Testament canon was based. These creeds and doctrines must be differentiated from the later Roman Catholic creeds and doctrines. The Roman Catholic Church adopted the apostolic creeds and doctrines, as did the other orthodox denominations, though with new additions on both.

Let us come back to the issue of Christmas. Many stories are in circulation about the origin of Christmas. You have heard repeatedly that it is a heathen rite. I will also show you the origin of that misinformation later. In July 64, two-thirds of Rome burned. Nero laid the blame on the Christians and persecuted them with unmatched viciousness in history. It was during this Nero's reign as emperor that Linus became the leader of Church of Rome. According to Geoffrey Hanks, the usual form of Church government at this time was the collective rule of elders and deacons. It wasn't till the end of the first century that the custom of one ruling elder called bishop became the practice in Church government.

Nero had wickedly driven Christians into hiding after killing the apostles and later his sister, because she was caught participating in the sacrament of Holy Communion. Her image, which the Roman Catholic Church believes is her uncorrupted body, is still standing in the Vatican monastery with three of her right-hand fingers raised in the sign of Trinity. The catacomb had become the home of Christians of Rome, never to show face in public. You will not blame them or consider their act as weakness if you remember that Nero executed his own mother. History said it was because she criticized his mistress, but Christian sources said it was because she asked him to relent on the persecution of Christians. Catacombs, by the way, are a network of subterranean chambers and galleries used for burial purposes by people of the ancient Mediterranean world, especially the early Christians. Toward the end of AD 67, Nero had completely driven the entire Roman Christian population into the catacombs, where they lived with their dead. This was the time of St. Linus's leadership of the Roman church.

So many stories are in circulation concerning the origin of the celebration of Christian Christmas. To me, the most interesting part of all accounts of its origin from all I have read or heard is that the day we celebrate Christmas was originally a day set aside for a pagan celebration. This is information that has gladdened me a lot. It is a common knowledge that it is the stronger that can bind the weaker and take over his possession. This is true both in the physical and spiritual. The Israelites left Egypt as slaves, wandered through the wilderness for forty years, exterminated the "original" occupants of the land of Canaan and possessed it. A pagan territory became God's territory. That is the stronger binding the weaker and taking his possession. In a parable Jesus illustrated how this principle operates in the spiritual. "Or else how can one enter into a strong man's house and spoil his goods except he first bind the strong man? And then he will spoil his house" (Matthew 12:29). So 25 December, originally a day the kingdom of darkness celebrates in honor of their god, has become a day the kingdom of light pulls out the entire world to celebrate the birth of her Lord. Hallelujah! This is a great achievement, a miracle indeed. I couldn't be prouder of my kingdom. Every Christmas, I celebrate two events: the birth of Jesus, and the victory of my kingdom against the kingdom of darkness over 25 December.

One of the sources of information on the origin of Christmas that interest me because of its sound logic is the one found in the *Bible Dictionaries*. I borrowed this book from a friend when I was working in Pomezia near Rome in the 1990s. Its account of the origin of Christmas made so much impression on me that I will like to share it here. I have also added to it from related observations and information gathered from associates and Roman Catholic Church historians like my very good friend Mr. E. Falappa.

According to this account, before the introduction of Christmas, each year, beginning on December 17, Romans honored

Saturn, the ancient god of agriculture, in a festival called Saturnalia. This festival lasted for seven days and included the winter solstice, which usually occurred on the last Sunday of the year on the ancient Julian calendar. During solstice, the Romans feasted, postponed all business and warfare, exchanged gifts, and temporarily freed their slaves. The year was AD 67; Saint Linus was just in his first year in office as bishop of Rome. Nero was still the emperor of the Roman Empire. Christianity had been driven into a coma, courtesy of Nero's severe persecution. The festival of Saturn would start on the 17th of December. The privileges the festival offered were too much a benefit for the Christian community to ignore, especially under their situation, and more also because there would be no break before solstice that year. The solstice occurred on December 25th that year. Saint Linus decided to call out all Christians from the catacombs for a crusade that would let the world know that Christianity was still alive in Rome. The privileges of solstice started that year by midnight of December 25th. Saint Linus called out all Christians in Rome to a lively procession from the catacombs, many of them in far-away Appian-way, to central Rome. The carol was so beautiful and colorful that by morning of the 25th, most children and women had joined. Nero was boiling in rage but could do nothing, because of the law governing the period of solstices. By the end of the day, the assembly had run back to the catacombs, and the children and wives of the elite, senators, and generals, went back to their homes. The next day, the 26th, normal business resumed in Rome. In the catacombs, there was apprehension. In the senate, there was confusion and bewilderment and silence, each looking at the other. "If we say to arrest and persecute those who participated in the Christian procession of the 25th, our children and wives would be involved," they reasoned.

By the noon, Christian occupants of cubicles in the catacombs became anxious and began to wonder what had happened to the occupants of the other cubicles, believing that arrest and persecution was eminent after the solstice. Quietly, they started passing boxes of gifts to each other's cubicles to determine the state of the occupants, like whether they had been arrested. To their amazement, no one had been arrested. That was the origin of Boxing Day of December 26th.

The next year, AD 68, probably as a result of disillusionment and shame over the victory of the Christians, the Gallic and Spanish legions, along with the Praetorian Guards, rose against Nero, and he fled from Rome, was declared a public enemy by the senate, and on June 9th, 68 AD, committed suicide near Rome. The victory of Christianity over the tyranny of Nero at the battle of December 25, 67, was sealed.

Those who told you that Christmas originated in the 4th century as the Christian substitute to the pagan celebration of the winter solstice without telling you the circumstance is only being mischievous. Ask them the origin of Boxing Day—a term not translated literally from its original Italian name, *Santo Stefano*, and its relationship with Christmas. *Santo* is an Italian adjective meaning *holy*; for example, *acqua Santa* means holy water. Boxing Day was literally picked to represent what happened on that 26th December when the Christians in the catacombs exchanged boxes of gifts in the catacomb cubicles as a way of communicating to determine the conditions of the others. On discovering that no one had been arrested or persecuted, they rejoiced in the Lord. God had used the participation of the sons and daughters and wives of the nobles, senators, and generals to tie the hands of Nero.

Christianity had conquered the Roman Empire, the ruler of the then world, to God's glory in Jesus's name. Christianity, however, still remained an illegal religion until in the 4th century AD, when Constantine the Great became the Roman emperor (306-337).

a deeper evangelism

Constantine the Great was the first emperor of Rome to be converted to Christianity. During his reign, Christians, previously persecuted, gained freedom of worship. He gave huge estates and other gifts to the Christian church. He established a capital in the eastern provinces, naming it Constantinople (now Istanbul, Turkey). With the freedom Constantine's conversion brought to the church, Christianity became a public pride.

Granted, the Gospel detailed the birth of Jesus Christ but did not give us the date of His birth, so true Christians do not know or assume knowledge of His exact birthday. However, the Roman Catholic Church, which the Catholics of Rome had become after acquiring state status under Constantine, in commemoration of the victory of 25th of December 67 over Nero, declared that day the Feast of the Nativity. That is how Christmas began according to the account I read from the CHURCH DICTIONARY.

It was a victory only a non-true Christian would take for granted. Christians like you and me were put into drums, bound with bitumen, and set on fire along the streets of Rome as human streetlights by Nero.

Boxing in Italian is *pugilato*. *Day* in Italian is *giorno*. For example, *giorno di paga* means *payday*. Boxing Day would have been *Giorno di Pugilato* instead of Santo Stefano. The English translation missed out the Holy—Santo. Just as *Christmas* in Italian is *Natece* and Christmas Day is *giorno di Natele*, so would Santo Stefano have been translated Holy Station. There is no Christ in the original Italian for Christmas. Natele is an adjective of one's birth. If we say *giorno di natele*, it means *day of birth*. So we have *vigilia di Natele* for that very important eve of 25th of December when St. Linus called out the Christians for the procession. We have *giorno di Natele* for the 25th of December, the day Christianity defeated Nero and the world he represented. The Holy Survival day, Santo Stefano, is the 26th of December, the day Christians in the catacombs passed gifts to one another. I have endeavored to bring out these translations to show that there was nothing in the original concept of Christmas celebrations that attributed the actual birthday of Jesus to December 25 except that the events surrounding this date were considered too precious by the church to be ignored, so it was adopted for the commemoration of our Lord's birth.

All the three events, the eve, the 25th, and the 26th of December, came together to make *Natalizio*; translated *Christmas* in English. You can now relax and enjoy the victory of Christmas now that you know how it came about. I believe God that I have been able to unblock one of the Christian wells the Philistines in our midst may have blocked in your life in Christ *Buon Natele*— Merry Christmas.

There are efforts today from many quarters including Christians to obliterate Christmas celebration either due to ignorance or a desire to reverse the victory for devil. These are the equivalent of the Philistines that infiltrated Israel.

Selwyn Hughes, of blessed memory, in the January 2005 issue of *Every Day with Jesus,* wrote on the topic "unblocking the wells" under the title "A Philistine Mentality."

> The Philistines, I am afraid, are amongst us still. Many of the wells from which our (apostolic) fathers drank are being stocked up with rubbish that passes for Christianity by those who substitute their own ideas for the truth of God. Thus the wells fail to serve their purpose. Perhaps no greater challenge faces the church of Jesus Christ at this time than identifying these blocked wells and cleaning away the rubbish so that once again all God's people have access to the fresh waters of truth.

These Philistines that have become owners of many bogus churches are fast moving away from the reality of the harsh sayings of Jesus as found in the Gospel. *Sin* is fast disappearing from their mouths. It is too harsh and makes the congregation uncomfortable, so they have to find some diversionary issues. "We must help God by hiding those harsh sayings of Jesus from the congregation so that members are not discouraged" seems to be their tactic.

They have forgotten that Jesus is identified in Scripture as *Skandolon*, the Greek word for *stumbling block*. Jesus told us in plain message that you either fall on this stone (God) and be broken, because "the sacrifices of God are a broken spirit; a broken and a contrite heart…" (Psalm 51:17), or allow it fall on you and be smashed to powder.

> And whosoever shall fall on this stone shall be broken but on whosoever it shall fall, it will grind him to powder.
>
> Matthew 21: 44

Good News Bible and some other translations omitted this harsh reality of the Gospel of Jesus Christ. We either accept His statements in totality, or we are not His followers. For sin, He came into the world in flesh. For sin, He faced the pains of the cross. To hide it is to crucify Him again and again. To hide sin means that redemption does not exist. How can you talk about salvation unless you first acknowledge the lethal reality of sin? In some quarters, these harsh teachings about sin are described in more euphemistic terms; adultery sounds ugly in the ear and harsh to the target, so call it "having an affair." Fornication is too abrasive; call it "premarital sex." And the so-called Church of Jesus Christ wobbles along in this fashion. The products are reformation that carries no spiritual value instead of regeneration and redemption. The Bible tells us that if we deny our sins, the truth is not in us, but that God is faithful enough to do what He said He would do—forgive and purify us if we admit and repent.

"If we say that we have no sin, we deceive ourselves and the truth is not in us" (1 John 1:8).

So should we, because we have admitted that we are sinners and have acknowledged our inability to help ourselves, continue to live in sin? God forbid. This has been the attitude and rationalization of many church goers. If this is so, the Bible would not have also proffered a remedy:

> If we confess our sins, He is faithful and just to forgive us our sins and cleans us from all unrighteousness.
>
> I John 1:9

Cornelius Plantinga wrote,

> "...self-deception about sin is a narcotic and produces a tranquillizing and disorienting suppression of our spiritual central nervous system.... When we lack an ear for the wrong notes in our lives, we cannot play the right ones or even recognize them in the performance of others.

We are not helping God, nor can we, by making His Word more palatable. Neither can we swell the population of His Kingdom by closing our eyes to impropriety in the church.

It has become an unwritten rule in some Christian quarters, that the congregation must not be offended by commenting on mode of dressing. This is part of the negative aspect of helping God mentality. In my church, Christ Church, Interdenominational, there is a dress code. It has, to a reasonable extent, reduced the incidence of mockers' presence in the church. I am not of any opinion on a particular type of dressing, for example, trousers are for men or women. The Bible message is this:

a deeper evangelism

> The women shall not wear that which pertaineth unto men, neither shall a man put on a woman's garment, for all that do so are abomination unto the Lord.
>
> Deuteronomy 22:5

Some quarters will tell you that it is Old Testament Law and we are no longer under the Law. Correct, but tithe is of the Old Testament Law also, and that same quarter emphasizes it above all other values. My view is that at the time of this instruction, both men and women in Israel wore long garments. The style is the difference. In Africa, both men and women were tying wrappers before shirts and trousers dominated men's dressing. The reason, I believe, is because men in the past were exclusively doing the climbing work and such jobs that requires freedom of the legs. Now such jobs are no more the exclusive of men, and trousers have also ceased to be exclusive to men. My friend's daughter was studying engineering in one of Nigeria's universities. Her father, on grounds of the passage above, forbade her from wearing trousers. During her industrial attachment, she was required to climb scaffolds. She went home and told her father that the boys always assemble at the base of the scaffold any time she climbs up, and of course, she has to because she has to pass. My friend, her father, rushed to the market and bought her a number of jeans trousers. What I think is important in dressing mode is not whether a woman puts on trousers or any other type of clothing, but the message in Matthew concerning the wedding feast:

> And when the king came in to see the guests, he saw there a man which had not on a wedding garment: And he saith unto him, "Friend, how comest thou in hither and not having a wedding garment?" And he was speechless. Then said the king to the servant "Bind him hand and foot, and take him away, and cast him into the outer darkness: there shall be weeping and gnashing of teeth."
>
> Matthew 22:11-13

That is what indecent dressing in the house of God could lead to. Whether it is trousers or any other type of dressing, the essential issue is whether it is fit for appearance before He who made us in His image. There is no doubt that some agents of the devil are sent to churches to distract the attention of believers in different forms, dressing being one. This is why only a non-serious church will close its eyes to the type of dressings that appear in their midst.

The attention on modesty, especially in dressing, seems to be directed more toward women, because men are mostly stimulated sexually by sight. Exposing to other men features that God has bestowed her for the exclusive delight of her husband is the limit a woman can lead a man in offence against God. The husband of such a woman may be dying in silence or may have made uncomplimentary comments that resulted in quarrel and decided to keep quiet. But is he truly keeping quiet? Of course not. Resentment creeps in and indifference results. Any little misunderstanding becomes overblown and can lead to anything, including break up. That is why the Bible says,

> Every wise woman buildeth her home, but the foolish plucketh it down with her hand.
>
> Proverbs 14:1

> In like manner also, that women adorn themselves in modest apparels, with shamefacedness and sobriety; not with braided hair, or gold, or pearls of costly array.
>
> 1 Timothy 2:9

Two issues are outstanding in this message of instruction from Paul. First is the issue of modesty, and second is the issue of prudence. Encarta Dictionary defines *modesty* as:

1. Humility: unwillingness to draw attention to your achievements or abilities.

2. Sexual reserve: reserve in appearance, manner, and speech, especially in relation to sexual matters.

It defines *prudent* as:

1. Having good sense in dealing with practical matters.

2. Careful in managing resources as to provide for the future.

Remove Paul, remove church, and remove your belief in God; who will not teach his or her child these two virtues, modesty and prudence? There is nothing to add or remove from the message of Paul in this passage concerning mode of dressing for the Christian. Let your dressing be in absolute sobriety.

In Europe and other cold areas, I observed that people of unsound mind overdress for the cool weather for maximum comfort, exhibiting maximum lack of modesty; but in Africa, person in their category almost go about naked, due to the hot weather, for maximum comfort, a case of absolute lack of modesty. The insane person is not sober, and so modesty and prudence are thrown to the winds.

That is what Paul is saying here, that we should not imitate the insane. It does not matter whether a woman is wearing trousers or not, though the style and fit are of essence. If we take the second definition of *prudent*, *careful in managing resources*, the message of Solomon in Proverbs 14:1 complements Paul's. Their concern is that we should not deprive the home, present and future, the means for sustenance due to our desire for flamboyance.

Our Gospel is a total package. It is interested in both our inside and outside. From how we treat the body to how we treat the soul. From how we appear before God to why we did. Anything within and around us that has the slightest possibility of keeping the Holy Spirit away from the Church should be done away with. Let no one be held responsible for the absence of the Holy Spirit in his or her congregation.

I have heard many Christians, some claiming to be born-again, extend the hand of fellowship instead of evangelism to people of other beliefs, especially Islam. Some so-called men of God even refer to them as "our Muslim brethren," not biological but in ecumenism. Are they your brothers in Christ or in Mohammed? I have even heard some churches sing praises to Allah. They want to help God expand His worship horizon. Who told you that God cannot make all mankind and even the beast worship Him if He needed it to be so? He has given us a free will, and if you knowingly include an unwilling mind into the house of the Lord, I believe that you will have some questions to answer.

Islam was singled out by Jesus Christ Himself while on earth, in prophecy, as a coming deserter to His mission.

> When ye therefore shall see the abomination of desolation, spoken of by Daniel the prophet, stand in the holy place (whoso readeth, let him understand) then let them which be in Judea flee unto the mountains...
>
> Matthew 24:15

This is the only passage in the Bible I have seen with a specific petition from the Lord to the reader. "Whoso readeth, let him understand." Have you given this a thought?

I should think the reason for the instruction is to alert us on the significance of this prophecy. The prophecy came just after Christ had prophesied that no stone shall be left on top of each other on the Holy Temple. So the holy place in reference is the Temple of God in Jerusalem. Today a Muslim Mosque, the Dome of the Rock is standing there.

Paul, in 2 Thessalonians, described the occupant of this desolation thus:

> Let no man deceive you by any means: for that day shall not come except there come a falling away first, and that man of sin be revealed, the son of perdition; who opposeth and exalted himself above all that is called God, or that is worshipped, so that he as God sitteth in the temple of God, shewing himself that he is God.
>
> 2 Thessalonians 2: 3-4

The oldest extant Islamic structure, the Dome of the Rock, stands on the sacred rock of Jerusalem Temple, where Muslims claim that Muhammad ascended to heaven. The prophecies above fulfilled. Our duty to God is to preach Christ to the Muslims and ask the Holy Spirit to open their eyes to see the Truth.

We cannot help God by any way, in any form, from anywhere. Help yourself by doing what He has commanded you to do through Jesus Christ, and He will not only give you help, but also a helper.

Do not let any man toy with your eternity for his or her selfish reasons. Your salvation is not in doctrine or creed but in Jesus Christ. Do not be an agent of division in the body of Christ. The Bible instructs in 1 Corinthians 2:5, "That your faith should not stand in the wisdom of men, but in the power of God."

Do not be afraid to judge your spiritual environment if you are convinced that you are in good standing with Jesus. The Bible says, "He that is spiritual judge all things, yet he himself is not judge by man" (1 Corinthians 2:1).

The Negative Spirit of Bacchus

Negative conditions are encountered in many occurrences and courses of life. In mathematics, it means less than zero. *Negative* is best explained in practical terms in mathematics. It carries the sign (-), and positive carries the sign (+), though usually absent. Negative indicates a value less than nothing, hence (-).

-1 + (-2) = -3 (one negative plus two negative is equal to negative three)

1 + 2 = 3 (one positive plus two positive is equal to three positive)

So what is wrong about negative? Let us look at the first equation. If you borrowed one dollar and lost it (negative) and borrowed another two dollars and lost it (negative) your indebtedness adds up to a negative value of three dollars. That you have lost both does not mean that the three dollars lost its worth. It is still the same value of the dollar you borrowed, even though you have lost both. The same with the second equation; if you earned one dollar and kept it (positive), and you earned another two dollars and kept it (positive), both add up to three dollars in worth, just as the ones you borrowed and lost (negative) retained their worth. If, however, you borrowed one dollar and lost it (negative), and earned another two dollars and kept it, your balance is one dollar in the positive, because you have to pay back the one you borrowed and lost. That is what mathematics teaches.

Physics explains *negative* as a reduction in value. Physics expects an object thrown down from above to gain speed on touching ground and expects an object thrown up to lose speed as it goes up. This is negative acceleration or positive retardation. Physics expects an object moving horizontally to continue at a constant speed without positive or negative acceleration, but positive and not negative displacement, unless influenced by an external force.

Philosophy explains *positive* and *negative* in relation to how we think and act in our natural environment and when under some influences. In nature, *negative* represents something or somebody undesirable: a person, thing, quality, or situation that is bad.

In medicine, it represents what is absent. When attached to the word *euthanasia*, it represents a practice of mercifully ending a person's life in order to release the person from an incurable disease, intolerable suffering, or undignified death.

In logic, it means opposing, denying, or contradicting a statement, proof, or argument.

In biology, it means moving away from source of stimulation such as light.

In photography, it represents a photographic image or film that shows black and white tones reversed and color as complementary.

In grammar, the word *negative* implies "No."

In Christianity, *negative spirit* implies all spirits, visible or invisible, that operate either in human or material form outside of the Holy Spirit, sometimes called the Holy Ghost. The name *ghost* and *spirit* often implies the same. However, the term *ghost* is applied more frequently to apparition, usually of a dead person, which varies in solidity from mere froglike appearance to replica of the dead person. On the other hand, the Holy Spirit or Holy Ghost is the third personality of the Divine Trinity, the other two being the Father and the Son.

The Holy Ghost is frequently represented with symbols such as the dove, symbolizing purity, peace, and reconciliation.

We can therefore comfortably define *spirit* as an important influence, somebody or something that is divine, or inspiring or animating influence.

Distilled or brewed liquors are any of various beverages of high-alcohol content, often called *ardent spirit*. As ancient as human civilization, alcoholic religious service has been associated with tradition.

Johann Wolfgang Von Goethe (1749-1832), a German poet, playwright, and scientist, in one of his poems on alcohol describes it thus: "I am the spirit that denies." So why should people want to serve the spirit that has confessed itself a denying spirit? Umberto Eco, an Italian writer and literary scholar provides the answer. He wrote in His book *Imitation* (1932), "The pleasure of imitation, as the ancients knew, is one of the innate in the human spirit." Alcoholic spirit is the imitation of the Holy Spirit. No wonder it is the innate spirit of the fallen man. That is why the world calls it *ardent* spirit; by interpretation, a passionate spirit.

W.B. Yeats (1865-1939) wrote in his poem *Human Condition,*

Wine (spirit) comes in at the mouth.
And love comes in at the eyes

a deeper evangelism

That's all we shall know for truth
Before we grow old and die.

Compare the fruit of the spirit of Bacchus and the fruit of the Holy Spirit in these passages and make your choice.

"Before me floats an image, man or shade, shade more than man, more image than a shade," W. B. Yeats continues. This is the fruit of the spirit of Bacchus: confusion, hallucination, imagination, and contradiction. But the true gift of delight, of exaltation, that sense of being more than human, which is the touchstone of the highest human excellence, can only be found in the fruit of the Holy Spirit:

> But the fruit of the Spirit is love, joy, peace, longsuffering, gentleness, goodness, faith, meekness, temperance.
> Galatians 5:22

According to World Health Organization notes on alcohol, the spirit of Bacchus brings madness, temporary as it may seem, but a disease called *incubus*, in which, when a person gets to sleep, he seems to have a heavy weight pressing on him, spirit oppressed, voice abolished, power to move impeded, throat obstructed almost to strangulation.

> Wine is a mocker, strong drink is raging; and whosoever is deceived thereby is not wise.
> Proverbs 20:1

That remarkable day of Pentecost, the Jerusalem crowd insinuated that the followers of our Lord were drunk, hence their boldness and utterances. They attributed the disciples' euphony to spuriousness, a state of mind usually induced by alcohol.

Others mocking said; these men are full of new wine.

Acts 2:13

Gleukos is the Greek word interpreted *new wine* here. It is a special kind of sweet and strong wine, distilled from the grape before it is pressed. That is what the people accused the disciples of Jesus of being full of. Peter was quick in refuting this ugly notion and introduced himself and the rest with him as fulfilling Joel's prophesy. They were, rather, filled with the real Spirit of God and not with the spurious spirit of alcohol, he told them.

Paul later, in Romans 14:17, wrote, "The Kingdom of God is not meat and drink; but Righteousness and peace and Joy in the Holy Ghost."

By "meat and drink," Paul did not mean the meat and beverages we eat and drink at meals in our homes, but the exotic meat the people of the world gobble while drinking in the beer parlors, usually to the exclusion of their families but to the pleasure of the daughters of Venus that customarily accompany them to such places.

A long text in condemning alcohol is found in Proverbs 23:29-32.

Who had woe? Who had sorrow? Who had contentions? Who had babbling? Who had wounds without cause? Who had redness of eyes? They that tarry long at the wine; they that go to seek mixed wine. Look not thou upon the wine when it is red, when it gives his color in cups, when it gives itself *aright*. At the last it bites like a serpent and stings like an adder.

The rejection of the spirit of alcohol soon became lost along the timeline of the church. During the totalitarianism of the old Roman Catholic Church, a deadly and most powerful and pervasive spirit had become well entrenched in the church. This was among the reasons the roaring Reformers, like John Wycliffe, Jon Hus, Martin Luther, John Knox, and others, began to fight the blasphemy and hypocrisy of the medieval church. With a functional name of "spirit of Religion," this high-ranking demon has for centuries kept multitudes in spiritual darkness by deceiving them into believing they would be saved by their religion, irrespective of their life style. The proper name of this spirit, according to those engaged in spiritual mapping, is "Queen of Heaven," mentioned in the Bible in Jeremiah 7:18.

> The children gather wood, and the fathers kindle the fire, and the women knead their dough, to make cakes for the queen of heaven, and to pour out drink offerings unto other gods, that they may provoke me to anger.

Operating as the spirit of religion, the Queen of Heaven has apparently succeeded in disguising herself very skillfully as the Blessed Virgin Mary, and has thereby delighted in receiving the worship and obedience of millions today as she did during the era of complete darkness in the gentile world, before Paul's commission "to open their (Gentiles) eyes in order to turn them from darkness to light, and from the power of Satan to God" (Acts 26:18).

Many drinkers, which included me in the past, cannot control their drinking, even when it becomes the underlying cause of serious harm, including medical disorders, marital difficulties, job loss, or automobile crashes. Alcohol drinkers develop a craving, or a strong urge, to drink, despite awareness that drinking is creating problems in their lives. They suffer from impaired control, an inability to stop drinking once they have begun. They also become physically dependent on alcohol. When they stop drinking, they suffer unpleasant physical ailments, known as withdrawal symptoms, that include nausea, sweating, shakiness, and anxiety. Alcohol drinkers develop a greater tolerance for it—that is, they progressively need to drink increasing amounts to reach intoxication.

The force behind alcohol dependence is in the power of this demon called the Queen of Heaven. The World Health Organization (WHO) notes, and I confirm from experience, that other behaviors common in people who have become dependent on alcohol include seeking out opportunities to drink—often to the exclusion of other activities—and rapidly returning to established drinking patterns following period of abstinence.

My Bible says of woes drinkers bring upon themselves:

> Woe unto them that rise up in the morning that they may follow strong drink until night, till wine inflames them. Woe unto them that are mighty to drink wine, and mingle strong drink.
>
> Isaiah 5:11 and 22

Spiritual Effect of Alcohol

How does this powerful weapon of darkness—alcohol—come to the service of Queen of Heaven?

The Bible says:

> And I find more bitter than death the woman, whose heart is snares and nets, and her hands as bands; whoso pleaseth God shall escape from her but the sinner shall be taken by her.
>
> Ecclesiastes 7: 26

The spirit of alcohol was introduced into the church by this demon, Queen of Heaven, functioning as the Bacchus spirit, or Dionysus, god of wine and vegetation, who according to the pagan world, "showed mortals how to cultivate grapevines and make wine."

A son of Zeus, Bacchus (or Dionysus) is usually character-ized in one of two ways. As the god of vegetation—specifically of the fruit of the trees—he is often represented on Attic vases with a drinking horn and vine branches. He eventually became the popular Greek god of wine and cheer, and wine miracles were reportedly performed at certain of his festivals. Bacchus is also characterized as a deity whose mysteries inspired ecstatic, orgiastic worship. The maenads, or bacchantes, were a group of female devotees who left their homes to roam the wilderness in ecstatic devotion to Bacchus. They wore fawn skins and were believed to possess occult powers with which they charmed men.

Dionysus is popularly called Bacchus, a name referring to the loud cries with which Dionysus was worshiped at the orgies. These frenetic celebrations became occasions for licentiousness and intoxication. This was the form in which the worship of Dionysus became popular in Roman Italy, where the Dionysian cult was called Bacchanalia.

John Milton (1608 – 1674), the hymnist, wrote this poem on Bacchus:

> Bacchus that first from out the purple grapes
> Crushed the sweet poison of misused wine,
> After the Tuscan mariners transformed,
> Coasting the Tyrrhene shore as the winds listed
> On Circe's island fell; (who knows not Circe,
> The daughter of the Sun? Whose charmed cup
> Whoever tasted lost his upright shape,
> And downward fell into a grovelling swine.

Remember John Milton. In the epic poem Paradise lost, he dramatizes the biblical account of humanity's banishment from paradise and also wrote the sequel to Paradise Lost, called *Paradise Regained*, in which Jesus triumphantly resists Satan and regains the paradise lost by Adam and Eve. John Milton wrote this hymn:

> Let us with gladsome mind
> Praise the Lord, for He is kind
> For His mercies aye endure
> Ever faithful, ever sure.

Alcohol's intoxicating quality seems to have infused it with some element of spirituality. Many folktales about first experiences with alcohol emphasize the puzzling sequence of intoxication, deep slumber, and reawakening, comparing it with a journey to the land of the dead and back. Alcohol was used in naming, marriage, and funeral rites among pagans, whose perception of family and society encompassed the ancestors, the living, and those yet unborn. Any gathering important to the visible and invisible members of their family or community warranted the use of alcohol in libation. It bound their family or community and cemented their relations with the supernatural world of spirits.

Pervasiveness

Alcohol dependence affects a broad cross section of society around the world. Statistics show that alcohol dependence touches successful business executives, skilled engineers, mechanics, laborers, homemakers, and church members of all denominations. World Health Organization estimates that nearly 62 million people worldwide suffer from alcohol dependence.

In Asian nations such as Japan, where the Queen of Heaven reigns supreme, alcohol abuse has become a social concern over the last decade. In these countries, drinking almost is required when conducting business. Bars are an extension of offices, places where key decisions are made. A person who declines an invitation to a drink risks being denied promotion within the company.

Physical Effects of Alcohol

Ethyl alcohol, or ethanol, is present in varying amounts in beers and wines and in distilled liquors, such as whiskey, gin, and rum. When a person consumes alcohol, the stomach and intestines rapidly absorb it. From there, alcohol travels in the blood throughout the entire body, affecting nearly every tissue. Moderate and high doses of alcohol depress the functions of the central nervous system, including the brain. The higher the alcohol level is in the blood, the greater the impairment.

As a person becomes intoxicated, painful or embarrassing situations appear less threatening, and as drinking progresses, speech may become loud and slurred. Impaired judgment may lead to incautious behavior, and physical reflexes and muscular coordination may become noticeably affected. If drinking continues, complete loss of physical control follows, ending in stupor and possibly death.

Social Effects of Alcohol

Throughout most of history, society has viewed people who drink to excess as irresponsible, immoral, and of weak character. Until the mid twentieth century, the typical picture of the drunkard was of someone without steady employment, unable to sustain family relationships, and most likely in desperate financial straits.

Intoxication threatens not only the individual who drinks but also the surrounding community. According to WHO, alcohol-use disorders undermine global health, accounting for three and a half percent of the total cases of disease worldwide.

I once came across a public advert billboard that had a picture of a bottle of beer with boxing gloves on its two hands, canvas boxing shoes on its feet and standing in a pose like Mohammed Ali. An inscription below read, "Bacchus! Do not challenge him. He inflicts two deadly punches: one on your health and the other on your pocket."

As I woke up one day late, having wasted my night in drinking houses, I realized that a third punch was missing in that public advert. I got back home late and drunk and went to sleep, dead like a log, no chance to review my past assignment, no forecast on my coming assignment, no dreams, no visions, no meditation—just dead and heavy snoring. Loss of time is that missing punch; *And whose time?* I asked myself. God's time, of course, which I am only a steward of. What account will I give for His time? I decided to draw up a reminder to myself in form of a poem that I must give account of my stewardship of His time. Let me share this poem with you, which I titled *The Stewardship of Time*:

> Time has ceased to be mine, but His it has become
> Little steward of Time, have I become onto Him
> To give account of at the end of my stewardship
> As to what I did not do with it,
> Because I did what I ought not.
> Redeem the Time, for the days are evil;
> Arise instantly from dead, my spirit,
> Awake now from sleep, my soul
> For procrastination is the thief of Time,
> His Time which I have become a steward thereof.

Avoid these three punches, and you have heeded the wise advice of King Solomon in Proverbs 3:2: "For length of days, and long life, and peace shall they add to thee." Because there will be no more punches on your time, your health, and your pocket when you cut off any relationship with the spirit of Bacchus, not on doctor's instruction, but in the name of Jesus Christ.

Development of Alcohol Dependence

Alcohol-use disorders develop in a predictable pattern. Health professionals use three stages to describe this progression. In stage one, individuals drink primarily as a supplement to social situations. Drinking at this stage has not become the central focus of a person's activities.

A reasonable number of social drinkers advance to stage two. In this early stage of a drinking problem, many people do not show any signs of illness. But often, more severe problems develop with time and continued drinking. Activities that focus on drinking may take up increasingly larger amounts of time in the person's life, and as a drinking problem progresses, the intoxicated behavior becomes disagreeable and antisocial. A person may resort to drinking to relieve the physical discomfort of withdrawal symptoms. Most often, attempts to avoid the discomfort result in morning drinking to offset symptoms that develop after a bout of drinking the night before.

As drinking continues, drinkers cannot acknowledge that drinking and intoxication have become goals in themselves. Drinking may become a technique for coping with problems, many of which have been brought about by alcohol use. Drinkers may neglect responsibilities to their family, seriously damaging relationships with their partners and children. In many cases, their productivity at work declines, often resulting in job loss. Despite numerous negative consequences experienced as a result of their drinking, they remain in denial of their problem. They continue to claim to friends and family that they can stop drinking any time they want to. But in actuality, they find it increasingly difficult to control their alcohol use.

Stage three is the final stage. In addition to suffering from many of the problems experienced by individuals in stage two, an individual in stage three can no longer control his or her drinking. The usual outcomes are clumsiness, uncoordinated behavior and impairment of mental abilities such as judgment and memory; irresponsible behavior, euphoria; standing, walking, and talking difficulties; motor and emotional control centers are greatly affected; slurred speech, staggering, loss of balance, and double vision can all be present. Drinker in this category may become unconscious. Respiration may slow down and can stop altogether, resulting in death.

Defilement by Alcohol

Paul cautions us in Romans 12:1, saying, "I beseech you, therefore, brethren, by the mercies of God that ye present your bodies a living sacrifice, holy, acceptable unto God..."

Paul reminds us again in 1 Corinthians 6:16 that our body is not our property but the Temple of God: "Know ye not that ye are the Temple of God and that the Spirit of God dwelleth in you?"

The Spirit of God cannot dwell in a body that has become a habitation for the spirit of Bacchus. Let us be reminded that during the feast of Passover (Pesah), the Israelites abstained completely from yeast, eating only unleavened bread (Matzo, bread that has no yeast and therefore did not rise as the normal ones we eat). The essence is to make sure there is no yeast in the body to convert body sugar into alcohol. The body must be completely free from alcohol during this feast. If the internally generated alcohol in the body for its own use is considered defilement, then the introduction of alcohol into the body from external sources cannot be contemplated at all by the family of Christ. Listen to Paul in 1 Corinthians 3:17:

> If any man defile the Temple of God, him shall God destroy;
> for the Temple of God is Holy, which Temple you are.

The question that comes to mind is this: If Paul advised Timothy to take a little wine for his stomach's sake, how then is drinking alcohol defilement? A careful analysis of that passage will reveal that what Paul meant here is non-alcoholic wine. The message of the angel Gabriel concerning the coming of John the Baptist in Matthew 1:15 is that *he shall drink neither wine nor strong drinks.* By transposition, we can say, "Drink no non-alcoholic wine or alcoholic drinks at all," showing that wine as used in the Bible does not always imply strong or alcoholic drink. Jesus drank and turned water into wine, may be not strong drink. Till today, all entertainment drinks, including Coca Cola, are called wine in my part of the world. Paul did not say for Timothy's head but stomach. Alcohol as we know it has its effect in the brain, not the stomach. Paul knew the spurious nature of the spirit of alcohol, and it would have been his recommendation to timid John Mark when he deserted them in the missionary battlefield at Antioch, for his "courage's" sake. But Paul would not encourage the spurious. Rev. Obong N. Obong asked his congregation in one of his sermons if any were willing to ask God for Timothy's stomach frailty so as to share in this advice. Nobody was willing! And why do people, including Christians, delight in making reference to this passage out of context? There are three parts to this text; why concentrate on one?

> Drink no longer water, but use a little wine for thy stomach's sake and thine often infirmities.
>
> 1 Timothy 5:23

The first part says that Timothy should not drink water anymore at all. This is an abnormal instruction, and the only explanation is that something had gone wrong with available drinking water around Timothy's location. There were no water-treatment facilities then, so the only way to remain safe under such circumstance was to avoid drinking water completely. The second part instructs Timothy to take a little wine instead. Safety first! Paul knew that Timothy could not afford to substitute water with fruit drinks, which he called wine in general terms; hence, he said, "little," the most that Timothy could afford. People have tended to imply that the *little* there means to avoid intoxication. That is far from the truth. The *little* there was in consideration of cost. Water was free, but fruit drinks would certainly not be. If we combine the two parts, this position becomes more meaningful. Even a worst enemy will not advise you to give up water completely and take only alcohol. I can tell you from personal experience that alcohol dehydrates the body and that taking alcoholic drink without taking enough water can be fatal. Certainly Paul would not intend that for his son, Timothy. If we join the third part, which talked about Timothy's frail condition, we come to the conclusion that Timothy was already infected by the prevailing water-borne disease that was ravaging his location. It is only by bringing the three parts of this message together that we can appreciate Paul's concern over Timothy's situation and sympathize with him instead of making it a drinking-parlor topic.

There was a time in Nigeria when many northern Muslim states established breweries in their states, yet prohibited their Muslim indigenes from taking the product. What is the motive behind this? The religion spirit called the Queen of Heaven in Jeremiah 7:18 in action. The idea is for more and cheaper alcohol to become available to the Christian south and for the family of

Christ to defile themselves the more to the glory and pleasure of Queen of Heaven.

Remind me also that Martin Luther, "The Battle-Ax of Reform," and his wife, Katherine, owned a brewery at their time. Correct, according to church history. But we must not lose sight of the environment and time they lived. During the medieval era, if anyone was deemed a Christian, he belonged to the Roman Catholic Church. The church became delirious with power, and the abuses began to show up in extreme hypocrisy and blasphemy. During this time, apostolic Christianity became dead. Religious politics became the dominant spirit with emphasis on power, riches, and prominence. Alcohol became the medium for social interaction and "spiritual fulfillment." Fellowship (*koinonia* in Greek) became fraud.

Reformation brought a complete upheaval to this dark situation and, through great physical and spiritual strength, restored an atmosphere of freedom of relationship between God and His people.

It was during this difficult period that Martin Luther married Kate, and a brewery was one of her many chattels. I am sure that Martine Luther is interceding for us, asking that we should not be led astray by this lapse.

Find and compare the similarities between the painting of Bacchus celebrating and the painting of the Vatican's Sistine Chapel ceiling. It was the institution that created this Sistine Chapel ceiling painting that Martine Luther had just escaped from, an institution whose hegemony was the spirit of Bacchus.

Solomon, in his human wisdom, writes in Ecclesiastes 9:7, "Go thy way, eat thy bread with joy, and drink thy wine with a merry heart…" (I was citing this passage a lot in my days of captivity), but in divine wisdom, he saw all as "vanity," hence his assertion that a fool drinks to forget his sorrows only to have them confront him again when he becomes sober.

No wonder Apostle Peter, in his first Epistle general, chapter five verse eight, writes, "Be sober…for your adversary the devil as a roaring lion walketh about seeking whom he may devour." But how can someone who is led by the spirit of Bacchus be sober?

Spiritualism

In a quest to conform to the world's intellectualism, mankind has deliberately become obedient to Satan to the extent that many have made a complete turnaround to become agents and worshipers of the devil. In the past, people had worshiped idols, believing them to be God. But today, we have come face to face with those who worship the devil deliberately and want the world to believe it is the proper thing to do. I will start by appealing to your sense of judgment, because a lot of Christians have this tendency of rejecting and sometimes refusing to study works of certain academic disciples, such as some aspects of psychology, philosophy, and the like, that tend to discredit the Word of God. I was deeply into this rejection until just recently, when God opened my eyes to see its true panorama. This is how it happened, and I believe that this revelation is also for whoever is in this category.

My company was planning to acquire an underwater-video-image-enhancement tool. This would give us a great advantage over our competitors, because we would be able to show underwater videos of sub-sea oil-production facilities as clearly as if taken from topside. The inventors and manufacturers sent me a technical manual of the equipment. The first line read: "The human eye has an ability to see millions of colors. But when *evolution* developed this fantastic image sensor, something was sacrificed: our ability to see in darkness." Evolution! Charles Darwin again, right in my office? I was very discouraged and decided that we should not have anything to do with this tool. Somehow, I could not get it off my mind. So I decided to take the issue to He who knows all, and as usual, He wasn't far and responded immediately. He asked me if my quarrel was with the equipment, the developer, or Himself, who gave the knowledge to the developer. And I answered, "Lord, I am quarrelling with the developer, because he is giving your glory to the most ultimate evil."

"Then you are quarrelling with me by extension for giving this knowledge to who you have, in your myopia, considered unworthy," the Lord told me. "Have you forgotten that my charity is for all? Also, fault me for giving rain to unbelievers. I release knowledge in a manner that you cannot understand. It has to do with time and place. The individual through whom knowledge comes into the world, what you may call the media, is just an instrument of conveyance. But the ultimate glory in receiving knowledge from me is to have a handshake with me before that person departs this world; otherwise, receiving from me becomes an additional burden in evidence against him or her on the judgment day."

He brought into my mind names of some who received knowledge from Him and testified to His goodness before they departed from this world: Noah, Abraham, Moses, Peter, Paul, George Washington, Isaac Newton, Thomas Edison, Smith Wigglesworth, G. Washington Carver, Pope John Paul II, and so many others.

"So worry not about who receives from me. Rather, worry that whoever receives of me must allow the light of my Son to illuminate his mind so that he will have a handshake with me before he departs this world. Take advantage of my release of knowledge, irrespective of how it comes into manifestation. But woe unto that person if he departs without shaking hands with me." The Spirit of the Lord instructs me.

It was a long session, and at the end, God made it clear to me that every unbeliever, as long as he or she is still living on the earth, is a potential believer until his or her last breath. The Lord made me to understand that any insightful development He brings into this world through an unbeliever is brought in through a potential believer. If, however, he or she dies without fulfilling the ultimate obligation of acknowledging God, that punishment awaits him and not me.

Why is this story necessary? Because I am intending to bring out the personality of the fallen man from a source most Christians would consider anti-Christian. One cannot separate psychoanalysis from Sigmund Freud. If his knowledge is good, we have to accept it as coming from God, because the devil does not have and cannot give useful knowledge to anyone.

From psychoanalysis, we discovered the three personalities of the fallen man: the id, ego, and superego, which I like to call the trinity of man. We have seen the Trinity of God in the previous chapters of this book, how perfect in unity, in purpose, and in essence. We shall by no means try to compare the Trinity of God with this triune personality of man, which psychology, behavioral science, and religion have consensually identified as chaotic, always in conflict, and at all times against each other. Let's take a short definition of these three personalities.

Perhaps Freud's greatest contribution in understanding the carnal man was his postulation of the principle of psychic determinism, which states that human thoughts, feelings, and impulses, rather than random, are linked in a system of causally related phenomena, behind which lies some reason or meaning.

His central theme is the role of conflicts that arises in a person's conscious mind when one set of beliefs impacts negatively on another set of beliefs, bringing about emotional disturbance, which results in disappointment, anger, or frustration. Freud developed a fundamental psychoanalytic hypothesis that defines the "pleasure principles" as the tendency of humans to seek pleasure in avoidance of pain. He held the concept that the conflicts of early life arose as a result of innate human instincts or drives. He went on to derive how life tends to become an equilibrium of drives and reality. In 1923, he articulated his idea into a structural model that postulates that the human mind is essentially the three personalities of id, ego, and superego.

He called the unconscious human personality the id. According to this theory, the id is not concerned with morality or reality but seeks only to gratify the instinctual drives and operates solely for the purpose of pleasure. As awareness comes with time, parents, family members, and society become obstacles to the demands of the id. The ego begins to develop in the form of conscious perceptions, and reality begins to come into focus. As the weight of the influence the family and society exert on a person progresses, conscience, which Freud called "superego" begins to manifest with resultant frequent conflicts with the drives of the id. In some cases, the ego mediates to resolve the conflict in such a way that the id's impulses are fulfilled in a manner or behavior acceptable by society.

In summary, the id, according to Freud's psychoanalytic theory, is one of the three basic personalities of the human, which I earlier called the trinity of man, the other two being the ego and the superego.

The id represents the common, instinctual drive of the individual, which includes biological urges, wishes, and motives, and therefore represents the pleasure principles.

The Ego denotes the pivot of the personality element of the individual that reflects on the reality in consonance with the norms of society. Its main duty is to mediate between the unconscious impulses of the id and the perceived family and social standards of the superego. The ego, in philosophy, represents the conscious self, or "I."

The superego, in psychoanalytic theory, designates that personality of man that automatically modifies and tends to inhibit those instinctual impulses or drives of the id, which has the tendency of antisocial actions or thought.

I have tried to bring out this information, because it has helped me in dealing with vices I picked up in the course of growing up. Take, for example, smoking and alcoholism, night clubbing, sexual lust, or all the other indulgences the world regards as pleasurable or enjoyment. There are none of them that any parent will encourage his or her son or daughter to indulge in, not even the very ones that worship such vices.

I started smoking and drinking alcohol in school. My id did not recognize smoking and drinking as pleasure before I got involved, so my smoking and drinking could not have been as a result of id's instinctual drive. Rather, it was the desire of my superego that I join my mates so that I could become acceptable socially. From becoming socially acceptable, the id discovered the spurious pleasure in alcohol and hijacked it. So we can see that un-Christian indulgence can be propagated by either the id or the superego, man's inherent propensity to seek pleasure or to belong being the principal initiator.

I have taken you through this cycle to show that the only way to escape from the snare of the devil is to surrender one's life to Jesus. No two individuals are the same. The counsel that worked for one may not work for another. Jesus knows us individually and proffers solutions according to our individual requirements.

Let us look at how these malevolent properties of the id, ego, and superego struggle for control of the man's mind and its consequences, causes, and effects.

My Spirit-guided mind tells me that the perfect man God created in the garden of Eden had these three personalities working in harmony. The moment man in Adam and Eve received the baptism of disobedience to God from the devil, they were thrown into confusion. The id made Adam realize that Eve was naked, and from then has become the libido personality. The superego made Adam recognize his supposed inadequate dressing of fig leaves instead of a designer suit when God called him, and till this day has remained the restrictive personality. Poor ego, from birth and childhood, it begins to receive shocking treatments that seem to say, "You are not wanted." The child's natural ignorance or lack of knowledge of good and evil soon begins to receive resentment from the parents, who begin to suppress it with restrictions according to social norms. By the time the child comes of age, the society has completely diminished and intimidated the ego the child has to incline toward the id or the superego. His or her choice is limited, becoming either an introvert or an extrovert.

The influence of parents and society on the child brings to my mind the story of the young lion and goat.

After an evening of play together, the young lion went home, and the mother asked where he had been. The young lion answered that he was playing with the goat.

"Goat! Where is it?" the mother asked.

"He's gone home too," the young lion answered innocently.

"You allowed the goat to go, and you have come home to eat. Fool, don't you know that goat is our food? No food for you in this house till you bring his carcass here," his mother concluded furiously.

RETURN TO Smith Wigglesworth

When the young goat got home too, the mother asked where he had been. "Been playing with the young lion," the young goat answered.

"Lion!" the mother screamed. "Don't you know that it is because of the lion that you don't have a father? They kill us for food; don't ever go close to him again."

The next evening, the young lion came calling the young goat to come for play, hoping to take his carcass home to his mother. But the young goat shouted back from afar, "That thing your mother told you last night, my mother also told me." And that thing their mothers told them destroyed their innocent, child-like friendship and replaced it with greed and fear.

Even in good Christian homes, the tendency of God's ministers' children toward the id or the superego is also there except where there is a foreknowledge of these spiteful tendencies and proactive measures are taken. We have a clear example in the Bible, concerning the children of Eli in 1 Samuel 2:

> Now Eli was very old, and heard all that his sons did onto all Israel; and how they lay with the women that assembled at the door of the tabernacle of the congregation.
>
> 1 Samuel 2:22

Where is the ego in situations like this when the id is on a rampage? It must have become latent from intimidation and suppression arising from Eli's exalted and sacred position. This is a common occurrence in many church leaders' homes today.

With this surface knowledge of psycho-mechanisms of the natural man, it will become a lot easier for us to understand why and how people cheaply become prey to the devil irrespective of their high professional qualifications. The Bible tells us that Jesus came to destroy the work of the devil. We all believe it, but without full understanding. Our limited understanding of that pas-

279   a deeper evangelism

sage assures us that Jesus has come to relieve us of the infirmities the devil has inflected on us and to release us from the bondage of various kinds. Correct, but that is viewing that passage from the periphery. Paul's letters are quite clear on the deep meaning of this passage. To me, it is the greatest message of the entire New Testament epistles. It is our assurance that through Jesus, we can go back to the perfect man God created in Adam and Eve before the fall. The work of the devil that made God send His only begotten Son to die on the cross is not making people blind or lame or sick. It is not possessing people with demons. The work of the devil that God sent His Son to destroy is that venom the Bible calls *flesh* that the devil injected into man after receiving obedience from him in disobedience to his creator. God took away His breath from man, took away the tree of life, and gave man a period of time to spend in this world and depart from His sight. That is the work of the devil Jesus has come to destroy to bring man back into perfect relationship with God into eternity. By achieving this, Jesus would render all the efforts of the devil and his achievement in the garden of Eden useless. So you will not expect the devil to fold his dirty hands and look on. No, he will fight back, and that is what he is doing. Through Spiritualism, the devil has corrupted the desire of God for a liberated human spirit relationship with Him forever through Jesus Christ. The devil has given Spiritualism a godly coating that, on the surface, looks as if it is fulfilling God's desire for sending His Son to the world, but in reality, it is for the opposite.

With this deeper understanding of the reason God sent His Son, let us now take a profound insight at the devil's aspirations in institutionalizing such practices as Spiritualism. Let us begin by answering some questions that may become necessary in appreciating the devil's deviousness in trying to mask his purpose for establishing Spiritualism in our God-given instruction to worship Him in spirit.

1. In what form does God want us to appear before Him for a perfect relationship?

    The Bible is our only guide and says from the mouth of the Lord himself that God is a Spirit and that those who worship Him must do so in spirit and truth.

    But the hour cometh and now is when the true worshipers shall worship the Father in spirit and in truth; for the Father seeketh such to worship him. God is a Spirit; and they that worship him must worship him in spirit and in truth.

    John 4:23-24

    My Bible says that you *must* worship Him in spirit and in truth. This is the only form in which we are asked to appear before God in worship.

2. Where and how can we find this worship in spirit and in truth?

    The Bible says nowhere, neither in the mountains nor in Jerusalem, but that your body has become the temple of God, where spirit and truth for the worship of God reside. No more temple sacrifices, no more burning of candles and incense, no more incantations and rituals. At anytime, anywhere you consecrate yourself for the service of God, there the worship of God in spirit and truth is.

3. So what is the difference between Spiritualism and worshiping God in spirit?

    In fact, a lot. There is no meeting point at all. To some, worshiping God in spirit has become the type of garment or mood they wear; to others it has become the level of riches and pleasure that sur-

a deeper evangelism

rounds them. To others, it has become the amount of power—physical and spiritual—they possess. How can you reconcile the fact that to some, worshiping God in spirit entails putting on of long, white garments without footwear, and to some, it entails pretending to hate all that surrounds them, including Christians of other denominations? To others still, it is owning private jets, money, luxury vacations, designer wardrobes, sex, alcohol, and so on, and to others, it is magic and wonders, or it is punishing the poor physical body through flogging or starving it of essential nutrients. All these are not worshiping God in spirit, but spiritualism, summarised in two words: hedonism and asceticism.

4. So what is worshiping God in Spirit and in truth?

Our Lord Jesus gave us this instruction of worshiping God in Spirit and truth by telling us that the time has come to do so in reply to the Samaritan woman's response that the Jews demanded that God should be worshiped only in Jerusalem. By saying that the hour cometh and now is the time to worship God in Spirit and truth, Jesus is saying that after His departure and the arrival of the Holy Spirit, the believer does not need any more ceremonies of any type, either in the mountains, referring to Moses and the church in the wilderness, or as found in the temple of God in Jerusalem. By knowing Jesus, that is, if He also knows you, worshiping God in Spirit and truth has already been established, anywhere and anytime, your body being the new temple, your broken and repented heart the sacrifice in place of animals.

Let me throw more light into this simplicity of worship our Lord accentuates in the passage we read in John 4:24. We all know the devil came down from heaven. He saw and participated in the divine fellowship and rituals of heavenly worship. By extension, God asked the Israelites through Moses to worship Him accordingly, hence the ceremonies and rituals of the worship of God in the Old Testament. Spiritualism is the devil's alternative, an imitation of the ceremonial worship of God he saw in heaven.

If you have observed any satanic worship or have read about it you will agree with me that they are clothed with many rituals and ceremonies. This is what the devil saw in heaven and has brought it to bear on his subjects here on earth. Some who have had the boldness to come out will tell you that they never bargained for what they saw. Because the devil has corrupted the rituals and ceremonies in the worship of God, man became unable to draw the line between sacrifice and worship for God and the devil. Sacrosanct as these rituals and ceremonies in the worship of God may appear, Jesus has told us they are no more required in our worships, because the devil has not only adulterated the practice but has laid a snare for us with them. Those who are involved in true Christian meditation, staying close to a Spiritualist will tell you the level of interference they experience in their meditation. The same way the devil intends rituals and ceremonies from Christian circles to interject with those from his worshipers, so that he may, true to his nature, fraudulently receive worship from God's people. That is why the only acceptable sacrifice to God has become our broken and contrite heart and our bodies, His holy Temple, that must be presented to Him at all times as a living and worthy sacrifice. Any other sacrifices, any other temples, are abominations to God and mere fancies of our imagination. This is how Isaiah says it:

> Thus saith the Lord. The heaven is my throne, and the earth is my footstool; where is the house that ye build unto me? And where is the place of my rest? For all those things

hath mine hand made and all those things have been, saith the Lord; but to this man will I look, even to him that is poor and of a contrite spirit, and trembleth at my word?

Isaiah 66:1-2

He that killeth an Ox is as if he slew a man; he that sacrificeth a lamb as if he cut of a dog's neck; he that offereth an oblation, as if he offered swine's blood; he that burneth incense, as if he blessed an idol. Yea, they have chosen their own ways and their soul delighteth in their abomination.

Isaiah 66:3

I am the Lord; that is my name; and my glory will I not give to another; neither my praise to graven images.

Isaiah 42:8

Behold, the former things are come to pass, and new things do I declare…

Isaiah 42:9

These are few of the passages from the Bible that drum into our subconscious the fact that God does not desire rituals and ceremonies anymore in our worship of Him.

What Is Spiritualism?

Ask a spiritualist the tenets of his or her belief, and you will be treated with their seven principles, or the "Magnificent Seven," which were supposed to have been communicated through the mediumship of Emma Hardinge Britten, in 1871, and Robert Owen, who died the same year as the spirit.

Permit me to list these seven principles, because it will help you to understand how the devil has camouflaged the purpose of Jesus in order to make easy prey of those seeking God for their selfish reasons. They even called their denominations churches and included Abraham Lincoln as a denomination. The devil remains a liar, because we know that in the body of Christ, the church believes that our God looks for us. We don't search for Him or His knowledge. The Spiritualists are engaged in a hide and seek with their gods, while those whose names are in the Book of Life stand in the way of God to be found.

The Seven Principles of Spiritualism:

1. The Fatherhood of God.

2. The Brotherhood of man.

3. The communication of spirits and the ministry of angels.

4. The continuous existence of the human soul.

5. Personal responsibility.

6. Compensation and retribution hereafter for all the good and evil done on earth.

7. Eternal progress opens to every human soul.

Viewed on the surface, you may think that nothing is wrong with these seven statements of faith until you read them with Holy Spirit-guided mind. My advice is don't bother to go any deeper or try to find out more about Spiritualism until you have been washed in the blood of the Lamb and filled with the Holy Spirit.

What lures people into Spiritualism?

1. Firstly, Spiritualism is an escapist mentality from the reality of heaven and hell. It propagates the inherent desire in the fallen man to hide from God, which started with Adam. The wicked have a tendency of running away from the harsh reality of heaven and hell by wishing away God and evil. The Bible says, in

Proverbs 28:1, "The wicked flee when no man pursueth; but the righteous are bold as lion." It takes boldness to approach God. Wickedness cannot allow many to approach God, so in their folly, they tend toward avoiding Him. Besides, the powers and privileges associated with communicating with spirits of the dead has always appealed to man from the time he received the devil's radiation of disobedience to God in the garden of Eden: a desire to be like God.

2. Secondly, the seventh principle states that the human soul continuously comes back to the world in human form to correct the mistakes of its previous mission; in other words, you can live the way you like, because you are still coming back to correct your mistakes is an added appeal.

Jesus and His redemptive purposes are completely missing in their seven principles. They have presented a simulation of His mission with a coating of brotherhood. This is the line they throw out to the public. The progression of their membership is as mysterious as itself. Once you are in, you are gone. So my advice is that the sea does not drown who it does not see. Don't attempt to go and find out. Enchantment, casting of spells, and hypnotism are real, and these are their strongest membership-drive tools. You would agree with me if you know the background of some who have become victims, people that would not, under normal circumstances, be associated with such.

Have you not heard or read from the Bible that the sin of apostasy is not forgivable? Apostasy means having seen the light of Jesus and gone back to the devil. Do you think the precious blood of Jesus is not capable of taking away this sin just like any other sin if the offender repents? Why not? But the problem is that there is no chance of repentance. It compares with a situation where somebody is taken from light into a complete darkness, but instead of no vision at all, the person begins to "see" better than in the former light. What do you think will be the attitude of that person toward the former, genuine light? Resentment, of course, though the "seeing" in the present darkness is a mere simulation, through the arts of hypnosis. That is why the Bible, in Jeremiah 7, says that we should not pray for such, because God has said He will not hear. And the apostles, in their epistles, concurred.

> There is a sin unto death; I do not say that ye shall pray for it.
>
> 1 John 5:16

> For it is impossible for those who were once enlightened and have tasted of the heavenly gift, and were made partakers of the Holy Ghost, and have tested the good Word of God, and the powers of the world to come. If they shall fall away, to renew them again unto repentance; seeing they crucifying to themselves, the Son of God afresh; and put him to an open shame.
>
> Hebrews 6:4-6

Any sinner can be rescued with prayers and counseling—lust, alcoholism, murder, stealing—but not Spiritualism. But still we know that God's hand is not so short that it cannot reach any depth. By deliverance, and only deliverance, God can rescue a Spiritualist by making him or her willing to reject occult through intercessory prayers.

So we thank God for the deep knowledge of human behavioral patterns He has revealed to us in these last days. Whether we call it psychology or philosophy, it doesn't matter; what matters is the Christian value we can derive from it. Most of the demons Jesus and the apostles cast away were in the form of modern-day Spiritualism-induced delusion. What the Word of

God informed us concerning the sin of apostasy not being forgivable is not that there is any sin that is beyond the cleansing power of the blood of Jesus but that a person under the influence of the power of Satan is possessed and subjected to such a mental state that efforts toward bringing him or her to light will be in vain, due to what psychology has come to explain to us as delusion of grandeur or delusional disorder. *Delusion*, which means false belief firmly held by somebody, even when that person is aware that others recognize such belief as bogus, when applied to religious belief can be expressed in the form of paranoia, a kind of psychosis in which the person becomes irrational and consumed by a consistent delusion of persecution and spiritual grandeur. Sigmund Freud postulated that paranoia is an intellectual disorder with a primary symptom in the form of extreme distrust of others. It does not usually come from natural sources. To distinguish paranoia from other organic mental disorders, the American Psychiatric Association applies the term *delusional disorder*, which usually comes without the paranoia symptoms of other mental disorders such as depression, schizophrenia, and hallucination. Its main manifestation in a person is a clear evidence that the person has lost touch with reality, a condition known as *psychotic symptom*. Psychology concurred with the Bible that delusional disorder is not a common mental illness and that its treatment successes are very rarely, if ever, due to little research information. Delusional disorder is not natural. It is a spell cast on somebody through the bewitching power of the devil via the evil spirits or demons the devil's agents are in contact with. That is why medical science can do little or nothing to help a victim. That is why the Bible says:

> Put on the whole armor of God that ye may be able to stand against the wiles of the devil for we wrestle not against flesh and blood, but against principalities, against

powers, against the rulers of the darkness of this world, against spiritual [ism] wickedness in high places.

Ephesians 6:17-12

And because the victim of spiritually induced delusion, as in patients of other forms of delusion, is not and cannot become conscious of his or her condition, he or she will resist help from any source or in any form. The best form of treatment is to stay clear of any form of Spiritualism and Spiritualist activities. We have an assurance in 1 John 4:4 that greater is He that is in us than he that is in the world. Why should we want to have anything with the gods of this world if we have been assured that what we have is greater?

Much as it may be partly true that their mediums do "see" what they claim (I don't have any concrete proof), the truth is that what they see and hear from are demons appearing as familiar spirits of deceased ones. I said "partly" because most have been exposed to be the work of skilled persons, such as ventriloquists, who could make sounds in familiar voices from the ground or air. Partly also because some lucky ones, whom God rescued by grace, like Ben Alexander of Exposing Satan's Power (ESP) Ministries, claim to have been involved. He is a great resource in the war against the power of Satan on earth, having been deceived for the greater part of his life and youth by this wicked phenomenon. His book *Out from Darkness* is both a rescue and an evangelical resource. This is what he said: "When I was a Spiritualist, developing into a medium, I would go into trance; I would see long, dark tunnels with a bright light at the end of it shaped like a cross. It was a pleasurable sensation, and I would look forward to it. Also, at some of the séances I attended, the phenomena of the colored lights would appear. When I asked the 'spirit' about them, he said they represent spirits who were progressing to a higher plane of development (returning to the

world, according to their belief in reincarnation). The final destination, the spirit said, was to be absorbed by the Great White
Spirit and to be at absolute peace. These are delusions of Satan;
he wants us to believe them, so we will have no need for Christ."

The Bible also said,

> Now the Spirit (Holy) speaketh expressly, that in the latter
> times some shall depart from the faith, giving heed to
> seducing spirit, and doctrines of devils.
>
> 1 Timothy 4:1

We have a clear example in the Scripture of such demons appearing to mediums in the form of the spirit of the person intended.
In 1 Samuel 28, it seems as if Samuel actually appeared to Saul,
but in 1 Chronicles 10:13, it becomes clear that what appeared to
Saul was a demon as an imitation or familiar spirit of Samuel.
Counterfeit demonstrations by ventriloquists suggest how it got
its name, *owb*, a Hebrew word translated *bottle*. The name also
implies that the apparent spirit of the deceased seen is like an
empty bottle containing the demon in operation.

The question again is, why do people, especially those who
have seen the light of the Gospel, become prey to this seducing
spirit? I repeat the same answer; it is the error of going out to
look for God in a desperate desire to have their problems solved
or their pains taken away. Saul's encounter with the woman of
Endor, in seeking the spirit of Samuel, which I would rather you
read from your Bible in 1 Samuel 28:7-19, should serve as an eye
opener. Please, please do not stop with this passage. You may be
deceived into thinking that Saul actually spoke with the spirit
of Samuel. Read 1 Chronicles 10:13, and you will observe that it
was a demonic spirit that appeared as Samuel that he spoke with.

So Saul died for his transgression which he committed against the Lord, even against the word of the Lord, which he kept not, and also for asking counsel of one that had a familiar spirit to enquire of it.

Spiritualism is a euphemism for *occult. Occult* is a name derived from a Latin word that means the knowledge of secret or hidden things. The Spiritualist tends to conceal his true identity by pretending to belong to a church or fellowship. To some, anyway, it does not matter anymore if you knew their true identity; the devil himself has taken off his mask to the shame of the world in general and the soldiers of the Cross in particular. A doctrinal standard of Spiritualism is the incursion of a spirit realm, or the fourth dimension, into the three-dimensional system of the world. Most so-called Spiritual churches or fellowship are glorified occult.

Is Spiritualism Church?

No, Spiritualism is not a church at all. It is not a member of the body of Christ but rather an anti-Christ *religious organization.* The medieval Roman Catholic Church was a form of Spiritualist movement. Thank God for the charismatic movement that rekindled the otherwise extinguished fire and turned a dark horizon into light, and the anointing of Pope John Paul II, which further fanned the glow into flame. About ten percent of my television time now is on Roman Catholic Television networks. Sometimes I sit back and wonder what the body of Christ would have missed if the Roman Catholic Church was not revived, at least to the extent we see and appreciate today. A lot more is still coming in the name of Jesus.

Spiritualism began as an organized movement in the 1840s in America and eventually spread around the world, especially in English-speaking countries. It acquired the name and form of *church* in America under an affiliate called National Spiritualist Association of Churches. Its origin as an organization of mediumship is usually traced to the Fox sisters of Hinesville, New York, in 1848, after the sisters claimed that spirits of the dead communicated with them. Thirty years later, the sisters admitted their fraud, but the movement had become unstoppable, with tens of thousands of the middle- and upper-classes holding séances, showing spirit entertainment with numerous magical tricks, such as making sounds, objects appearing and vanishing, lights glowing from no source, moving objects without visible physical contact, etc. For them, these were clear evidence of "scientific proof" of life after death and a disproof of the Christian "superstitious nonsense" of heaven and hell. From their belief and practices, you will know that Spiritualism is not church but adopted the name to lure people in search of God for unscriptural purposes into their fold. Spiritualism, or Spiritism, whichever you choose to call it, believes that the human personality survives death and can communicate with the living through a medium that represents, for them, the equivalent of a Christian priest or pastor. They believe that when a person dies, the soul comes back in another body to continue the process of perfection. Their services are characterized by every variety of psychic power, from clairvoyance to telekinesis and telepathy. As should be expected, these acts were so attractive to the inquisitive world that repeated charges of fraud even flamed the spread as a proof of prophesied persecution. It was only in the 1920s, when magicians such as Houdini exposed the techniques and methods of deceits employed by mediums to fool even the holiest and the wisest, that the spread began to die down.

Spiritualist churches are, therefore, places where Spiritualism practitioners conduct their own type of worship services. It has no relationship with the church of Jesus Christ. Their services are usually conducted by a medium in place of the Christian pastor. There is usually an opening prayer, followed by an address in the form of our sermons, hymns, and finally, a demonstration of mediumship. By intuition, the medium claims a contact with the spirit of the dead, which they refer to as "opening up." Finally, a presentation of survival evidence to relatives and friends of the deceased, whose spirits the medium has contacted, is made. Their sermons are in a form of trance lecture, dealing with metaphysics or principles of daily living. This is often followed with a demonstration of clairvoyance, in which the medium would receive impressions or would hear voices and relate the message to the audience. Spiritualists teach from the Bible and other religious books and claim to have the nine miraculous gifts of the Holy Spirit of 1 Corinthians 12. They have their Jesus, who is not to them a Son of God, but a medium of the highest order.

Spiritualism practices a Spiritualist healing service in a form where the medium directs healing energy to a patient from a higher source by using his or her hands to affect repairs of defective body function. Claims are sometimes made of full or partial recovery, which does not surprise us, because the Bible says,

> For they are the spirits of devils, working miracles, which go forth unto the kings of the earth and of the whole world, to gather them to the battle of that great day of God Almighty.
>
> Revelation 16:14

Their seminaries are called *development circles*, where mediums develop their ability by sitting regularly with new student psychics. Meditation plays a significant role in their training practice and often includes the breathing practices of Buddhists. To attain a higher level of existence, the Spiritualist includes in his or her practice a form of prayer with phrases like Hail Mary, Shama, Yisrael, or Salah, and other names with God, Jesus,

YHWH, or Allah, depending on the practitioner's background, mood, or situation. A meditation technique known as *imaging* is also common. The practitioner employs it to "meet" his or her guiding angel, connect with the dead, to receive protection or support from their gods, or simply to calm the mind.

Spiritualists believe in the idea that the creator of all things is the universe and therefore do not really adhere to any particular religion but draw inspiration from other religious traditions, mostly Christianity and others with deep, mystical traditions, such as Hinduism, Buddhism, Sufism, etc.

Their original seven principles were extended to nine in their Six Articles of Declaration of Principles of 1899 to accommodate the beliefs of the then-modern Spiritualist.

Spiritualism is still in full force today in the form of churches and fellowships, or Brotherhoods (with sisters as members), and can be found almost everywhere in the world.

It is neither a Christian church nor a Christian fellowship. Their beliefs and ideas are quite contrary and, in fact, are completely opposite but definitely not equal to Christianity. They believe in communicating with the spirits of the dead. They believe that the human spirit continues to grow from one human body to another until it reaches perfection. Their idea is that afterlife is not a permanent thing but one in which the spirit of the dead continues to evolve into a higher plane. These two primary beliefs lead to their third belief that spirits of the dead are capable of providing the living information concerning moral and ethical issues, as well as the nature of God and the afterlife environment. This is what they mean when they talk about their spirit guide—their reliance for worldly and spiritual guidance.

Every Christian should avoid any association with Spiritualism and understand and regard it as witchcraft and evangelize against it. It is the devil's innovation to destroy the work of Jesus on the cross. The Bible warns, "Do not turn to mediums or wizards; do not seek them out, to be defiled by them"(Leviticus 19:31, RSV).

When Spiritualism emerges in a Christian environment, it tends to camouflage itself with the common features of Christianity, ranging from liturgy, such as Sunday services and fellowship with God in prayers and hymns, to moral value systems. Do not be deceived, don't even try to go and find out, because you may be hypnotized or put under a spell. Those who knew you before will not believe it is the same you they are talking with. You will be the only person that will not know you are no more what you used to be physically, mentally, and spiritually. You will even begin to pity those who are concerned about your situation, as if they are lost. May it not happen to you or your loved ones, in Jesus's name. The negative spirit of Spiritualism is real. Spiritualists do not believe that the way we live and end our life in this world bears consequence on God's assignment of our souls in eternity in heaven or hell; rather, they see afterlife as a hierarchical system of "spheres," by which the individual soul is continuously in a progression to perfection. The Christian Bible is not their source of knowledge of God, neither can it be, because the living Bible is Jesus Christ, the Word of God, the truth they have become deaf to hear, the Way they have become blind to see, and the Life they have denied themselves of.

The Appeal of Spiritualism

Why did mediumship and Spiritualism have its early appeal on the middle and upper class? Why does it appeal to people at all? The reason, I think, is because Spiritualism concentrates its activities in the minds of its victims. Psychoanalysis, as we saw earlier in this chapter, identifies the three personalities of the human being as id, the pleasure seeker; ego, the mediator; and superego, the society consciousness. Bear in mind that Spiritualism is a religion whose basic tenet and practice is communication with the dead. Some Spiritualists are nominal Christians who attend séances only; others are committed members who attend regular services as well as séances. To both, the idea of a contact with their dead loved one is exciting, especially the supposed comfort of obtaining information regarding the cause of their death and guidance from a loved one that is in a position (as a spirit) to reveal situations regarding the things on earth. The fascination of the mysteries of psychic environment is not just a youthful exuberance but a natural tendency of the fallen man. With this in mind, it becomes easy for us to map out strategies and campaigns to evangelize the world concerning Spiritualism. We now know our targets, and we know what to tell them.

Spiritualism presents an environment that misleads people into believing they can attain the wisdom and knowledge of God (does it remind you of the story of the forbidden fruit in Genesis?) through mediumship and the cyclical re-emergence of their spirit into this world. This falsehood appeals to the id, and it begins to crave for it. In an unbalanced mind, either from parental or societal suppression of the ego, or as a result of a shy and timid superego, this appeal is transformed into desire or mind-set, and action to actualize it follows. Once a person steps in, he or she loses control. Spiritualism is the true opium of the sinner, because it spuriously hides the pains of the belief in absolute death, the devil, hell, heaven, and of course, judgment.

How do hypnosis or enchantment become effective? By exposing one's mind to satanic waveforms through the spiritual "Internet." How else do viruses enter into your computer? The catalyst for the process is the absence of essential, mind-fortifying facilities and activities, the same way virus intrusion into the computer is made possible by the absence of anti-virus programs. We therefore can summarize the two weapons of Spiritualism as hedonism and asceticism.

Both hedonism and asceticism are products of the same father: the devil. As I have said before, the devil is not omnipresent and therefore requires many agents and spirits to cover the world. His agents are everywhere, in the church, classroom, laboratory, libraries, homes, air, land, and water, but he is not everywhere at the same time. So he needs many spirits and agents, called demons.

Encarta Dictionaries defines *hedonism* as *seeking of pleasure; devotion, especially a self-indulgent one* and *to seek pleasure and happiness as a way of life.* In philosophical terms, *hedonism* is a doctrine that holds pleasure as the highest goal or the source of moral value and *asceticism* as *a self-denying way of life; austerity and self-denial, especially as a principle way of life.*

The word *hedonism* is derived from the Greek word *hedone*, meaning *pleasure.* From a philosophical view point, it represents a postulation that pleasure is the sole and ultimate purpose of life and its pursuit the end and ideal of conduct. In ancient Greece, where the doctrine originated, two important theories were expounded. The Cybernetics, known as egoistic hedonist, incline to a doctrine that believes that the gratification of one's immediate personal desires, irrespective of its consequences on others, is the supreme goal of human existence. To them, knowledge is the ability to satisfy the pressing sensation of the moment, and therefore, any attempt to formulate a system of moral values that denies the desirability of present pleasure for reason of the pains it will cause in the future is not just futile but foolishness. The Epicureans, or the rational hedonists, are inclined to the doctrine that true pleasure is attainable only by reason and to achieve this demands some level of asceticism by way of discipline and prudence. Consider the two or just one of the doctrines fully developed in any person, and you have a Spiritualist next door.

Asceticism is also derived from a Greek word, *askesis*, meaning *self-denied*. The doctrine of asceticism stresses to the believer that self-denial and renunciation of earthly pleasures is a compulsory requirement in order to attain a higher level of spirituality, intellectuality, and self-awareness. It usually demands fasting, certain levels of celibacy, abstinence from food, drinks (including non-alcohol), and sexual activities (legitimate or not). It demands the induction of physical pains and discomfort, such as endurance of extreme conditions such as cold and heat and other self-inflected punishments. The doctrine encourages periodic withdrawal from the material environment for meditation. This is what Paul says of such:

> ...forbidding marrying, and commanding to abstain from meat, which God hath created to be received with thanksgiving of them which believe and know the truth..."
> 1 Timothy 4:3

Neither hedonism nor asceticism is an attribute of the Christian whose life is not to become a slave to outward demands and desires. To be a Christian is to be Christlike by acquiring that inexplicable empowerment that makes him a truly free human.

Are you still searching for the Spiritualist? That's one at your doorstep if clothed in his regalia of hedonism and asceticism. He is that man or woman who does not know Jesus as the Son of God. He knows Jesus quite all right, everybody knows Him, but he does not know Him by His name that is above all other names. He calls Him grand master, the prophet, the teacher, Rabbi, and so on, but he does not know Him by His true name—Word of God that became the Son of God, the Redeemer. Oh, how I weep, join me daughters and sons of Zion, join me and weep for the miserable souls who do not know the Word of God and His true name.

Allow me a little theological digression here for the edification of the church. Do you believe in the divine Trinity? I believe God that you do. Do you believe that this Trinity is made up of God the Holy Spirit, God the Son, and God the Father? This is a belief of the privileged, those whose names are written in the Book of life. But this Trinity existed before creation. "Let us make man in our image…" If Adam and Eve had not disappointed God and brought curse upon humanity, would there have been need for a Redeemer to come into the world to reconcile man with God? Certainly not, and that is to say that there would not have been Jesus and, by extension, a Messiah, Christ, or Son of God, because there would not have been need for blood sacrifice to redeem man. Therefore, we can say that these are the names of God that were given to us by prophecy and wisdom of God, of He who would come to rescue man from the curse inherited from Adam and bring him back into intimate relationship with God. The Son of God was not His name from the beginning; otherwise, the Bible would not have put it in future tense in the prophecy of His coming. "He shall be great and *shall be called* the Son of the Highest" (Luke 1:32).

Satan knows the Trinity of God in full detail. He served Him when he was still the faithful archangel Lucifer, the morning star. Apostle John the beloved tells us in chapter one verse one of the Gospel he wrote that this person of the Trinity we now know as Son is, at the beginning, the Word of God.

> "In the beginning was the Word and the Word, was with God and the Word was God."
>
> John 1:1

Therefore, the three-in-one God Lucifer served is the Spirit, the Word, and God—yes, and God. It does not in any way suggest that the Word or the Spirit is not God. You will see what I mean

a deeper evangelism

in the next few lines. I have always believed that sometimes, it becomes necessary to bring in a kind of sanctified creative imagination to bear on some Bible accounts. This is one such time. Take water, which exists in three states, for example. If ice is required for an application that requires water in that state, and ice is produced from a reservoir of water and taken for that application, while in the form of ice, it may have changed in physical appearance, but its chemical properties remain that of water, or H_2O. On melting and returning back into the reservoir, it mixes back with what is left in the reservoir after it was taken out as ice. Somebody who came after it has returned into the reservoir will not know unless told that a portion of that water had left as a solid and had come back without any sign to indicate so. Also with vapor, which, when it goes out from the same bulk of water to drive a turbine, and when the job is finished, will condense back into the bulk without any indication that it has gone out as air. Now suppose the vapor and the ice left for missions, and you became thirsty. What do you drink? You would take water from the same reservoir where ice and vapor have left and drink. So there is still water, unchanged in name and all other properties, left in the reservoir after two phases have left. Water consists of vapor, ice, and water, not as components, but as one. That is the way to look at the Trinity and be able to see clearly the homogeneity of God: the Spirit, the Word, and God as one God. This is how the Bible puts it:

> Now there are diversities of gifts, but the same Spirit and there are diversities of administration but the same Lord (Word) and there are diversities of operation but it is the same God which walketh in all.
>
> 1 Corinthians 12:4-6

And these three—Spirit, Lord, and God—is one God; as ice, steam, and water is water.

If somebody who is ignorant about ice saw it as a solid, left, and then returned, and you told him it had been poured back into the reservoir after it melted, he would say that he doesn't understand what you are talking about. He would not believe. That is ignorance; it is not a respecter of person. It does not care how many degrees you have, or how many things you have invented. If Bill Gates should go to some parts of Africa or Asia today, there are many situations he too would say, "I don't understand; I don't believe it." So do not be discouraged when they tell you the same about the Trinity of God. "I don't understand; I don't believe it," is a disease caused by ignorance, which only wisdom can cure. Knowledge is not wisdom; rather, wisdom is the ability to utilize both knowledge and ignorance to achieve the highest possible goal. So it is only wisdom that can cure disbelief and wrong belief.

We may not have come into full terms with the message and significance and symbolism of water as provided to us in the Bible regarding our understanding of the Godhead. It is mentioned far more than any other material in the Scripture, mostly in spiritual symbolism. Examples are:

> Concerning the person who does not walk in the counsel of the ungodly: "And he shall be like a tree planted by the Rivers of water."
>
> Psalm 1:3

> Therefore with joy shall ye draw water out of the wells of salvation.
>
> Isaiah 12:3

On the restoration of the land of Israel: "And the parched ground shall become a pool, and the thirsty land springs of water."

Isaiah 35:7

"Jesus answered, 'Verily, verily, I say unto thee, Except a man be born of water and of the Spirit, he cannot enter into the kingdom of God.'"

John 3:5

Jesus used water symbolically many times in the Gospel:

1. Mathew 10:42, Mark 9:41, John 3:5
2. John 4:10
3. John 4:14
4. John 7:38
5. Acts 1:5

I think Christian scholars should use the nature of water to throw more light onto the Trinity. This is a substance that even when you have taken away two of its three phases, the remaining is still of the same original composition, physically, materially, and chemically. When the vapor or solid phase returns into the bulk, there is no sign whatsoever to indicate that it had existed in entirely different form.

So God the Word becomes unto us Son of God. It is our assurance that in Him we have become sons and daughters of God. It is this name that confuses the devil. It is the name the Spiritualist would rather die than acknowledge, because his or her name is not written in the Book of Life. Jesus is the wisdom and the manifestation of the power of God (1 Corinthians 1:24). The Bible, in John 1:2, says, "All things were made by Him and without Him was not anything that was made." This is the power the devil is afraid of, the reason he is relentlessly recruiting men and women into his army to oppose the power of the Word—Jesus Christ. What do you think happened on the day of Pentecost concerning Peter's sermon in tongues?

If you were there with a Frenchman, an Italian, a Greek, a Jew, and others, and each of you were taking notes as Peter was talking, at the end, you would have taken your notes in English, the Frenchman in French, the Italian in Italian, the Greek and the Jews and the others in their different languages. The Frenchman, you know very well, does not understand English but managed to say to you, "Peter, goodu tuku," and showed you his notes.

Just then, the Italian, who speaks his Italian and both English and French, came and said to you, "My friend, sorry you did not understand that wonderful message Peter delivered in Italian..."

Then you cut in, "No, No, I understood him well; he spoke in English. These are my notes."

"Let me see." The Italian collected your notes, and to his surprise, the same message he heard in Italian. He collected the French man's notes and saw the same message. What happened? The language Peter spoke and they heard is the Word, which was from the beginning. King David prophesied of it thus: "There is no speech nor language, where their voice is not heard" (Psalm 19:3). Peter did not speak a particular language, but Jesus the Word. Whenever you are speaking under the anointing, you are not speaking a language but Jesus. When Bill Graham brought salvation to President George Bush, it wasn't the language he spoke that saved Bush, but Jesus, the power in the word he uttered. Toward the end of 2007, Benny Hinn was conducting a training meeting for pastors on TBN. He was teaching on the subject of Holy Spirit. That was the day he said Jesus had to pray to the Father before the Holy Spirit was allowed to come.

With this, we can trace the date. I was writing and watching him on the television. At the end, he said, "You, you," pointing as if it were at me, "sitting there watching, you have pains in your right ear; you're healed in the name of Jesus." I may not have said it exactly the way he did. I had been having severe pain inside my right ear for some while, and it kept progressing. So as he said that, I instinctively touched my right ear—no pains. I pressed harder, and still no pains. I applied pressure into my ears by drawing down my jaw muscles, and still no pains. I went on my knees and claimed my healing. Till today, I have not had any pains in that ear. This is not intended as a testimony, though there's nothing wrong if it becomes one. The point I am trying to make is that it is not the language spoken by Benny Hinn that healed me but the power in the word—Jesus. If you blow away a piece of paper with your breath, the force is not in your mouth, but in the breeze from your lungs, which you did not see. The power that healed me was not in the mouth of Benny Hinn but in the Word he spoke. And that power is Jesus Christ, the Son of God. He is the Word of God in action. He has come into the world a first time and destroyed the work of the devil. He is coming again to destroy the devil himself. The devil is not relenting. Since he does not have the power to destroy Jesus, he has shifted his war to His achievements. Pick up your Bible and see that from the time the devil learnt a Redeemer was coming, he has been out to destroy Him before He comes to destroy him and his works. Why do you think the genealogy of Jesus in Matthew 1 differs from the account in Luke 3 after David? The answer is found in the same Luke chapter three in verse twenty-three: "And Jesus himself began to be about thirty years of age (being, as was supposed, the son of Joseph) which was the son of Heli." Joseph was the legal son of Heli by virtue of his marriage to Mary, the biological daughter of Heli. That was the dart God threw to the devil in the wrong direction. He pursued the genealogy of Jesus through David, Solomon to Joseph, while God had prepared the coming of Jesus through David, Nathan to Mary. Remember that Matthew's account started from the beginning with Abraham and ended with Joseph as the son of his biological father, Jacob.

> And Jacob begat Joseph, the husband of Mary, of whom was born Jesus, who is called Christ.
>
> Mathew 1:16

Note that the singular, was, refers to Mary. While Luke's account started from the last with Joseph as the legal, not biological, son of Heli and ended with Adam. This is where and how the two accounts diverged: "And Jesse begat David the king, and David the king begat Solomon of her, that had been the wife of Urias." This is the Matthew account.

We know how David acquired the mother of Solomon that was on line as the great grandmother of Jesus. The devil was waiting. "I will challenge God. Yes, I will put it to Him that Jesus cannot be called holy with such a dirty background." The power in the Word of God, Jesus, took a clean path in Nathan and left the devil to pursue Solomon and his mother: "Which was the Son of Mattatha, which was the Son of Nathan, which was the son of David, which was the Son of Jesse" (Luke 3:31b-32a).

When the birth of Jesus came, and the devil found out he had deceived himself, he set up his next action plan against Jesus. He knew he did not have the power to harm Jesus, but there was someone who could do it: Herod, for fear of his throne. So he revealed the birth of Jesus to a group of Spiritualists in the east, using the star to lead them to Herod and Herod to the infant Jesus. Have you wondered why the star did not lead them straight to Bethlehem but instead led them first to Jerusalem to alert Herod? Is this not enough evidence that astrology is

a deeper evangelism

satanic? The devil was fooled again except that innocent infants were massacred by Herod.

The devil is a fighter and must fight to the last. Never try to have anything to do with him, because he will never allow you to have peace again. So he waited for an opportune moment when he could catch Jesus in an unwary state. The right moment came, after forty days and forty nights of fasting. Remember that we have examined the dangers of abstention under asceticism. That is when you are very vulnerable to spiritual attack. Be careful when you fast, especially at the point of breaking the fast. Remember, that was the time the devil chose to attack Jesus. "Hi, Son of God, did you say you are? How come you are looking so hungry and tired? Of course you should, after forty days and forty nights of fasting. Are you waiting for someone to bring you something to eat? Ha-ha-ha... I thought you are the Son of God? Where is the power if you cannot make these stones to become food for you to eat?" Jesus ignored him. The significance of these temptations, we are told in Bible lessons, is that if Jesus had succumbed to the devil, God forbid, He would have given an impression of His mission as being one of a conquering Messiah instead of a suffering one. Quite correct and true, but that is not the main issue. The devil wanted obedience and worship from Jesus. This was the offence that brought curse on humanity, which Jesus has come to redress. If He became guilty of it also, what would have been the remedy? Our central belief is that Jesus came into the world to destroy the work of the devil. What do you think this work of the devil is? Blindness, deaf and dumbness, lameness and paralysis, leprosy and unclean spirits? These are what we generally believe are the works of the devil Jesus came to destroy. He could have destroyed all these from heaven with a word. The work of the devil He came to destroy is the curse on humans brought about by the devil when he deceived Adam and Eve to worship him in obedience and disregard God in disobedience. That was the same condition he wanted to commit Jesus into.

In Genesis 3:19, we see the concluding part of the curse on man: "In the sweat of thy face shalt thou eat bread till thou return into the ground; for out of it wast thou taken; for dust thou art, and unto dust shalt thou return." Man received the death penalty and lost the provision of God to live forever. Why do you think God created the universe? Exhibition of power? No, it was for man to have trillions upon trillions of miles of space to move around, as he was supposed to live forever.

> And the Lord God formed man of the dust of the ground and breathed unto his nostrils the breath of life, and man become a living soul.
>
> Genesis 2:7

This was the perfect man God created with a life of His own breath, the Holy Spirit, so that he would live forever. Yes, man was to live forever, in physical communication with God. We know this because God's visit to Adam and Eve after their disobedience indicated a physical condition through the physical description of the weather: "In *the cold of the day*." The curse took all away, and God clothed man in a coat of skin and took His breath away from man so he does not live forever again and drove him away.

> Unto Adam and also to his wife did Lord God make coats of skin and clothed them. And the Lord God said Behold, the man is become as one of us to know good and evil and now, lest he put forth his hand, and take also of the tree of life and eat and live for ever. Therefore the Lord God sent him forth from the garden of Eden.
>
> Genesis 3: 21-23a

A long passage but a very necessary one, because it is the inability to put this passage in its proper perspective that has left the world wallowing in ignorance concerning the purpose of God in sending his Son into the world to atone for the sins of humanity. By not appreciating this passage for what it represents, the world has continued to be enveloped in skepticism that denies us a proper explanation as to why God had to subject His own Son to a death on the cross; and the devil is delighted in our inability to offer proper explanation. Let's try and digest the passage this way:

1. When God clothed man with skin, there was blood. So the curse God put on man did not come without blood. God cursed man and drove him away from His presence with blood on his head and will logically require blood to clean man up before bringing him back to His presence. There is nothing in the Bible to assure me that the fallen, worldly man is the same man God created originally in his image and likeness. What I am sure of is that when a man is set free from the curse of Adam, he becomes a new, Christlike creature, and if Christlike, an image and likeness of God. I therefore believe it is wrong for the entire humanity to claim to be the image and likeness of God. It is an exclusive prerogative of a true Christian.

2. Certainly it wasn't human skin God clothed humanity with but that of an animal. The power of gossip and the sensation it brings has been in existence from old. The devil was aware of the treatment God had given to the fallen man. After man received a curse and animal-skin "baptism," he degenerated both spiritually and mentally and, of course, in stature. The devils began to gossip that man had been degraded to animal. That was the gossip communicated to Charles Robert Darwin in 1836 in the Galapagos Island toward the end

of his voyage in the *Beagle*, by the demon of his mediumship, who mischievously told him that man got to his present form evolving from animal. At any time the concept of evolution crosses your mind, know it that you are craving for the devils' gossip.

Let us take this Charles Darwin's mediumship and devils' gossip a bit further. It appears to me, the Spirit's answer to the evolutionists and a challenge to their advocates. Evolution is not science, not history nor geography. It is a belief, like any other religion. It is the religion of the gods of this world, supported and promoted by his agents in the courts of human law and disseminated by a political system populated by wicked rulers. They have falsely regarded evolution as science in fulfillment of Paul's prophecy in 1 Timothy 6:20, "O Timothy, keep that which is committed to thy trust, avoiding profane and vain babblings, and *oppositions of science falsely so called*." Has evolution not become science falsely so called? Where is the proof required of a scientific theory? Our weapon against them cannot be carnal, because we fight not against flesh and blood, but principalities, powers, rulers of the darkness of this world, and spiritual wickedness in high places. Our weapon is the Sword of the Spirit, the Word of God. "For the word of God is quick, and powerful and sharper than any two-edged sword, piercing even to the dividing asunder of soul and spirit, and of the joints and marrow..." (Hebrews 4:12). The battle has begun.

Does it occur to parents and guardians that any time their wards are being taught the so-called theory of evolution in school, the children are being taken to a Spiritualist congregation of mediumship? Is the trend the world is fast heading toward, especially the young ones, not supposed to be a serious indication that something has gone wrong with our school system?

From the teaching of evolution in schools, our wards and children have believed and categorically affirmed that a certain AD 1874 caricature I saw somewhere represents their grandparents. The devil remains a liar.

The many shootings in schools today are one of the many products of teaching children the devil-sponsored concept of evolutionary process as the origin of man. The students have been indoctrinated into a belief that man evolved from animal. "So what does it matter killing an animal, even if it looks different, and calls himself another name—human," is the mentality behind these reckless killings. That is just one of what the devil wants to achieve with this misinformation, and the society has given it to him on a platter of gold, not by ignorance but as her contribution to the spread of the gospel of Satanism. Its founder, Charles Robert Darwin, was trained in theology at the University of Cambridge after he dropped out from medical school of Edinburgh University. His father was disturbed in the spirit over his joining the *Beagle* voyage of 1831 and almost prohibited him for fear it might lead him away from a future in his calling as clergy. How his father would wish he had succeeded in stopping him, because it was in this voyage that the mediumship that led to his notebook and the paper he presented to the Linnaean Society in London, concurrently with a similar paper by Alfred Russell Wallace, occurred. How come two people of different backgrounds, at different locations, could come up with same idea on the same issue at the same time? It is unnatural. The perception of evolution is not natural. If you have ever engaged a Spiritualist in an argument concerning his or her beliefs, you will agree with me that Satan has endowed them with supernatural intelligence similar to what was awaiting the Gospel of Jesus in Athens on Paul's arrival. But the Word of God assures us that what is in us is greater. The apostles and early Christians proved this statement right by making nonsense of the intelligence of the world with the Gospel of Jesus. We do not have to worry about their earthly intelligence. All we need to do is to open our armory and bring out our weapons and disarm them. Engaging in debate with them to prove the falsehood of evolution and other such folly beliefs is glorifying their master. With the power of the Holy Spirit, let us expose Charles Robert Darwin and his disciples for what they are—mediums and Spiritualists—and thrash out their power to enchant the world. Paul did that to many such institutions in his time. Apostle John brought down the great temple of Diana in Ephesus. Smith Wigglesworth, an illiterate plumber, brought Spiritualists to their knees on the floor of his meeting halls anytime they intended to disrupt his service. To Smith Wigglesworth, it is a shame to even think of doing an open battle with the devil, a banished criminal. That is giving him honor he does not deserve. So why should we even contemplate engaging his agents in any form of open debate? We should bark orders at them to be still. Be convinced about this and try it. How did we come to know Saul's Roman name, Paul? This is how Luke reported the indecent in Acts of the Apostles 13:9-10:

> Then Saul who also is called Paul, filled with the Holy Ghost, set his eyes on him (Elymas) And said; O full of all subtlety and mischief, thou child of the devil, thou enemy of all righteousness, wilt thou not cease to prevent the right ways of the Lord. And now behold, the hand of the Lord is upon thee, and thou shalt be blind...

This is how the Bible teaches us to deal with the messengers of evil. Smith Wigglesworth believed it, and it worked for him.

When God decided to bring back man to Himself, blood was required to break the curse made with blood, and if that blood must expiate for the sins of all humanity, it must have no sin of its own. Such blood could not be found on earth, because all have been contaminated by the blood of Adam and Eve. But God's love for mankind was unquenchable, and the only source of blood free from sin is in God Himself. Hence, the voice Isaiah the prophet heard in chapter six verse eight: "Also I heard the voice of the Lord, saying who shall I send, and who shall go for us? Then said I, 'Here am I, Send me.'" If you study Isaiah well, you will see that he enjoys impersonating Jesus.

This is how the Word came into the world as Son of God and the world did not recognize Him. Please, let the Holy Spirit persuade you to read the immediate verse after this "send me," and you will see that Isaiah was referring to Jesus. Below is another example of Isaiah impersonating Jesus in His mission of coming into the world:

> I have not spoken in secret from the beginning: from the time that it was, there am I: and now the Lord God and His Spirit, halt sent me.
>
> Isaiah 48:16

This is Isaiah again talking about Jesus in first person.

What do you understand by "old things passing away and all things made new in Christ Jesus"? Not the alcohol of the past, not the cigarette one smoked and had dropped or drugs one did in the past or the uncontrollable sexual lust one has been delivered from when one accepted Jesus as one's personal savior. No, not those "little" lyings and cheatings one has given up. These are the symptoms and proof that old things have passed away and an indication that one's alienation from God is over, that the animal-skin coat one was clothed with and the blood of animal on one's head and the limited number of years to live have all been taken away by the blood of Jesus, that one has been restored to the perfect man God created with a life of His breath, a clothing of His aura, and life without end, in replacement of life sustained by blood, water and oxygen.

> Therefore if any man be in Christ, he is a new creature; old things are become new.
>
> 2 Corinthians 5:17

It is unto the true Christian only that old things that separated humanity from God have passed away. When God found faith in the heart of Abraham, He also found a person through whom He would bring a seed into the world to break the curse and reconcile man with Him. But first He would raise a nation from the same Abraham that would begin the practice of atonement before the final sacrifice. That seed is Jesus, who on that fateful Good Friday, hung on the cross and became a curse on our behalf.

> For he that hanged is accursed of God.
>
> Deuteronomy 21:23

He is known to us as the Son of God, and that is our privilege, a name available only to the chosen. Yet Spiritualism has as number one in its seven principles the Fatherhood of God. A father without a progeny? They cannot mock God; rather, they are exhibiting their confusion. When one becomes used to the spirit of imitation, when one becomes used to negative spirits, one is bound to become confused. But we have the spirit of truth, so we know whom we have believed. He is coming back to take us as brothers and sisters to where He has prepared for us in His and our Father's mansion after He has finally destroyed the devil. We have the assurance from the Bible that He is coming back to us as a Brother. Romans 8:15: "For ye have not received the spirit of bondage again to fear; but ye have received the spirit of adoption whereby we cry Abba, Father." Daddy, Daddy, Daddy. This is

a deeper evangelism

my assurance that Jesus is coming back to me as a Brother. The Bible tells me that God has begotten me again after Jesus resurrected me from the death I inherited from Adam.

> Blessed be the God and father of our Lord Jesus Christ, which according to his abundant mercy hath begotten us *again* into lively hope by the resurrection of Jesus Christ from the dead.
>
> 1 Peter 1:3

> Blessed assurance, Jesus is mine
> O what a foretaste of glory divine
> Heir of salvation, purchase of God
> Born of His Spirit, washed in His blood.
> Frances Jane Van Aislyne (1820-1915)

And it is in this premise that the devil has deployed his last days' army in the battle of the brotherhood of man. The devil's foreknowledge of the coming Brotherhood of Jesus has led him into establishing a counterfeit brotherhood of man as a camouflage to sneak in and spy on our liberty.

The first coming of Jesus was to destroy my curse so that I can go back into the original, perfect father-son relationship with God as was in the garden of Eden before the fall. It was not intended to destroy the devil but his works only; hence, the demon that said his name is Legion in Matthew challenged Jesus's faithfulness if He had come to destroy them before the time. And Jesus, the Faithful God, did not destroy them before the appointed time but, rather, allowed them to live, though not in the humans He had come to release from curse but in pigs.

I have been assured that in His second coming, I am going with Him as a Brother, because He has released me from curse. I saw when He took it upon Himself to the cross. I saw when the filth of my curse separated Him from His own, when He cried,

"My God, My God why have you forsaken me." I heard when the Father and the Holy Spirit told Him that they cannot come near Him because He was a curse and full of sin. My sin, my curse. I saw when He took my curse into hell and destroyed it. I heard Him. I heard when He said, "*It Is Finished.*"

Conclusion

Jesus declared in Luke 12:41 and 59 that He has come to send fire on the earth. He asked if we think that He has come to bring peace then answered no, that He has come to bring division. The real refiner's fire (Malachi 3:2) that separates the pure from the impure, fire that divides families into pure and impure, fire that divides friends and relations into pure and impure. Fire that is burning and blazing in the broken and contrite hearts of those whose lives have been changed through the mystery of the fire baptism of the Holy Spirit. Above all, the fire that overwhelms all other fires that are kindled and fanned by the evil passion of the devil directed against God and all that are godly. That is the fire that should burn in today's church now and redeem her of confusion and worldliness.

Ralph Waldo Emerson (1803-1882), American essayist and poet, son of William Emerson, onetime minister of First Church of Boston, with a past of seven ancestors of ministers, a graduate of Harvard University at age of eighteen, wrote, "To secure strength, nature implants cruel hunger and thirst, which so easily overdo their offices and invite disease."

Hunger and thirst can overdo their offices one hundred and one times in the lives of the worldly, but the fire of the Holy Spirit keeps them in check and under control in the lives of those who have been washed in the blood of the Lamb. Do you know Him? Have you met Him?

My Brother in the family
My Friend in the society
My Savior in the world
My Guardian in this temporal

My God in the abundance
My King in the heavenly
My Lord in the Spiritual
My Breath in the eternal

He could not be held by nature
He faces all directions at all times
He is in no place at any time
But at every place in all times

He is indescribable
He is incomprehensible
He is infinite
He is inexplicable

You must encounter Him personally
In order to know Him
The Way Truth and Life
My Lord and My God

Chigbu Okoroafor